WHAT CAN I DO
IN R.E.?

A consideration of the place of Religion
in the twentieth-century curriculum
with suggestions for practical work
in schools

MICHAEL GRIMMITT

MAYHEW-McCRIMMON
Great Wakering

First published in Great Britain in 1973 by
MAYHEW-McCRIMMON LTD
Great Wakering Essex England

Reprinted 1976, 1977
Second edition 1978
Reprinted 1982

Second edition
ISBN 0 85597 261 0

Printed in Hong Kong by
Permanent Typesetting & Printing Co. Ltd.

'Religious Truth is normal experience understood at full depth; what makes truth religious is not that it relates to some abnormal field of thought and feeling but that it goes to the roots of the experience which it interprets.'

—M.V.C. Jeffreys, *Glaucon*

'The name of this infinite and inexhaustible depth and ground of all being is God. That depth is what the word God means.'

— Paul Tillich, *The Shaking of the Foundations*, SCM Press, 1949.

Contents

Contents

Acknowledgements

Grateful acknowledgements are made to the respective publishers for quotations from the following books and articles:

B.B.C. Publications: L.P. record No. RESR 9, *The Hopwood Family;* sleeve note by Ralph Rolls.

Child Education : Elizabeth Wilson, "World Religions in the Infant School", Autumn, 1970.

Collins Fontana: Ninian Smart, *The Religious Experience of Mankind,* 1971.

Edwin Cox: *Aims in R.E.,* a paper given to the London Society of Jews and Christians, 1970.

Evans Brothers Ltd & Methuen Educational Ltd : Schools Council Working Paper Number 36, *Religious Education in Secondary Schools,* 1971.

Faber & Faber Ltd : Ninian Smart, *Secular Education and the Logic of Religion,* 1968.

George Allen & Unwin Ltd : R. S. Peters, *Ethics and Education,* 1966. Thor Heyerdahl, *The Ra Expeditions,* 1971.

Harper & Row Inc., New York : Paul Tillich, *Dynamics of Faith.*

Heinemann Ltd : John Wilson, *Education in Religion and the Emotions,* 1971.

Holt, Rinehart & Winston Inc. : Carl Sandburg's poem "Fog" from *Chicago Poems.*

Hutchinsons Ltd. : Alan Durband, *New English,* Book 3, 1967.

Learning for Living, The Journal of the Christian Education Movement, published by SCM Press Ltd : Joan Clark, "The Junior School", Vol. 10 No. 3, January, 1971.

Macmillan Ltd : T. O. Ling, *A History of Religion East and West,* 1968.

Oliver & Boyd Ltd and Moray House College of Education : D. McIntyre & A. Wainwright, *Curriculum and Examinations in Religious Education,* 1968.

Penguin Books Ltd : Paul Tillich, *The Shaking of the Foundations,* 1962. John Wilson, Norman Williams & Barry Sugarman, *Introduction to Moral Education,* 1967.

Routledge & Kegan Paul Ltd : R. G. Goldman, *Religious Thinking from Childhood to Adolescence,* 1964. R. G. Goldman, *Readiness for Religion,* 1965. Edwin Cox, *Changing Aims in Religious Education,* 1966.

SCM Press Ltd : H. Loukes, *New Ground in Christian Education,* 1965. J. A. T. Robinson, *Honest to God,* 1963. I. T. Ramsey, *Religious Language,* 1957. I. T. Ramsey, ed. : *Words about God,* 1971.

The Shap Working Party & The Community Relations Commission : W. Owen Cole, "Some approaches to the teaching of World Religions in Schools" in *Education for a Multi-Cultural Society; World Religions; Aids for Teachers,* 1972.

The Times Educational Supplement : Colin Alves, an article, 24 March, 1967.

Preface

I hope that this book may be of value in helping students and teachers to find their own answers to the question which forms its title. Various considerations have determined its form and content, the most significant being the need to show the practical relevance of the Theory of Education to the task of teaching Religion in schools and the need for a book which can form the basis of a short Professional or In-Service course for non-specialist teachers of R.E. A particular feature of the book is its application of curriculum development techniques to R.E., and so, perhaps, it may be appropriate to summarise its Objectives as follows :

To provide students and teachers—especially non-specialists in R.E.—with an opportunity to :

1 acquire knowledge of current educational thinking and practice in the teaching of religion in schools.
2 recognise the relationship between a sound philosophy of Religious Education and successful classroom practice.
3 practise and acquire the skills involved in designing and implementing schemes of work and lessons in R.E. in accordance with educational criteria.
4 become sensitive to the need to examine their own attitudes towards R.E. in the light of Objectives 1, 2 and 3.

I would like to record my gratitude to those whose writings have greatly contributed to my own thinking on the subject of R.E., especially to Professors P. H. Hirst, R. S. Peters, N. Smart, Mr J. Wilson and to the late Right Rev. Dr I. T. Ramsey under whom it was my privilege to study for a short period. If through brevity, over-simplification or misunderstanding I have been guilty of misrepresenting their ideas, or the ideas of anyone else mentioned in this book, I offer my sincere apologies and beg their indulgence. I would also wish to extend my apologies to any person from whom I may have unconsciously borrowed without permission or acknowledgement.

May I record too my gratitude to friends and colleagues who have so willingly given of their time and thought to the problems that have inevitably arisen during the writing of this book. I would especially like to thank Mr Michael Cockett and Mrs Jennifer Gilbert for their help and advice on many points and also Mr Reg Chrimes, Mr Joseph Crossley, Mr Dick Roberts and Mr Albert Makinson. I owe a special debt of gratitude to Mr E. W. Loadman and the staff of C. F. Mott College of Education Library for the excellent service they have given me and to the students of the

College's Experimental Unit for their constructive criticisms and valuable suggestions. Finally, I would like to thank my wife without whose support and encouragement in countless ways this undertaking would never have been completed.

M.H.G.

Liverpool
June 1973

Preface and Introduction to the Second Edition

What Can I Do in RE? was written in 1973 in an attempt to bring together current thinking about the curriculum and changing estimates of the place and purpose of Religious Education within it. Since that time the debate about the nature, aims and future of R.E. has continued with a vigour and intensity that few might then have foreseen or expected. Undoubtedly the major impetus for this came with the publication of the *City of Birmingham Agreed Syllabus and Handbook* in 1975. In a relatively short period of three years, this syllabus, with its endorsement of the value to R.E. of the phenomenological approach to religious and non-religious belief-systems, has had far-reaching effects on both public and professional thinking about the subject.

For example, since 1975 no fewer than twenty-six reports, statements and pamphlets on R.E. have appeared from various voluntary and professional bodies concerned with the future of R.E. (see list on page 277), and the subject has been a recurring item for debate in the House of Lords and at a number of significant public meetings. Furthermore, four Local Education Authorities in addition to Birmingham have issued new agreed syllabuses in the past three years and many more have now begun to re-consider the adequacy of existing ones. Parallel to such developments has been the continuing work and influence of the Schools Council.

In 1973 I commented enthusiastically on the early work of the Schools Council Project on R.E. in Secondary Schools and called for an extension of the insights and techniques of the phenomenological approach to primary school R.E. and assistance in identifying the "key-concepts" and "structure" of religion as essential pre-requisites to successful curriculum decision-making in R.E. (see pages 88–92). Gratifyingly, both these requests have now been met: the first by the work of the Schools Council Project on R.E. in Primary Schools, especially through its handbook, *Discovering an Approach* (1977), and the second by the publication of the Schools Council R.E. Committee Bulletin, *A Groundplan for the Study of Religion* (1977). In addition, the major part of the curriculum materials scheduled for publication by the Secondary Schools R.E. Project are now available under the title *Journeys into Religion* (1977).

In view of such developments, why a second edition of *What Can I Do in RE?*? There are several reasons. Firstly, there is as much a gap in 1978 as there was in 1973 between the theoretical debate about the nature and aims of R.E. and actual classroom practice, and many teachers, especially non-specialists, still find it very difficult indeed to bridge that gap. The comments of students and teachers who have been using *What Can I Do in RE?* during the last five years, and of those who have been concerned with their training, provide good grounds for believing that the *Conceptual Framework for R.E. in Schools* which the book offers (see page 50) can give assistance here. Secondly, despite recent developments, the two practical approaches it advocates (*The Existential Approach* and *The Dimensional Approach*) can be seen as being not only consistent with present-day trends in the subject but also they provide at least one possible solution to the difficulties of relating the study of religious phenomena to the immediate experiences, interests and thinking of children and young people. To this end we still await "A Groundplan for the Study of Significant Childhood and Adolescent Experiences" to put alongside *A Groundplan for the Study of Religion* to help us ensure that R.E. is as much to do with the 'dialogue with experience' as with the 'dialogue with living religions'. The research which Edward Robinson describes in *The Original Vision* (1977) seems to be pointing us in directions worthy of careful consideration in this respect. Thirdly, everything else apart, it is a fact that students and teachers are still asking, "What can I do in RE?" and still needing all the encouragement they can get to find their own answers to that question.

No changes in the original text have been made in this edition but a considerably larger, up-to-date select bibliography has been added incorporating books and materials for pupils and teachers as well as sections on audio-visual aid suppliers and publishers. The bibliography is intended to serve as a guide for teachers seeking classroom books and materials appropriate to a given age-range which might confidently be used, or adapted for use, within the approaches proposed by this book. Full details of the most significant publications on R.E. up to 1978 have been included for those who wish to acquaint themselves with recent developments.

I would like to express sincere thanks to my secretary, Carol Williams, for her many acts of kindness as well as for typing the additional material for this publication so expertly, and to my colleague, Geoffrey Robson, for providing a list of recommendations on children's literature and for his excellent support during the last two years.

Birmingham   M. H. G.
March 1978

Summary of Chapter Contents

The paradoxical position of religious teaching in the English educational system. The only compulsory subject but the worst taught subject. Reasons for its low classroom status. The attitudes of teachers, employing authorities and pupils to religious teaching. The failure of Agreed Syllabus R.I. The need for a radical reappraisal of our thinking about religion, of its contribution to the child's educational development, of the ways in which the subject might be taught, of how teachers might be trained, and also of what we mean when we speak of "successful" teaching of religion.

The impetus for change in the teaching of religion in schools. Three aspects of change unique to the mid 20th century. The "New Theology". The "Death of God Theology". The task of re-defining "God" in terms which correspond to the thought-forms, language and experiences of 20th century man. Tillich's notion of God as "Depth". Awareness of the peculiar nature of religious language and of Religion as a "unique mode of thought and awareness". The contribution of contemporary theology to an "approach" to religious teaching in schools.

The demand for the content of the school curriculum to be justified on educational grounds. R. S. Peters and the selection of educational criteria. Three educational criteria to be applied to religious teaching. The demands of Curriculum Development. The work of Piaget and J. S. Bruner. The need to teach the key-concepts, principles and the "structure" of any Form of Understanding rather than an assortment of unrelated facts and pieces of information. The integrated curriculum.

The major determinants of social change. The need for R.E. to broaden and deepen "universal perspective" so that it becomes one of "universal understanding". Technological aims and premises which can eclipse man's personal freedom and individuality and blunt his sensitivity to the priority of human needs. "Authentic" existence in the 20th century. The task of restating personal identity and personal choice in contemporary terms. The development of a perspective from which to examine the claims, demands and values of the "technological society" and the "alternative society".

A simplified model of the Curriculum Process. The aims of education. The aims of R.E. The application of the three educational criteria to R.E. Confusions arising out of a failure to distinguish between educational grounds and ecclesiastical, spiritual, historical, moral and cultural grounds as a justification for religious teaching. The questionable position of equating teaching Christianity with educating children in Religion as a unique mode of thought and awareness. The assumptions underlying the terms, "Scripture", "Religious Knowledge", "Religious Instruction" and "Divinity". The task of finding aims which are educationally valid within a state system of education serving a pluralist, multi-racial and multi-cultural society. The analysis of aims given in the Schools Council Working Paper No. 36, *Religious Education in Secondary Schools*. "The Confessional or dogmatic approach"; "The Neo-Confessional or neo-dogmatic approach". The distinction between the role of the Church and the role of the state school in matters of religion. The difference between "Instructing" and "Educating". The task of the state school to educate children in Religion and in Religious Understanding. The strengths and weaknesses of "The Personal Quest approach" associated with Loukes, Cox and Alves. "The Phenomenological or undogmatic approach" and the views of Ninian Smart. The differences between Paul Hirst's concern with "teaching about religion" and Smart's position. The application of the three educational criteria to the "phenomenological approach" to R.E. The difficulties presented by the "phenomenological approach". The problem of inappropriate courses in Religious Studies at Universities and Colleges of Education. The problem of changing teachers' attitudes to religious teaching in school. The need to accept World Religions as an integral part of R.E. at all stages—primary and secondary.

"Recognition of Pupil Characteristics" as the second stage in the Curriculum Process. A summary of the work and findings of Jean Piaget. How and why a child's thinking differs qualitatively from that of an adult. Stages in cognitive development. The rationale underlying the stages. The educational implications of Piaget's theory of "schematic learning". The essential tasks of the teacher in assisting the child's cognitive development. The investigation of children's religious thinking by R. J. Goldman. A summary of Goldman's work and findings. The strengths and weaknesses of Goldman's research. His questionable assumption that a child's ability or lack of ability to discern *Biblical* concepts is indicative of his ability or lack of ability to form *religious* concepts. Making sense of a highly complex *interpretation* of man's feelings, acts and experiences expressed through mythological, metaphorical, poetic and, occasionally, historical categories, is not necessarily the same as forming "religious" concepts. The need for a wider interpretation of William James' definition of religion. A critical estimate of Goldman's recommendations for R.E. in schools. Considerations to be borne in mind when devising curricula for R.E. The need for work in schools to be underpinned by a sound "philosophy of R.E.".

The need for an approach which (i) seeks to create in pupils certain capacities to understand and think about religion as a unique mode of thought and awareness, (ii) starts with the child's own "feelings, acts and experiences" and (iii) helps children to build conceptual bridges between their existential experiences and the central concepts of religion. The value of a "conceptual framework" instead of a syllabus. Diagram showing the relationship between the *Existential Approach* and the *Dimensional Approach*.

Level One : an explanation of the rationale underlying the *Existential Approach*. Mature religious concepts as the outcome of man's reflection on his own and other's life experiences. The theological and educational justification for the approach. The processes involved in the validation of religious concepts. Further comments on Tillich's sermon, "The Depth of Existence". Reflective thinking and the analysis of the depths of all experiences as a "theological" activity.

Their special characteristics and purpose. Providing children with an opportunity to practise a particular *skill*—that of reflecting at depth on their own "feelings, acts and experiences". The avoidance of religious language and distinctly "religious" subject-matter. The purely "secular" nature of *Depth Themes*. *Depth Themes* as a planned educational activity involving selection on the part of the teacher. Themes which promote "disclosure of self", "disclosure of others" and "disclosure of relationship between self and others". The four aims of a *Depth Theme*. *Depth Themes* as a common "secular" basis for R.E. and M.E. Their relationship to Wilson's moral components, EMP and PHIL. The contribution of *Depth Themes* to laying the foundations for an understanding of religious concepts. The *depth* at which a *Depth Theme* is explored is determined by "pupil characteristics". The planning of a *Depth Theme*, like any educational process, to begin with the careful identification of aims and objectives.

The possibility of initiating children into Religion as a unique mode of thought and awareness through an understanding of religious language and its function. The division of "Knowledge" or "Thought" into different "modes" or "forms" each with its own distinctive "structure", its own set of unique concepts and principles, its own symbolic means of communication and its own peculiar forms of "proof" or "verification". Mathematical, Scientific, Ethical, Aesthetic, Religious Understanding and so on. Analysis of statements illustrating these forms. A detailed analysis of the

statement, "Jesus is the Way, the Truth and the Life".
A consideration of the peculiar nature of religious
language and religious assertions. Language which,
on the surface, appears to be "matter-of-fact" or
"descriptive" but which functions more like the
language of poetry. Religious language as the language
of commitment. The contribution of I. T. Ramsey.
Language which evokes "disclosures". A consideration
of "self-disclosure" and disclosure situations. The
parallel between the logical behaviour of the tautology,
"I'm I" and the logical behaviour of the word "God".
"I" as a reference-point against which to understand
and talk about what a person is asserting. "Cosmic-
disclosures". "God" as a reference-point against which
to understand and talk about the perspective which
follows from a cosmic disclosure. Using the the word
"God" to confine discussion to a perspective of commitment and mystery. "God" as a word which is
expressive of the *kind* of commitment with which a
person responds when he is confronted by a cosmic
disclosure—a "religious" commitment. A consideration
of the nature and function of symbolism. Religious
symbols which fail to disclose truth to man in the 20th
century. Religion, like science and the arts, engaged
in an evolutionary process that affects its modes of
expression and communication as much as the ideas
and concepts underlying it.

The implications of this discussion for the teaching of
religion in schools. *Symbol and Language Themes.*
Their relationship to *Depth Themes* and their special
characteristics and purpose. Their concern with promoting understanding of the nature and function of
symbols and the ability to use them. Themes which
concentrate on the context out of which religious symbols have grown. Themes which involve children in
examining the symbolism found in religious feasts,
festivals, ceremonies, ritual and myths. Presenting religious festivals as "dramatised theology". The importance of looking outside the Judaeo-Christian tradition.
Educating children in the use of evocative, metaphorical and mythological language rather than judiciously excluding all traces of it from the content.
Learning to see religious language as the language of
commitment which seeks to evoke in others a sense of
the mystery that the religious man calls "God". In-

troducing elementary philosophical analysis into schools. The aims of *Symbol and Language Themes*.

(c) *Situation Themes*

The possibility of extending the common ground between R.E. and M.E. while ensuring that work contributes positively to the development of Religious Understanding as well as fostering moral insight. The psychological and ethical problems associated with modifying attitudes. The difficulty of encouraging the transfer of the capacity to make moral judgments into the sphere of moral conduct. The importance of encouraging pupils to recognise the need for devising and adopting principles which can provide guidelines for moral decision-making. The social climate of the school and the opportunities it provides for pupils to introject attitudes and values of worth to their moral development. The need for teachers to underline and extend this by a teaching programme specifically designed to foster worthwhile attitudes and values. The suitability of *Depth Themes* as the "core" of such a programme in the primary school. The need for these themes to be augmented in the secondary school by a scheme which makes provision for the children's more complex experiences and their greater capacity for moral judgments. *Situation Themes*. Providing children with an opportunity to examine and discuss situations which call for a moral choice or judgment to be made. Themes which present examples of persons acting and behaving in accordance with the beliefs and values that they happen to hold about themselves and about others. Examples of material suitable for use in *Situation Themes* and criteria for its selection. The value of the Schools Council Nuffield Humanities Curriculum Project and the Schools Council Moral Education Curriculum Project. The relationship of *Situation Themes* to Wilson's moral components, DIK, PHRON, KRAT 1, GIG 1. Reservations about KRAT 2. The contribution of *Situation Themes* to the development of Religious Understanding. The question, "Is there a logical connection between Morals and Religion?" A consideration of John Wilson's position in *Education in Religion and the Emotions*. Themes which confront children with persons adopting a particular attitude and a course of action because of the religious beliefs that they hold. Themes which point children beyond actions and attitudes to the beliefs that underlie them and which motivate the person to act in accordance with certain principles. Themes which confront children with "religious" responses to feelings of love, hate, fear, guilt, joy, awe, and so on, and which lead them to accept or admit to their own experiences of such feelings and come to some conclusions about the sort of responses they might reasonably adopt towards them. The aims of *Situation Themes*.

Some final observations on the *Existential Approach*.

Introduction; further comments on the Schools Council Working Paper No. 36, *Religious Education in Secondary Schools,* and on the "phenomenological approach" to R.E.

Level Two : an explanation of the rationale underlying the *Dimensional Approach*. The six inter-related and inter-dependent dimensions of religion—experiential, mythological, ritual, social, ethical and doctrinal. The aim of the *Dimensional Approach*—to initiate children into Religion as a unique mode of thought and awareness by (i) familiarising them with its six dimensions, (ii) presenting selected religious concepts by way of the six dimensions, and (iii) helping them to build conceptual bridges between their own experiences (developed within the *Existential Approach*) and what they recognise to be the central concepts of religion. The importance of recognising the way in which the experiential dimension provides the justification for the existence of the other dimensions. The problem of relating "religious material" to the developmental pattern of children's thinking overcome, initially, by emphasising that "understanding" religion is not only a matter of grappling with certain concepts at an intellectual level but also being aware of the sort of feelings or emotions which are involved in religious belief. Sensitising children to the feelings which underlie religious beliefs and practices as a first priority rather than giving them an accurate grasp of religious teaching. The criterion for selecting material for use with children—that which is best able to evoke in them a sense of religious experience and a perception of how adherents to a religious faith feel about life. The logical priority of material illustrating the experiential, mythological and ritual dimensions over material illustrating the social, ethical and doctrinal dimensions. The grouping of material into three "areas" to be introduced in stages parallel to work within the *Existential Approach:* that is, (1) experiential, mythological and ritual material; (2) social and ethical material; (3) doctrinal material. A description of the special characteristics of :

A consideration of the implications for work with children.

The importance of educational Objectives. Relating the choice of Objectives for a Scheme of Work to (i) the general aim of R.E., (ii) the structure of religion, and (iii) pupil characteristics. Objectives appropriate to the stated aims of *Depth Themes, Symbol and Language Themes* and *Situation Themes.* Devising Knowledge, Skill and Attitude Objectives.

Using "religious material" and teaching it in such a way as to convey its "theological significance" to children. Choosing and stating aims which reflect and identify particular theological insights. Translating these aims into objectives.

An example of aims and objectives of a Scheme of

xxi

INTRODUCTION

The Failure of Religious Instruction

There is something paradoxical about the position of religious teaching in the English educational system. As a result of Part 2 section 25 of the 1944 Education Act, "religious instruction" is the only subject which appears in the curriculum by law. Yet it is generally agreed by pupils and teachers alike that R.I., as it came to be known after the 1944 Act, is about the worst taught subject in the curriculum! Is it possible that there is some sort of connection between the subject's legal status and it's classroom status? Are we dealing here with cause and effect? That does appear to be the case.

Because of Part 2 section 25 of the 1944 Act, "religious instruction" has to be included in the timetable of state schools, and yet in very few, if any, schools has it been accorded parity of esteem or status with other subjects. Rather it has been seen by pupils and teachers alike as an unfortunate but obligatory "chore", and accordingly has been given the barest minimum of time allocation.

Furthermore, despite the statutory status of R.I., very little emphasis has been placed on a teacher's professional training in this subject—largely as a result of the misguided belief that, "Anyone can teach R.I. You just open the Bible, read them a bit and then get them to write/draw about it". Would anyone dare to say that about any other subjects in the curriculum? About French, Physics or Maths for instance?

If you doubt that this attitude still persists have a look at some of the secondary teaching posts advertised in the *Times Educational Supplement* and note the frequency with which a post, say in English or History, carries the statement, "Willingness to take R.I. an advantage". Note too how many posts specifically in R.I. also expect candidates to offer other subjects, such as English, French, Music and Games! So, possession of training specifically in R.I. is rarely a first priority in the minds of appointing authorities when interviewing candidates for posts. This is similarly the case with appointments to Primary schools. Here appointing authorities *assume* that

1

a candidate is not only willing but also professionally able to deal with a class's R.I.

As a result, religious instruction has been taught in state schools over the years largely by teachers who have been either untrained or only partially trained in the subject. Their attitudes to R.I. have varied. Some have been anxious to teach the subject well and have approached it imaginatively and sympathetically. Others have been either uninterested, openly opposed to it, or worst of all, over-zealous for it! The latter have tended to be the type of teacher whose one burning purpose in life is to convert the whole of 3B to the Christian faith! Usually they have achieved the reverse effect! It is not surprising then, that the quality of religious teaching in our schools has been, and, in many schools continues to be, very much inferior to that of other subjects in the curriculum.

Perhaps even more appalling than this is the fact that in many of our state schools R.I. amounts to nothing less than an exercise in sheer indoctrination—the teaching of beliefs as if they were facts. At the same time, for the vast majority of pupils, the lesson is associated with the repetition of over-familiar Bible stories, incredible miracle stories, bewildering parables, Saint Paul's journeys, the Virgin Birth, chunks of Jewish history, maps of Palestine, sermonising, irrelevance and the discomfort of sitting on a hard seat waiting for break or History, dinner-time or Geography, or, best of all, home-time and escape into the "real" world outside.

For some this will appear to be an exaggerated and cynical caricature of the state of the subject in schools and the teachers who teach it. For others it will be an accurate reflection of what, in their own experience, religious instruction is like in many of our schools. If we were brave enough to ask our pupils for their reaction to the religious teaching they receive, what do you think they would say? It is unlikely that they would be complimentary; very few would consider that the R.I. lesson is the highlight of their week! Ironically, research has shown that after receiving ten years of traditional, agreed-syllabus religious instruction, from five to 15+, pupils are almost completely uninformed about the Christian faith and have largely failed to grasp any of the key religious concepts. In other words, there are strong grounds for believing that the effect of the traditional R.I. syllabus and approach on children's religious thinking is to cause it to become increasingly retarded as they progress through the stages of formal education so that the majority leave school "theologically illiterate" at 15+. What is even more disturbing is that they leave school either having rejected religion as meaningless, childish and irrelevant or feeling totally apathetic or distinctly antagonistic towards religious claims or statements or towards any religious position. In actual fact they have often rejected *religion as defined and taught by the schools,* and this is fre-

2

quently far from being what religion actually is! Could there be any greater indictment of the way in which they have been taught than this? Perhaps even more to the point, does all this add up to a watertight case against retaining "religious instruction" within the state school system?

The simple answer here would be "Yes"; and yet such an answer would carry the implication that religion, or the "Form of Understanding" called "Religious Understanding", is an unimportant aspect of man's knowledge and experience and is not something about which an educated person should be informed. Atheists and agnostics as well as those committed to a religious belief would find this difficult to accept. And so, inevitably, we are forced to pursue a line of thought which leads not to the wholesale rejection of teaching religion in schools but to a radical re-appraisal of our thinking about religion, about its contribution to a child's educational development, about the ways in which the subject might be approached and taught, and about the ways in which teachers may be trained to teach the subject successfully. We must also think carefully about what we mean when we speak of "successful" teaching of religion. This book attempts to contribute to this process of re-appraisal.

Further reading

Surveys of R.E. in schools in chronological order

Institute of Christian Education : *Religious Education in Schools* (N.S.; S.P.C.K., 1954).
University of Sheffield Institute of Education : *Religious Education in Secondary Schools* (Nelson, 1961).
H. Loukes : *Teenage Religion* (SCM Press, 1961).
H. Loukes : *New Ground in Christian Education* (SCM Press, 1965).
J. W. Daines : *Meaning or muddle?* (University of Nottingham Institute of Education, 1966).
E. Cox : *Sixth Form Religion* (SCM Press, 1967).
C. Alves : *Religion and the Secondary School* (SCM Press, 1968).
P. R. May & O. R. Johnston : *Religion in our schools* (Hodder & Stoughton, 1968).
Dom Philip Jebb : *Religious Education: drift or decision?* (Darton, Longman & Todd, 1968).
Church of England Commission on R.E. in Schools : *The Fourth R* (N.S. & S.P.C.K., 1970).
Schools Council Working Paper No. 44 : *Religious Education in Primary Schools* (Evans/Methuen, 1972).

Other observations on R.E. in schools

D. Dewar: *Backward Christian Soldiers* (Hutchinson, 1964).
A. G. Wedderspoon (Ed.): *Religious Education 1944-1984* (Allen & Unwin, 1966).
K. Gibberd: *Teaching Religion in Schools* (Longmans, 1970).

Chapter 2

Theological, Educational and Social Change

The impetus for change in the teaching of religion in our schools stems not simply from our awareness of the failure of traditional "religious instruction" but also from three aspects of change unique to the mid 20th century. These are : theological change, educational change and social change. Together they have created a force which, in the last eight or ten years, has led to a remarkable revolution in the field of religious teaching. A radically new and different approach in both content and method is indicated and symbolised by the deliberate adoption of the title, "Religious Education" or R.E. The significance of this title—not entirely new as a label for religious teaching—will only become apparent if we first examine briefly those three aspects of change which have led to its adoption.

Theological change

Like all other academic disciplines, theology has been subjected to a great deal of change and development in the 20th century. Not unexpectedly this change has been very much in keeping with the revolutionary and critical character of the present age. Born out of the writings of theologians such as Bultmann, Bonhoeffer and Tillich, and popularised by Bishop John Robinson's book, *Honest to God* and the resultant *Honest to God Debate,* the radical "New Theology" has had the effect of calling into question not only the usefulness of the traditional framework through which the Christian faith has expressed itself for nigh on 2,000 years, but also the validity of those theological concepts upon which the whole of Christian doctrine rests.

The radical nature of theology in the 20th century is perhaps best illustrated by "The Death of God Theologians" (e.g. Thomas Altizer, William Hamilton, Paul Van Buren and so on) who, as their title indicates, start from the premise that "God is dead"—a premise that is designed to expose both the ineffectiveness and irrelevance of traditional ways of speaking about "God" for 20th

5

century man, and also to call in question any procedure by which "God" may be "known".

Alongside this preoccupation with the task of re-defining "God" in a way which corresponds with the thought-forms, language and experiences of modern man, there is, too, considerable debate among theologians about the "form" in which the Christian Gospel may find expression in the 20th century. Largely through the influence of Bultmann, the "New Theology" has accepted the need to "demythologise" the New Testament account of the birth, life, death, resurrection and ascension of Jesus (and that means abandoning miracle stories, demons, nativity and resurrection accounts as *historical facts*) so that the central message of Christianity (itself at doubt) may speak to 20th century man in his existential situation.

It is not difficult to see, from this brief account of developments in contemporary theology, that such radical changes in the way in which the Christian faith is expressed and interpreted must inevitably find their way into the classroom. Here their implications are enormous. They throw doubt immediately upon the value of teaching children the traditional Christian thought-forms for these are seen by the new theologians as positive hindrances to understanding Christianity in the 20th century. (The number of pupils who reject the Christian faith as "meaningless" would appear to bear this assertion out.) Yet the form of expression, drawing heavily on existentialist philosophy, which they seem to advocate as a relevant replacement is far too complex for use with pupils in school.

Consider the problem of communicating to children the following definition of God, given by Paul Tillich :

The name of this infinite and inexhaustible depth and ground of all being is God. That depth is what the word "God" means. And if that word has not much meaning for you, translate it, and speak of the depths of your life, of the source of your being, of your ultimate concern, of what you take seriously without reservation. Perhaps, in order to do so, you must forget everything traditional that you have learned about God, perhaps even the word itself. For if you know that God means depth, you know much about him. You cannot then call yourself an atheist or unbeliever. For you cannot think or say : Life has no depth ! Life is shallow ! Being itself is surface only. If you could say this in complete seriousness, you would be an atheist; but otherwise you are not. He who knows about depth knows about God.

The Shaking of the Foundations, pp 63f,
"The Depth of Existence".

This may not serve as a definition of God which a child could *verbalise* in the way in which it is expressed here, but it can serve,

6

as we shall see in Chapter 5, as the rationale for a relevant and effective *approach* to R.E. both at primary and secondary stages.

The changes which have occurred in theology in the 20th century would appear, at first sight, to have considerably increased the problems and complexities of religion and religious belief. Yet it should be noted that modern theology has taken as its predominant concern the problem of *communicating* religious concepts in a way which has meaning for modern man. In this sense modern theology should have greater meaning for modern man than has, for example, New Testament, Patristic, Medieval or post-Reformation theology. After all this theology has grown out of a situation with which he is intimately familiar, namely, life in a technological and scientific age.

In an attempt to aid theological understanding modern theology focuses attention firmly on the peculiar nature of religious language and seeks to find models, images and symbols which have the effect of "disclosing", or pointing man towards, the type of theological insights which have meaning today. We must not be surprised if the models, images and symbols selected are what we would call "secular" for secular forms of expression are more likely to have a case value for us than outdated and obsolete "religious" ones.

Most important of all, modern theology attempts to arouse in man an awareness of how "Religious Understanding" differs from other "Forms of Understanding" (mathematical, scientific, historical and so on), and how the type of tests which may be applied to religious concepts are very different from those which may be applied, say, to scientific or historical concepts. In short, modern theology tries to illuminate the nature of religion and to show it for what it is— a special way of looking at and talking about the experience of living—living in the 20th century.

If we can overcome the initial barrier of its unfamiliarity (and it is only unfamiliar because we are only familiar with pre-20th century theology!) we will find that modern theology has much to offer us in our task of devising a form of R.E. which is meaningful and relevant to the children we teach. Its contribution, though, may be even greater in terms of *approach* than in terms of content.

Educational change

It is inappropriate in a book of this type and size to attempt to provide an outline of all the many developments which have recently occurred in the theoretical study of education. It may be useful at this point, however, to identify certain educational principles which are immediately relevant to our task of re-appraising the nature and contribution of R.E. in schools, and, at the same time,

7

to clarify some of the educational terms which are likely to arise when we begin to apply educational techniques to R.E.

At a time when knowledge is expanding rapidly and new disciplines are beginning to emerge it is not surprising to find educationists insisting on the need for every subject to justify its inclusion in the school curriculum on *educational grounds*. What exactly is meant by this?

The main difficulty here is in determining what constitutes "educational grounds". Clearly this is dependent upon one's definition of "education" and that involves making a number of value-judgments which, in turn, are dependent upon the culture of the society providing the education and upon the particular view of the child's nature which happens to be acceptable at one time. Not surprisingly, therefore, attempts to define "education" as a specific process only serve to increase the number of definitions and decrease the possibility of common agreement about the nature of education. A more helpful approach is to identify several criteria—*educational criteria*—which "education" needs to meet or fulfil if it is to be "education" and not merely "instruction", "training", or "indoctrination".

Professor R. S. Peters has made a number of comments and observations which provide some useful guidelines for thinking about "education". In *Ethics and Education* (Allen & Unwin, 1966, p 50) he speaks of "education" as being concerned with "initiating" young people into "what is worthwhile". He considers "what is worthwhile" to be, ". . . specific modes of thought and awareness such as science, history, mathematics, religious and aesthetic awareness together with moral, prudential and technical forms of thought and action". This view seems to imply that certain "modes of thought and awareness" are "worthwhile" for their own sake; they have an intrinsic value which is sufficiently important to justify their inclusion in the curriculum.

Peters is anxious to emphasise, however, that, ". . . the central uses of the term 'education' are confined to situations where we deliberately put ourselves or others in the way of something that is thought to be conducive to valuable states of mind". In other words, "education" requires that the outcome of being initiated into a "mode of thought" should be in some sense valuable or worthwhile to the person concerned; it should make a difference to him and that difference should be considered desirable. It is, then, the *capacity* of a "mode of thought and awareness" to *contribute valuably and also uniquely to the child's cognitive (intellectual), emotional, social or physical development* which constitutes its *educational validity*.

This observation prompts the question, "In what *sense* can we speak of a "mode of thought and awareness" contributing both

8

valuably and uniquely to a child's development?" The division of "knowledge" or "thought" into different "modes" or "forms" implies that each one has its own distinctive "structure", its own set of unique concepts and principles, its own symbolic means of communication and its own peculiar forms of "proof". Is it, then, valuable for the child to know his way about the different "modes" or "forms" just because they are there? Or is it because each one contributes something special and distinct to his development as a person? There would appear to be very strong grounds for supporting the second reason.

Peters argues that for something to count as "education" a minimum of knowledge and understanding must be involved and also "some kind of cognitive perspective". "Cognitive perspective" results from an ability to forge new links between what is known (and what is felt) so that one is able to view both knowledge and experience from a multi-dimensional or ever-changing perspective. In this process new knowledge, if it is properly assimilated, constantly throws light on, widens and deepens one's view of things. Thus, the *educational justification* for incorporating a particular "mode of thought" into the curriculum needs to be sought in that mode of thought's capacity to *widen and deepen* the child's cognitive perspective in a unique way—to add yet another dimension from which he can interpret his experience. It is in this sense—in widening and deepening cognitive perspective—that we can speak of a certain "mode of thought and awareness" contributing valuably and uniquely to the child's development.

The development of "cognitive perspective", however, does not depend simply on different modes of thought and awareness being presented to the child, it depends too on *how* these are presented. Professor Peters has commented that, ". . . education at least rules out some procedures on the grounds that they lack wittingness and voluntariness on the part of the learner". Thus the teaching of beliefs as if they were facts would constitute "indoctrination" rather than "education". Such procedure fails to promote *understanding* on the part of the child, and without understanding there can be no development of cognitive perspective. The *educational validity* of a mode of thought, or of a subject, also depends, then, on how far it is possible to teach it in a way which ensures understanding and promotes cognitive perspective.

From these observations it is possible to identify at least three *educational criteria* which subjects need to meet or fulfil if their inclusion in the school curriculum is to be justified on *educational grounds*. The criteria may be expressed in question form:

1   Does this subject incorporate a unique "mode of thought and

awareness" which is "worthwhile" to man's understanding of himself and his situation?

2 Does this subject serve to widen and deepen the child's cognitive perspective in a unique and valuable way and so contribute to his total development as a person?

3 Can this subject be taught in ways which ensure understanding and actively foster the child's capacity to think for himself?

In due course (Chapter 3) we will need to apply these educational criteria to religious education. Its ability to fulfil them will determine whether or not it should, on educational grounds, continue to occupy a place in the school curriculum.

Another recent development in education, closely connected with the notion of educational justification, is "Curriculum Development". This is best regarded as a set of techniques or principles which are used in planning learning situations in terms of their educational worth. So often the content of a lesson or a series of lessons is chosen simply on the basis of what comes next in the syllabus, or "what goes down well with the children" or even what the teacher enjoys teaching! None of these ways of determining content necessarily ensures that the content is really worth learning and that it has any distinctly valuable contribution to make to the pupil's educational development. In other words, unless care is taken the value of lessons becomes very much a hit and miss affair. Teachers can go through the motions of teaching and pupils through the motions of learning and yet the end product may be of little if any educational significance.

Curriculum Development demands, therefore, that prior to teaching anything, we decide (on the basis of our knowledge of the subject and of the children in our class) on a number of *educational objectives* which we wish to achieve through our teaching, and that we state these in precise terms (often called "behavioural terms") *before* going on to select content and method which is best suited to their achievement. Note how the choice of content and method(s) (the "curriculum") follows from our objectives and not vice-versa; a curriculum should be specifically designed to achieve educational objectives. The objectives selected may be *Knowledge Objectives* (what knowledge the children will acquire through the lesson), *Skill Objectives* (what skills they will develop or practise in the lesson) and *Attitude Objectives* (what attitudes, values, sensitivities or feelings they will develop through the lesson).

The rationale underlying this technique is the view that it helps us to ensure that what we teach is educationally worthwhile and that at the end of a learning situation we are in a position to *evaluate* the success of our teaching by seeing (from what the child-

10

ren can do) if our objectives have been achieved. Teaching and learning thus become far more systematic and progressive; the curriculum "develops" in accordance with what are seen by the teacher to be the "needs" and "interests" of his class. Learning becomes a more purposeful and successful activity. Clearly we will need to apply Curriculum Development techniques to religious education. (See Chapter 7.)

The areas of educational change and development so far considered have brought us into contact mainly with the philosophy of education. Two other aspects of development which must be mentioned stem from studies in the psychology of education. Like the developments considered earlier, these also have far-reaching practical implications for religious education.

We must attribute a great deal of our knowledge of how children think and how they learn to the work of Jean Piaget and J. S. Bruner. (See Chapter 4.) Both these psychologists have emphasised the crucial part that the formation of *concepts* plays in developing the child's capacity to think, understand and learn. Whereas simple information or "facts" are relatively easy to understand and learn, the task of forming concepts, which underlie these facts and in which the facts cohere, is notoriously difficult. Even more difficult is the task of seeing the relationship of one concept, or a set of concepts, to another concept. Yet it is from the latter that the capacity for formulating principles develops. (The highest forms of thought depend upon principles).

The practical implications of this are that teachers need to be aware of the *key concepts* which, when related to each other, form the *principles* of a subject or academic discipline. This complex arrangement of concepts and principles is known as a subject's *structure* and it is this which needs to be taught to children rather than an assortment of unrelated facts and pieces of information. It is only on this basis that true understanding and learning can occur. We will need to consider, therefore, which are the key concepts, principles and the structure of religion and then determine by which means these may best be taught to children.

Finally reference needs to be made to the growing demand for different subjects in the curriculum to be *integrated*. (We see this in the adoption of the "Integrated Day" by some Primary schools and of "Inter-Disciplinary-Enquiry" or "I.D.E." by some Secondary schools.) There are strong psychological reasons for rejecting the division of knowledge into man-made subject areas—especially in the case of Primary school children who have, according to Piaget, a "global" view of knowledge as being indivisible and continuous. This raises the question of how far it is possible for religious education to be integrated with other subjects and still enable key religious concepts to be understood.

There is a great danger when commenting on social change of over-simplifying a very complex phenomenon. It is desirable, therefore, in this context, to restrict comment to some aspects of social change which have immediate practical implications for the development of religious education.

Certainly science has been one of the major determinants of social change in the last 30 years. Very significant is the way in which it has changed our view of the universe and diminished, through advanced telecommunication systems, the size of our world. As a result we are probably more aware of events occurring in parts of the world thousands of miles away from us (not to mention parts of the universe) than our immediate ancestors were aware of what was happening in their own local community. It is impossible, therefore, for us to live in isolation, unaware of how other men feel, think and act. Science has given us a "universal perspective" on life; it has made us conscious of those with "life-styles" different from our own. The increasingly multi-racial and multi-cultural nature of our own country has further widened this perspective. It may well be the task of religious education to broaden and deepen this "universal perspective" so that it becomes one of "universal understanding".

Science, however, has also been responsible for narrowing perspectives. At the same time as raising standards of living in this country it has contributed to the development of a society with a narrowly materialistic outlook. It has cultivated a mistaken belief in the power and ability of technology to solve all man's problems. The pressure which present society exerts on individuals to contribute, occupationally and ideologically, to its continued development and to accept its technological aims and premises, has had the effect of eclipsing man's personal freedom and individuality and blunting his sensitivity to the priority of human needs other than the material ones. Consequently, there is a growing feeling, especially among young people, that man in a technological society has become a means to a rather dubious end and that personal existence can only become "authentic" or meaningful if he breaks free and determines his own identity, his own values and, most important of all, his own purpose. Religious education should be able to help young people to clarify such problems in their own minds and examine the implications of different lines of approach.

Disillusionment with society and a demand for "personal freedom" seem to have a cause and effect relationship. Current forms of expression of this feeling include "dropping out", rebelling against (especially through sex, drugs, pornography and violence) and experimenting with "alternative forms of living" such as that of the commune. The pervasive philosophy of "Do your own thing"—especially evident in Pop-culture—represents a serious attempt to re-state in contemporary terms, the value of personal identity and personal choice and so correct the imbalance created by the technological emphasis of society. At the same time it reflects a radical change in the basis of morality. Young people today, especially those of average and below average ability, need help in developing their *own* perspective from which to examine the claims, demands and values of the "technological society" *and* the "alternative society". Only if they are able to exercise personal discrimination and make informed choices, especially in matters of belief and action, will they be in a position to prevent themselves from being exploited. Religious education may, therefore, play an important role in helping them towards personal autonomy based on a critical awareness of alternatives.

These observations on theological, educational and social change—brief and inadequate as they are—should not only convince us even further of the need for a radical re-appraisal of our thinking about religious teaching, but also provide us with a number of guidelines to assist us in this task. It is these guidelines which underlie the observations which are offered in the following chapters of this book.

Further reading

Theology

T. J. J. Altizer and W. Hamilton : *Radical Theology and the Death of God* (Penguin, 1968).

P. M. Van Buren : *The Secular Meaning of the Gospel* (SCM Press, 1963).

J. Robinson : *Honest to God* (SCM Press, 1963); *Exploration into God* (SCM Press, 1967).

W. Strawson : *Teachers and the New Theology* (Epworth, 1969).

Education

R. D. Archambault (Ed.) : *Philosophical Analysis and Education* (RKP, 1965; articles by R. S. Peters and P. Hirst).

R. F. Dearden : *The Philosophy of Primary Education* (RKP, 1969).

A. Harris : *Thinking about Education* (Concept Books, 1970).

P. H. Hirst and R. S. Peters : *The Logic of Education* (RKP, 1970).

R. S. Peters : *Ethics and Education* (Allen and Unwin, 1966).

R. S. Peters (Ed.) : *The Concept of Education* (RKP, 1967; articles by R. S. Peters and P. Hirst).

Sociology and Social Ethics
M. J. Cockett (Ed.): *ROSLA, School and Christian Values* (Mayhew-McCrimmon, 1972; chapter by M. H. Grimmitt).
R. S. Downie: *Roles and Values* (Methuen and Co. Ltd, 1971).
J. Wilson *et al*: *Introduction to Moral Education* (Penguin, 1967; Part IIB by B. N. Sugarman).

Chapter 3

Can we justify the teaching of religion in schools on educational grounds?

A consideration of Aims

In view of the increasing importance of Curriculum Development in education it is appropriate that we follow its techniques in our preliminary thinking about the development of religious education, as well as in our practical work of planning R.E. lessons. After all, Curriculum Development is specifically concerned with ensuring that what we teach has *educational validity* and so, if we are seeking to justify the inclusion of religious teaching in the curriculum on *educational gounds* it is likely to be of decisive importance in assisting us towards this end.

Set out below is a simplified model indicating a series of stages which we might follow when preparing a lesson.

A Simplified Model of the Curriculum Process

1 Selection of Aims. (The overall aim of the subject or Scheme of Work.)
2 Recognition of Pupil Characteristics. (Developmental age, interests, needs, experience, the social context in which they live and are taught.)
3 Selection of Specific Objectives. (Identification of Knowledge, Skills and Attitudes consistent with the "structure" or key-concepts of the subject.)
4 Selection of subject matter appropriate to 1, 2 and 3.
5 Structuring of subject matter. (In accordance with learning theories.)
6 Selection of method(s) appropriate to 1, 2, 3, 4 and 5.
7 Creation of the "learning situation". (Putting the lesson into effect.)
8 Evaluation of the lesson in terms of Aims and Specific Objectives. (Did I achieve them?)

Aims

When we talk about "Aims" in education we are really talking about *intentions* and *purposes*. There is no difference between saying, "The aim of education is . . ." and "The intention or purpose of education is . . .". It is important to note, however, that aims, intentions and purposes are very closely connected with values. It would be strange to do something intentionally if we did not attach some value to what we were doing. Similarly our choice of aims in education depends very largely upon what we believe the function of education to be, and that involves making a value judgment. As well as influencing our choice of aims, our definition of education will also determine the curriculum, the syllabus to be followed in each subject and the way in which we teach it (i.e. our "approach"). In other words, decisions made about the *aims of education* as a whole affect our decisions about the *aims of subjects* included in the curriculum.

Educational aims, therefore, are really designed to help us to answer the question, "Why?"—"Why am I teaching this subject, this fact, this concept, this skill and so on?" They also help us with the question, "How?"—"How shall I teach this subject, fact, concept, skill and so on?" because *how* we teach something, our "approach", is governed by what we hope to achieve. It is upon the basis of sound educational aims, then, that a sound educational superstructure (made up of subjects, syllabuses, schemes of work, lessons and so on) depends. Worthless educational aims or, worst of all, no educational aims, result in worthless teaching. So, time spent thinking about educational aims is time very well spent. Several books dealing with educational aims and objectives have been suggested at the end of this chapter.

The Aims of R.E.

We now need to turn to a consideration of the aims of religious education. While doing this it is essential that we bear in mind the three educational criteria, noted earlier, which a subject needs to fulfil if its inclusion in the curriculum is to be justified on *educational* grounds. The three criteria are :

1   Does this subject incorporate a unique "mode of thought and awareness" which is "worthwhile" to man's understanding of himself and his situation?
2   Does this subject serve to widen and deepen the child's cognitive perspective in a unique and valuable way and so contribute to his total development as a person?
3   Can this subject be taught in ways which ensure understanding and actively foster the child's capacity to think for himself?

The different reasons given in the past for including religious

teaching in the curriculum have rarely been "educational" ones. Rather the subject has been advocated on what may be called *ecclesiastical/spiritual, historical, moral and cultural grounds.* As we have seen, the reason given for including a subject in the curriculum largely determines the type of teaching approach adopted and also the content of the subject. In religious teaching we will also find that the title given to the subject reflects the teaching approach.

The following reasons have all been used at some time or another to justify having religious teaching in the school curriculum :

1 Because in the late 19th century its inclusion in the curriculum was the only way of reaching a compromise between Church and State. (Ecclesiastical or historical justification.)
2 Because this is a Christian country and it is only right that every child should be brought up in the Christian faith. (Ecclesiastical or cultural justification.)
3 Because Christianity is true and without a knowledge of it men and women will live impoverished lives. (Ecclesiastical/spiritual justification.)
4 Because a child who has a religious faith is more likely to behave in a moral way than a child who has not. (Moral justification.)

Time and space does not permit us to examine all the assumptions which underlie these statements but one or two observations are appropriate. With the possible exception of the fourth statement, all contain the tacit assumption that the content and approach of religious teaching should be Christian. All imply that the outcome of the teaching should be that the child will have a commitment to the Christian faith. All assume that the task of the school in relation to religious teaching is identical with that of the Church. It is very doubtful if any one of these assumptions can be justified on *educational* grounds.

There may be some who would wish to contest the above conclusion by pointing out that Christianity does in fact meet the first two educational criteria and, with a bit of care, can meet the third. Certainly Christians do believe that their faith is a *unique* mode of thought and awareness and that it does contribute to cognitive perspective in a *unique* and valuable way. Several points may be made about this view. Firstly, that it rests on a *belief*—a belief held by some and hotly denied by others. Accordingly, if this argument was accepted then the very same argument could be used to justify the inclusion of every other religious faith, humanistic and atheistic philosophies, political ideologies and even witchcraft and magic. Secondly, that it equates the Christian faith with "Religious Under-

17

standing"; it assumes that the two are synonymous. In actual fact, of course, the Christian faith is just one of many different *expressions* of Religious Understanding and it is the latter which is the unique mode of understanding rather than the former. In other words, if we are going to justify the curriculum in terms of unique modes of thought and awareness we must make sure that we incorporate the whole of the mode—Religion—and not just part of it—Christianity.

We will need to develop this final point further in due course, but first let us look at some of the assumptions which underlie the different titles given to religious teaching in schools.

"Scripture" implies that the intention or aim of the subject is to provide the child with an opportunity to "read, mark, learn and inwardly digest" passages from the Jewish and Christian Scriptures —even if their content is largely unintelligible to him. The justification for this approach is ecclesiastical/spiritual; it rests on the belief that the Bible is the revealed Word of God and as such should be taught to the child. The aim, therefore, is to provide the child with "spiritual edification" and lead him to a confessional commitment to the Christian faith. It is apparent that for the vast majority of pupils this approach only serves to add to their confusion about religion, promote boredom and reinforce their belief that religion has very little relevance to "real" life. Despite the title—"Scripture"—it is assumed that the Qur'an, the Bhagavad Gita, the Granth, Buddhist Scriptures and so on are to be excluded.

"Religious Knowledge" or *R.K.* has much in common with "Scripture". The title, however, implies the learning of a body of "factual information" associated with religious belief—Jewish/ Christian belief. It often implies, too, the learning of "religious beliefs" as if they were pieces of factual information. The latter constitutes indoctrination. For the most part the aims of R.K. are the same as those given for "Scripture" and once again "knowledge" of other faiths is assumed to be unnecessary.

"Religious Instruction" or *R.I.* implies the one-way process of *instructing* the child in a body of "religious knowledge"—i.e. Jewish/Christian beliefs. Not only is it questionable to put the words "religious" and "knowledge" together (can we speak about "knowledge" in religion in the same way as we speak about "knowledge" in History or Physics, Geography or French?), but the verb "to instruct" is best reserved for facts and skills. (Again, what are the "facts" of religion? Do we include beliefs? If so, do we teach beliefs as if they were facts? To do so would be to indoctrinate). The aims of R.I., then, have much in common with the aims of R.K. and Scripture.

"Divinity", often adopted in grammar schools, smacks of academic pretentiousness. It is a title which implies that lessons

18

are spent in learned discourse about the nature of the Divine and other theological technicalities. The aim here would appear to be that of promoting "theological" understanding—a reasonable aim —but as courses are usually watered-down versions of the type of theological syllabus offered in theological colleges for intending ministers of religion, the child's "theological" understanding remains much as it was—extremely limited. The title further serves to reinforce the child's belief that religion and life are mutually exclusive. Often though, "Divinity" is used as an academically respectable synonym for "Scripture", R.K. and R.I. and in terms of content and approach there is little to choose between them. It is rare to find that consideration of Hindu, Muslim and Buddhist concepts of the "divine" feature in "Divinity".

"Scripture", "R.K.", "R.I." and "Divinity" therefore, are titles which beg a large number of philosophical questions and typify, in the majority of our schools, approaches to religious teaching which are narrowly Bible-based or Bible-centred. They reflect an assumption that religious teaching should be Christian, should lead children towards a Christian commitment and that the Bible is the text-book "par excellence" for achieving these ends. In a recently published Schools Council Working Paper (Number 36, *Religious Education in Secondary Schools,* p 4), three aims which typify what the report calls "The Confessional or dogmatic approach" to religious teaching are recorded. These are :

1   "The aim is not simply to present the Bible as a record of historical events but to bring children into an encounter with Jesus Christ . . ."

    (North Western C.S.E. Board R.K. syllabus)

2   "The theme is Christian discipleship . . . which may be defined as a way of life based upon faith in Jesus Christ whom God sent to be our Deliverer and through whom man can enter into a special relationship with God."

    (East Midlands C.S.E. Board R.K. syllabus)

3   "This syllabus aims at presenting to young people the challenge of the personality of Christ . . ."

    (West Yorks and Lindsey C.S.E. R.K. syllabus)

Can aims such as these be accepted as being educationally valid within a state system of education serving a pluralist, multi-racial and multi-cultural society?

Although these three aims are taken from recent "teacher-based" C.S.E. syllabuses considerable doubt about the Bible-centred "Confessional" approach has been expressed for some time. The mid 1960's saw the revision of a number of Agreed Syllabuses by L.E.A.'s in terms of the capacities, needs and interests of children. In like vein the Newsom (1963) and Plowden (1967) reports advocated a more liberal or "open-ended" approach to religious teaching and were not unsympathetic towards extending the content to include, though marginally, faiths and ideologies other than the Christian one. There was also a concern expressed that recent findings of educational research should lead to improved methods and techniques of teaching religion. The work of Dr R. J. Goldman led to a much greater appreciation of the difficulties that children have in forming religious concepts, and consequently attempts were made to devise schemes and materials which would assist children in this area of cognitive development. (See Chapter 4.)

This replacement of the Bible-centred approach by the Child-centred approach marked an important advance in re-appraising religious teaching in schools. There was, however, very little attention given to working out an educationally acceptable philosophy to underlie this new "developmental" approach to religious education. In other words, the thinking began with *content* rather than with *aims,* and not surprisingly the syllabuses produced in the 1960's and many of the child-centred schemes and materials published at the same time, are now being subjected to much criticism. The central objection to them is that they are still confessional in both outlook and approach; like the earlier Bible-based syllabuses they see the aim of religious teaching in terms of leading the child towards a confessional commitment to the Christian faith. This objection is made even more legitimate by the fact that the "across-subject" approach, with its emphasis on the child's own experiences, tends to "disguise" its concern to inculcate a Christian view of man and the world. Non-Christians are justified, then, in seeing this approach as being an even more insidious form of indoctrination than the more openly confessional approach outlined earlier.

The Schools Council Working Paper on R.E., therefore, refers to this approach to religious teaching as "The Neo-Confessional or Neo-Dogmatic approach". Below are a number of statements, some quoted in the Working Paper, which are typical of the sort of aims that are consistent with this approach.

1 "I would lead children to integrate all they are learning and doing in all subjects within a world view of God as creator and as the person who cares about his people . . ."
   (R. J. Goldman, *Readiness for Religion,* p 197.)

2 "Christianity should be taught because it is true; because it answers the deepest needs of human nature, and without a

20

knowledge of the love of God and a relationship with him men and women will live impoverished lives . . ."

(R. J. Goldman, *Readiness for Religion*, p 59.)

3 "This syllabus is not only concerned with Christianity as an abstract concept but with what it means in every sense to be a Christian and to be religiously committed."

(Inner London Agreed Syllabus, *Learning for Life*, 1968.)

4 "It is the prime object of religious education—to awaken children to the spiritual dimension, to show that religion belongs to life, to show that the life Jesus lived, His death and resurrection, and the stories which He told are of present importance because they are eternal; . . . to open a path to a freely chosen commitment to the way of life that millions have trod through so many centuries; to make the Bible live again as the Word of God to His world."

(Kent Council of R.E., *A Handbook of Thematic Material*, 1968.)

5 "Children should be taught to know and love God and to practise in the school community the virtues appropriate to their age and environment."

(Plowden Report, *Children and Their Primary Schools*, 1967.)

6 "Children should not be confused by being taught to doubt before faith is established."

(Plowden Report.)

Can aims such as these be accepted as being educationally valid within a state system of education serving a pluralist, multi-racial and multi-cultural society?

From this brief examination of the Confessional and Neo-Confessional approaches to religious teaching, it should be apparent that the main *educational* objection to both of them is that they see the aim of religious teaching in terms of leading the child towards a confessional commitment to the Christian faith. The reason why they adopt this aim is that they assume that the task of the school in relation to religious teaching is identical with that of the Church. Thus, the first step towards developing an approach to religious teaching which is educationally valid is to recognise that the roles of the state school and the Church are different. How do their respective roles differ?

People attend Church, and a particular denomination of the

Church, voluntarily; they go for the purpose of being *instructed* in those aspects of the Christian faith which are believed by its *adherents* to be necessary for their salvation. In short, they go expecting either to be initiated into Christian faith and belief or to have their already accepted Christian commitment sustained and deepened. Under such circumstances—*adult* circumstances—it is entirely appropriate that the religious teaching they receive in Church is both "confessional" in outlook and doctrinal and denominational in content.

Children, on the other hand, do not attend school voluntarily, and, in spite of the conscience clause (of which many parents are ignorant) are a captive audience in religious education lessons. They are also an immature audience. The vast majority, therefore, either by virtue of their pluralistic background or their age, are uncommitted to religious belief. To use these circumstances to *instruct* children, especially young children, in the tenets of the Christian faith with the intention of moving them towards a religious commitment is as questionable educationally and morally as it would be to instruct them in the tenets of Marxism with the intention of moving them towards a political commitment. It is not that Christianity or Marxism should be avoided in the state school classroom—far from it—but that in dealing with these subjects the emphasis should not be placed on "instructing children in" a particular faith or ideology with a view to securing their commitment, but on "educating children for" an *understanding* of *Faiths and Ideologies* of which Christianity and Marxism are but two of many existing examples. Once again we see the importance of incorporating the whole mode of thought and awareness in the curriculum rather than just one aspect of it. In short, the state school, unlike the Church, has the responsibility of *educating children in Religion and in Religious Understanding.*

This awareness of the need to distinguish between the respective roles of the state school and Church and to focus attention on Religion and Religious Understanding has led, in recent years, to the development of two main lines of approach to religious teaching, both of which abandon the confessional standpoint. The first of these has been called "The Personal Quest approach" and it is largely associated with the names of Harold Loukes, Edwin Cox and Colin Alves.

This is an approach which sees religion as being concerned primarily with providing an interpretation of life in terms of meaning and purpose. "Religious Understanding" therefore, is an awareness and appreciation of the religious interpretation of life, especially the importance it assigns to a sense of mystery. On this basis Religious Education is seen as providing children with an opportunity to examine the "religious interpretation of life" and engage in a *personal* quest for meaning, purpose and value. Set out below are a number of statements which indicate aims consistent with this view.

1　"The aim of religious education in a county school is to enable a boy or girl to have a proper understanding of what is meant by a religious approach to life. . . . It is not the purpose of religious education in the county school to bring about a commitment to the Christian faith . . ."

Social Morality Council,
(*Moral and Religious Education in County Schools*, 1970 p 13.)

2　"The aim of religious education should be to explore the place and significance of religion in human life and so to make a distinctive contribution to each pupil's search for a faith by which to live."

(Church of England Commission on R.E. in Schools—The Durham Commission— *The Fourth R*, 1970.)

3　"There is a growing feeling that R.E. ought to be, in the jargon of today, 'open-ended'. This means it should have as its aim the giving to children of a religious view of life and then allowing them freely to make up their minds how that view shall express itself in belief and practice."

(Edwin Cox,
Changing Aims in Religious Education, 1966.)

4　"The aim of R.E. is to help pupils to understand the nature of our present secular, pluralistic society, to help them to think rationally about the state and place of religion in it, to enable them to choose objectively and on sound criteria between the many conflicting religious statements that are made in a pluralistic society, and to work out for themselves, and to be able cogently to defend, their own religious position or their rejection of the possibility of having one."

(Edwin Cox, *Aims in R.E.*, a paper given to the London Society of Jews and Christians, 1970.)

5　"The purpose of religious education is to help our pupils build up a worthwhile sense of direction in life, to help them achieve a valid perspective on the whole business of living . . . Religious education is fundamentally concerned with the education of attitudes, not with the study of cultures, nor with the assessment of systems of belief (though, of course, both the latter play their part in the former). It is concerned with the pupil's development of a faith in which to travel through life."

(Colin Alves, an article in
The Times Educational Supplement,
24 March, 1967.)

6 "Religious education, in brief, is about the life our children learn about, the depth of the life they learn about on the surface, the whole of the life they learn about in fragments. At root religious education is a conversation between older and younger on the simple question, What is life like? . . . Life . . . can be encountered only in dialogue, between persons who have had some experience in living it and persons who are beginning to engage in it; and the dialogue will turn on what he and they have found or can find together."

(Harold Loukes,
New Ground in Christian Education, 1965.)

Especially valuable in these statements of aims is the recognition of the crucial importance of the child's own experiences as the starting points for religious education. *Mature* religious concepts, as expressed in and through traditional religious symbols and language, are essentially the outcome of man's reflection on his own and other's life experiences. To begin the child on this process of reflection is to involve him in the same activity, though at a simpler level, that is characteristic of the theologian. Thus the subject-matter of religious education becomes life itself and the aim to help the child to analyse his own experiences at greater depth and with clearer insight. (See *New Ground in Christian Education*, Chapters 8 and 11.) This approach coheres firmly within the "child-centred" view of education for which there is strong philosophical and psychological (i.e. educational) support. It would seem, then, that so far this approach can be justified on educational grounds.

There are, however, aspects of "The Personal Quest approach" which remain questionable. Edwin Cox ends his book, *Changing Aims in Religious Education*, with the following words:

At the present time of uncertainty and rethinking, it (i.e. R.E.) must be a search in which teacher and student "feel after truth and find it", as far as their experience and understanding allow. But it is a search based on the belief that the past experience of the human race can provide helpful signposts, that honest thinking can lead to truth, and that life has been given us with point and purpose by a personal power greater than man, and is not "a tale told by an idiot, full of sound and fury, signifying nothing".

Thus, despite its "open-endedness" this approach has an underlying premise that life is "given . . . with a . . . purpose by a personal power". Is this so very different from the "world view of God as creator" within which Goldman would lead children to integrate all they are learning and doing? (See p 20) Certainly Cox is anxious to avoid any suggestion that R.E. should steer children towards a confessional commitment, and yet he would appear to entertain a very strong hope that the child's "quest" will lead him to this position. The same impression is given by his reference to "The inculcation of favourable attitudes" to religion. Is it not possible to avoid "loading" this approach with a particular set of beliefs and values and simply concentrate on providing the child with an opportunity to explore a whole number of alternative "frames of reference", atheistic as well as theistic? In that way the approach would pay more than lip service to the notions of "personal" and "quest". In all fairness, however, it should be mentioned that Cox advocates the inclusion of world religions and atheistic philosophies in R.E. though he weights the syllabus, especially in the Primary school, very heavily with specifically Christian teaching.

A similar criticism may be made of Harold Loukes' position, even though his definition of "religion" and "religious" is very broad. Although he refuses to restrict "religion" to one subject and would lead children to explore the "religious dimension" of all subjects and all experiences, he sees the Christian tradition as providing the framework within which this exploration should take place. Is it realistic to expect children not to see this as advocating the Christian interpretation as *the* interpretation towards which life's experiences inevitably point? His particular conception of "The Problem Approach" with four stages—that is : raising the problem; analysis of the problem; the Christian judgment on the problem; application of the Christian judgment (See *Teenage Religion*, Chapters 4 and 5)—would appear to reinforce this view. One wonders how Loukes can insist that "Convinced Christians can claim no monopoly of the search for living truth" and yet only use the Christian tradition in his teaching. By implication, then, the "Personal Quest" becomes a "Christian Quest".

Before leaving this approach it is, perhaps, relevant to ask how far it is legitimate, from an educational point of view, to speak of R.E. as making a distinctive contribution to "each pupil's search for a faith by which to live" or to "the pupil's development of a faith in which to travel through life". Here we encounter an underlying premise which many would wish to question—namely, that it is both necessary and desirable that a pupil has a *faith* to guide him through life. Two points may be made. Firstly, if the word "faith" is being used in these quotations as a synonym for "philosophy of life" or "life-style" then once again we see the need for providing the child with an opportunity in R.E. to encounter and explore the broadest possible range of philosophies rather than a single "religious" position. If the word "faith" is equated purely with religious belief, even in a broad sense, then we are restricting the child to one distinctive world view. This, as we have seen, has questionable educational validity. Secondly, although education is concerned with assisting the total development of the child in which attitudes play a considerable part, in matters of belief it is just as questionable to infer that there is merit in having a "faith"—any faith—as it is to infer the merits of a particular faith.

The nub of the problem would appear to be that even in the case of "open-ended" approaches there is still an underlying assumption that R.E. should not simply be concerned with helping the child to find his way about Religious Understanding as a Form of Understanding, so enabling him to view life from yet another angle, but that in some sense it is part of R.E.'s responsibility to convince him that if he adopts a religious position he will be all the better for it. There is a strong case for R.E. in state schools abandoning this latter responsibility, for that belongs to the child himself, and concentrating entirely on the former. If R.E. teachers could adopt the attitude of a shopkeeper with wares in his window which he is anxious for customers to examine, appreciate and even "try on" but not feel under any obligation to buy, then many of the educational problems connected with R.E. would disappear. It is this attitude which underlies what the Schools Council Working Paper No. 36 calls, "The Phenomenological or undogmatic approach", and it is to a consideration of this that we now turn.

This approach, as its title suggests, takes "Religion" as its field of study and seeks to show what is distinctive and unique about religion as a (unique) "mode of thought and awareness". In this sense it meets the first of the three educational criteria, outlined earlier (p 16) which it was suggested were necessary if a subject is to be included in the curriculum on valid educational grounds. In other words, it is an approach which recognises that the study of religion should be governed by the same educational principles as any other subject. Thus, aims consistent with this approach may be expressed in the following ways:

1   "The aim of R.E. is to promote understanding of the nature of religion itself as a distinctive way of interpreting experience".

2   "The aim of R.E. is that of creating in pupils 'certain capacities to understand and think about religion'."

(N. Smart, *Secular Education and the Logic of Religion*, 1968.)

Just as it is the task of the teacher of mathematics or history to show what is unique about mathematics and history as modes of thought and to help pupils to think mathematically or historically, so it is the task of the teacher of religion to show what is unique about religion and to help pupils to think religiously or, a better term, theologically. This is entirely in keeping with the view of education as "the initiation of young people into what is worthwhile" which we examined in Chapter 2. So far, then, there are no educational objections to this approach.

Professor Ninian Smart, who is a leading exponent of the approach, has been careful to point out that the "Phenomenological approach" to religion is not only concerned with providing information about the practices and beliefs of different religions. In his words, "R.E. must transcend the informative". Consequently it is inaccurate to identify this approach with, say, the approach advocated by Professor Paul Hirst, namely that R.E. should be concerned with "teaching about religion" rather than "teaching religion". This latter view sees R.E. as an academic exercise, dispassionate and objective. Smart, on the other hand, argues that one is not initiated into an *understanding* of religion if one knows only its "explicit" or external features. Initiation demands an awareness or personal experience of the "implicit" or inward elements of religion—like feelings of awe, wonder and love and the need to express these feelings in worship. Furthermore, it is the "implicit" or "feeling" side of religion which evokes questions about life's ultimate significance, its values, meaning and purpose. To ignore the "implicit" side of religion is to remove from examination and consideration that aspect which provides the very basis and reason for religion's existence. It is also to make the aim of initiating a person into Religious Understanding, in the fullest sense of the term, an impossible one.

On the surface these observations about the importance of initiating pupils into the feeling side of religion appear to imply a process not dissimilar to that of conversion. And yet, in subjects like music, art, literature and drama we have exactly the same concern—to initiate pupils into the "feeling" dimension of these arts. In these fields we would not dream of questioning the educational validity of such an approach as we recognise that without it we can never hope to create true understanding in our pupils. The same is precisely true of religion. Just as the intention of a music, art or poetry "appreciation" lesson is to promote sensitivity, on the part of the

27

pupils, to the "essence" and "nature" of art so a lesson dealing with the implicit side of religion should have the intention of promoting a similar type of sensitivity to the essence and nature of religion—not for the purpose of conversion or for securing commitment but for promoting understanding.

A further concern of an "appreciation" lesson is that of helping pupils to learn how to "step into the shoes" of, say, a composer or a poet and see and feel what he, the composer or the poet, sees and feels. This too is an essential pre-requisite to understanding any art form or the work of an artist. So it is of religion. Only when we can "bracket out" ourselves, our pre-conceived notions and our particular values and concentrate on what, for example, a Muslim feels when he prays to Allah or a Jew feels when he celebrates the Feast of Passover, will we begin to appreciate and understand the essence of Islam and Judaism. In none of this is it legitimate to say that we are trying to *convert* pupils to a particular artistic or religious position. In art appreciation we do not concentrate exclusively on the paintings of one artist and in religion we ensure that a wide range of faiths and ideologies are represented. At all times we should be trying to help pupils to do far more than *describe* the piece of music, the painting, the poem and the act of worship—we should be encouraging them to ask, "What is it that is important to him? What sort of feelings and beliefs does he have that prompt him to do as he does? What is his intention?"

Professor Smart, whose work and thought underlies much of the Schools Council Working Paper, emphasises the importance, to the phenomenological or undogmatic approach, of *presenting* religion in such ways as "to bring out the meanings and values to the participants". It is an approach which recognises that religion is multi-dimensional and that an effective study of religion must contain reference to at least six inter-related and inter-dependent dimensions. Smart lists these as : doctrinal, mythological, ethical, ritual, experiential and social. He contends that each one of these provides a different starting point for the study of a given religion. In addition, however, attention needs to be given to non-theistic or atheistic philosophies for these too are belief-systems which should be understood. Although "comparison" is not an essential feature of the phenomenological approach to religion, certainly in the senior forms of the Secondary school pupils should be given an opportunity to face up to such a question as, "Is there a dichotomy between religious and secular belief systems or is it that they are part of a continuum and that the difference between the two is to be found in the way that they *express* their beliefs?" Any intelligent attempt to answer this question needs to be based on a clear and accurate understanding of the nature of religion, of the distinctive characteristics of religion and of individual faiths, and the particu·

lar bases upon which secular ideologies rest. The phenomenological approach is designed to promote this sort of understanding.

We now need to consider how far the Phenomenological or undogmatic approach to R.E. provides educational justification for including the subject in the school curriculum. Even the most cursory glance at the *aims* of the approach enables us to see how completely *educational* they are in comparison with the aims of other approaches. There can be no doubt that this approach has the definite intention of *educating pupils in Religion and Religious Understanding* and as such fully deserves the title *"Religious Education"*. We have already seen that in taking "Religion" as its field of study and in seeking to show what is distinctive and unique about religion as a "mode of thought and awareness" the approach meets the first of the three educational criteria outlined earlier. By implication it subsequently meets the second criterion—that of widening and deepening the child's cognitive perspective in a unique and valuable way and so contributing to his total development as a person. But what about the third criterion? Using the phenomenological approach, can this subject be taught in ways which ensure understanding and actively foster the child's capacity to think for himself? It would appear that in this respect the approach may encounter certain difficulties.

The first of these is to relate the approach to the capacities of younger children—those in the Infant and Junior schools in particular. At first sight the phenomenological approach appears to lack what is so commendable in Loukes' approach—appeal to the child's own situation and experiences. And yet, with care, every one of the six dimensions of religion (doctrinal, mythological, ethical, ritual, experiential and social) can be related to the world of the Primary school child. Of course some dimensions can more easily be used than others. For example, the mythological, the ritual and the experiential dimensions provide a wealth of material for use with young children. We must try and avoid the notion that, in the Infant and Lower Junior school, one needs to be teaching distinct belief systems, each with its own personal identity and characteristics. Rather one is teaching children to become aware of the phenomenon called "Religion" and how it grows out of our reflection on our own experiences of life. Different aspects of different faiths are used as illustrations of this and not as distinct religions to be "studied" in an academic sense. We shall see later how important it is to approach the content of R.E. *developmentally* and so cater for the changing experiences and capacities of the child. In this way the phenomenological approach becomes a "child-centred" approach with all its attendant educational benefits.

The second difficulty—indeed the major difficulty—concerns the teacher. The ideal teacher, so far as the phenomenological approach is concerned, is one who is ready to portray sympathetically and without bias *any* viewpoint which he may be required to teach. Professor Smart writes :

> The test of one who is teaching reasonably in a society such as ours is openness, not what his commitments are. The Humanist teacher should give some imaginative grasp of religion, just as the Christian teacher should be able to elicit from his pupils an appreciation of the forces of Humanism. The Christian should be able to teach Buddhist studies and to do so without judgmental attitudes . . .
>
> (*Secular Education and the Logic of Religion,* p 98.)

These observations, more directly related perhaps to the secondary school teacher, illustrate the considerable need for change in two areas; in the theological education and training of teachers and in the attitudes of teachers to religious teaching in schools.

It is useful here to distinguish between the specialist teacher of R.E. who tends to orientate towards the Secondary school situation, and the non-specialist R.E. teacher, i.e. the one who has not studied religion as a Main subject at College or University but who is expected to take R.E. with his or her class. With regard to the former, the phenomenological approach is likely to make much greater and broader demands on his knowledge than his traditional theological education is able to accommodate. A course which provides an opportunity for detailed study of Biblical Theology, Greek and Hebrew, Ecclesiastical History, Christian Doctrine and perhaps Christian Ethics and only a very limited insight into the Philosophy, Sociology and Psychology of Religion and World Religions, is, as far as the phenomenological approach is concerned, biased in the wrong direction. Happily, some Universities and Colleges of Education are now becoming aware of this and modifying their courses. With regard to the non-specialist teacher of R.E. there is the very real problem that the phenomenological approach lies beyond their competence—unless, of course, they are prepared to read widely in World Religions, Philosophy of Religion and so on. In addition to the considerable demands that the approach makes on knowledge it also requires a high degree of creativity, imagination and flexibility on the part of the teacher if it is to be taught successfully. Certainly this approach abolishes the view that "Anyone can teach R.E." ! Possible solutions to this problem include the radical reappraisal of professional R.E. courses in Colleges and the design of a "two-level" phenomenological approach, the first level being within the competence of the non-specialist and the second more suited to the specialist teacher.

If anything, the problem of changing teachers' attitudes to religious teaching in school is the more crucial one. Educational research has shown, time and time again, that the success of innovations (mixed-ability teaching, integrated day, family-grouping and so on) is determined to a considerable extent by teachers' attitudes. If a teacher believes in a form of organisation or in the capacity of a child to succeed, his expectations tend to be self-fulfilling. The need for openness and breadth of vision that the phenomenological approach to R.E. demands requires an adjustment in attitude on the part of many teachers. The change in emphasis and content away from Christianity towards Religion is likely to be seen by many teachers as unnecessary and undesirable. The acceptance of World Religions as an *integral part* of R.E. *at all stages* is likely to take time and be the cause of disputes and disagreements among school staffs. But the longer this takes the more our society becomes pluralist, mult-cultural and multi-racial and so the need for change becomes even more necessary.

Whichever method is adopted, one must ultimately, in principle, regard Christianity as a World Religion, and teach it as such. The "half-way stage" of treating Hinduism, Islam, and perhaps Buddhism as appendices, is unsatisfactory. Agreed that Christianity is the predominant religion of our culture, and the one which has influenced it most. This will influence the Religion syllabus in terms of content : it must not be allowed to influence it in terms of approach.

> (W. Owen Cole : "Some approaches to the teaching of World Religions in Schools", in *Education for a Multi-Cultural Society; World Religions: Aids for Teachers,* Shap Working Party, published by The Community Relations Commission, January 1972.)

Further reading

Education
R. G. Cave : *An introduction to Curriculum Development* (Ward Lock, 1971).
D. Jenkins, R. Pring and A. Harris : *Curriculum Philosophy and Design* (The Open University, 1972).
A. and S. Nicholls : *Developing a Curriculum: A Practical Guide* (George, Allen & Unwin, 1972).
H. Taba : *Curriculum Development; Theory and Practice* (Harcourt, Brace & World, 1962).
D. K. Wheeler : *Curriculum Process* (ULP, 1967).

Education and Religion
D. W. Gundry : *The Teacher and the World Religions* (James

Clarke & Co. Ltd, 1968).

J. R. Hinnells (Ed.) : *Comparative Religion in Education* (Oriel Press, 1970).

E. G. Parrinder (Ed.) : *Teaching about Religions* (Harrap, 1972).

C. Macy (Ed.) : *Let's Teach Them Right* (Pemberton Books, 1969).

N. Smart : *Secular Education and the Logic of Religion* (Faber, 1968).

J. Wilson : *Education in Religion and the Emotions* (Heinemann, 1971).

Articles

W. Owen Cole : "Religion in the Multi-Faith School", *Learning for Living*, Vol. 12, No. 2, November 1972.

P. H. Hirst : "Christian Education : A Contradiction in Terms", *Learning for Living*, Vol. 11, No. 4, March 1972.

N. Smart : "Comparative Religion Clichés", *Learning for Living*, Vol. 12, No. 2, November 1972.

J. Wilson : "Religious Education and Ultimate Questions", *Learning for Living*, Vol. 11, No. 5, May 1972.

See also Vol. 11, No. 1, September 1971 *Learning for Living*, for a number of articles on Curriculum Development and R.E.

Chapter 4

The Contribution of Development Psychology to Religious Education

In accordance with the Curriculum Process Model, set out on p 15, our consideration of *Aims* needs to be followed by *"Recognition of Pupil Characteristics"*. We shall find, when we begin to plan R.E. lessons, that this will require careful analysis of the needs, interests and experiences of the particular children in our class so that we can devise lessons or "learning experiences" which are educationally relevant to them. In addition, however, we will need to be aware of the different ways in which children think at different stages of their development. Only when we have this awareness will we be able to select content and methods which have meaning for the children and which serve to foster their development. This relationship between children's thinking and *how* and *what* we teach will become apparent if we look briefly at the work of Jean Piaget in the field of developmental psychology.

The value of Piaget's work for education is to be found in the insight it provides into *how* and *why* a child's thinking differs *qualitatively* from that of an adult.

A How

Piaget's research has led him to posit the existence of *Five Stages* in the development of a child's thinking, each with its own distinct characteristics. In the summary below it is important to see the ages given for each stage as rough approximations and not as rigid demarcation points.

1 *Sensori-motor stage* (birth to 18 months/2 years)

The child:
(a) Exercises reflexes.
(b) Co-ordinates actions and perceptions (1-4 months—chances on an action and repeats it; 5-8 months—repeats actions that change his environment, some anticipation

33

of his own actions; 9-12 months—sets aside an object to reach another; 12-18 months—explores and experiments overtly; 19-24 months—covert rather than overt trial and error—actions now internalised).

(c) Learns that objects are conserved (i.e. that an object continues to exist when it is out of sight).

2 *Pre-conceptual or pre-operational stage* (18 months to 4/5 years)

(a) Represents one thing by another (i.e. developing the capacity for symbolic function, especially with the onset of language. This means that he can grasp a number of events as a whole and that his range of thought extends outside his immediate environment).

(b) Plays games of pretence.

(c) Learns letters; may read and write.

(d) Is still unable to form accurate concepts (i.e. classify objects and so on, and use the "class" name. Thinking is *transductive,* i.e. if two objects are the same in one (obvious) respect then they are considered to be identical in all respects. This confusion of genetic and specific concepts may be seen when a child misapplies the term "Daddy" for "man" or "dog" for "sheep" and so on).

(e) Thinking is also egocentric (i.e. he makes experiences conform to his view).

3 *Intuitive stage* (4/5 years to 7 years)

(a) Forms concepts in and through action (i.e. through first-hand experience).

(b) Depends on perceptual judgments (i.e. he "centres" on some striking but not necessarily important feature, and is unable to "decentre". Thinking is not reversible—he cannot work backwards and so discover faults in reasoning).

(c) Sees only one relationship at a time. (Hence his inability to reverse.)

4 *Concrete Operations stage* (7 years to 11/12 years)

(a) Depends more on mental "operations" than upon physical actions, though the latter persist.

(b) Forms classes and series. (The child is now able to "reverse" thought and "decentre" away from deceptive perceptions. He uses both inductive and deductive logic but such use is limited to *concrete* situations, actions,

34

sensory data and so on. Thus, *conceptual thought* is now possible provided the concepts can be demonstrated concretely.)
(c) Can hold two relationships in his mind at once.
(d) Corrects distortions in thinking (due to over-reliance on appearances) by reference to past experiences. Conservation now possible, e.g. substance (7/8); length (7/8); time (8/9); weight (9/10); velocity (9/10); area (9/10); volume (11/12).

5 *Formal Operations stage* (11/12/13 years onwards)

(a) Forms and uses abstract concepts (i.e. reasons increasingly in verbal propositions).
(b) Makes hypotheses which he tests.
(c) Plans ahead.
(d) Looks for general laws and principles which he can apply.

B Why are there these stages in the development of a child's thinking?

The rationale underlying Piaget's developmental psychology is his *schematic* view of the nature of motor and mental operations. This emphasises the importance of certain adaptive processes which are brought to bear by the child on his experiences. He considers that such processes are the result of the interplay of what he calls "Assimilation" and "Accommodation" which are influenced by both maturational and experiential factors. Through this mental activity the child builds up "Schemas" and all new experiences are brought within, and interpreted by existing schemas (acting as a unitary mass). Although the schemas or schemata are dynamic (i.e. capable of modification and change) they are by nature "progressive" (i.e. they are built up through assimilation and accommodation from simple beginnings to more complex, highly integrated entities). In other words, by "Abstracting" what is common from each new experience the child needs to "reconstructure" (Piaget's term) the existing schemas.

Thus, when faced with a new problem of learning, the child approaches it by imposing upon it an "anticipatory schema". If this coincides closely with the demands of the present problem the solution will be reached easily. If there is less common ground the schema will need to be altered or, in Piaget's words, "reconstructured". To do this the new elements will need to be assimilated and this in turn will require the abandonment of some former elements (i.e. the process called "accommodation"). The reconstruc-

35

turing will be complete when the new learning is mastered. The changed schema will now be more comprehensive and more relevant to the solution of the new problem as well as to the earlier ones. In its turn this new schema will become an anticipatory schema for the solution of the next new problem and so the process continues ad infinitum. Thus thinking and learning advances by a series of schemas which increase in complexity and flexibility as they abstract, assimilate and accommodate new elements.

The concept of conservation applied to substance affords an excellent example of this process. If we present a child whose thinking is characteristic of pre-conceptual stages with a ball of plasticine, roll it into a sausage and ask him, "Is there more plasticine in the ball, or in the sausage, or is there the same amount in both? he will answer, "More in the sausage" or "More in the ball", depending on whichever happens to *appear* larger to him. The child's response is prompted, therefore, by his centering on one particular perceptual feature—length, for example—and ignoring others—weight and mass, for example. This is an illustration of "egocentric" thinking. Consequently, if he is asked to justify his choice he will do so by words such as, "Because it is". His inability to "reverse" thought prevents him from "translating" the sausage back into the ball even if he has observed how the sausage was formed. Furthermore, adult verbal explanation will not cause him to modify his view. In other words, his anticipatory schema is too rigid and defies modification. With time, though, maturational factors will contribute to the onset of reversibility and to the capacity to hold two relationships in his mind. This, combined with his experience of plasticine and allied substances, will eventually cause him to become aware of the inappropriateness of his explanations. By abstracting features from his experiences and relating them to the task of the ball and the sausage, he will reconstruct his schema. Thus he eventually accepts the concept of conservation. By this time he has reached the stage of Concrete Operations.

One further illustration, this time characteristic of the thinking of a child in the Concrete Operations stage, may serve to clarify what is, after all, a complex theory. A child of seven/nine might be asked to say what is wrong with the following statement. "In an old graveyard in Spain, they have discovered a small skull believed to have been that of Christopher Columbus when he was ten years old." Although a child in this stage is able to put two or more aspects of a situation together and hold them in his mind at once, and although he is able to examine statements for inconsistencies he is *still* restricted to *concrete* facts and cannot move away from the *contents* of the concrete situation. Thus his reply is likely to be along the following lines : "It is wrong because you should not dig up graveyards, they are holy places."

What are the educational implications of this theory of "Schematic Learning"?

Although Piaget's findings have implications for *what* we teach and when we should teach it, by far the most important outcome of his work is the insight he provides into *how* we should teach something. Without attempting to answer this question fully, we might note the following points :

1   If the child learns "schematically" he needs to be taught "schematically". Subject matter, even purely "factual" subject matter, needs to be presented in such a way that the child may discern its "structure"—the way in which facts relate within the subject, how these cohere within concepts and how concepts relate to form principles. Teaching which reveals structure greatly assists the child with the process of abstraction, assimilation and accommodation—the basis of learning. It also assists "transfer" of understanding both within a subject and between subjects. Piaget's findings have presented teachers with the challenge of devising new methods and techniques of teaching which reveal structure—a challenge which so far has been taken up most readily and successfully in the field of mathematics teaching (e.g. the Cuisenaire and Dienes structural systems).

2   Piaget's work (like that of J. S. Bruner) has high-lighted the central position which is occupied in thinking and learning by concept-formation. Successful learning is characterised by the ability to form accurate concepts, be they numerical, linguistic, historical, geographical, scientific or religious. Indeed, whether or not a child is able to think numerically, linguistically, scientifically or theologically depends on his ability to form, understand and use concepts intelligently. Thus, Piaget has indicated to teachers the outstanding need for them to first of all identify the key-concepts within a subject and then devise effective means of helping pupils to develop them. It is regrettable that in many academic fields, including theology, very little thought and work has been expended on this crucial task.

From these observations it may be useful to list what appear to be the essential tasks of the teacher in assisting the child's cognitive development :

1   To identify the key-concepts within a subject. (In fairness to the class teacher it should be pointed out that this task, because of its great complexity, is one that should be under-

taken by the leading experts of a subject or academic discipline, e.g. University Professors and research workers. We shall see later how great the need is for professional theologians to involve themselves in this priority work in the field of Theology and Religion.)

2 To present subject matter "structurally" with particular emphasis on concept-formation, ensuring that both content and methods of presentation are appropriate to the developmental levels of children in their class. (Hence the importance of knowing and being able to recognise the characteristics of Piaget's five developmental stages.)

3 To bring the child face to face with the inadequacy of his existing schemata.

4 To offer him guidance in the process of abstracting, assimilating and accommodating. (For example, by presenting a concept in as many different ways as possible and providing for the use of the concept in different and varied situations. Hence the value of the "Spiral" curriculum.)

In conclusion, one should note the implications of Piaget's work for curriculum development. We have already seen how his findings have immediate relevance to the content and this will influence, even if only indirectly, choices of objectives. Patterns of school and classroom organisation also fall within his influence; for example, our present concern with "integration" of curricula has caused the adoption of different grouping procedures all designed to facilitate learning in the ways which we have been examining. Furthermore, Piaget's work has focused attention on the importance of social relations and language to cognitive development; on the necessity of providing the right sort of environment and conditions for maturation; on the importance of *intrinsic* motivation, and, although he does not explicitly advocate activity or experience-based methods, his research would appear to provide for their justification. Clearly modern education owes much to this man.

It now remains for us to attempt to relate these findings in the field of developmental psychology to R.E. We are fortunate in having available the research findings of Dr Ronald Goldman who, starting from Piaget's description of children's thinking, undertook a detailed examination, in the mid-60's, of children's notions about religion in an attempt to discover whether these followed the same pattern. His findings are recorded in his book, *Religious Thinking from Childhood to Adolescence* (R.K.P., 1964). Dr Goldman found that religious thinking does follow Piaget's developmental pattern and that "religious thinking employs the same modes and methods as thinking applied to other fields". He draws the conclusion that "The implications of this fact are very far reaching for religious education", and his later book, *Readiness for Religion* (R.K.P., 1965) represents an attempt to translate those implications into practical terms. Set out below is a summary of Goldman's findings.

It should be noted that Goldman discerns stages between those described by Piaget. A particular feature of religious thinking is the longer period during which Concrete Operations persist and the subsequent delay that this causes in a child reaching the Formal Operations stage. Goldman gives the stages of religious thinking as :

1 Pre-operational/intuitive thought from early childhood to 7/8 years.
2 Concrete Operations stage from 7/8 to 13/14 years.
3 Formal (abstract) Operations stage from 13/14 years onwards. (Here the stages are given in terms of mental rather than chronological age.)

The characteristics of children's religious thinking may be classified for convenience in the following ways :

1 *Pre-Religious Thought* (Infants 5 to 7+ years)

  (a) A fairy-tale level of religion. God, Father Christmas and fairies on an equal footing.
  (b) God is man-like; he is seen in purely physical and human terms.
  (c) Prayer is magical.
  (d) Religious words are used without understanding.
  (e) Physical and fantasy ideas are merged.

Ideas of God

  "God is the man in the moon. He has a round head and he has bent ears. He lives in a round home."
  "I think God might live up in space. I think he might clean up his house sometimes. I think he might eat something like bread and sausages when he is hungry."
  "God is in the sky and you can't see him. He flies around. Sometimes he stops behind a cloud to have something to eat. He goes down to land at night to see shepherds and to talk to them."

  (*Readiness for Religion*, p 80.)

2 *Sub-Religious Thought Stage 1* (Early Juniors 7 to 9 years)

  (a) God beginning to move out of fairy-land.

39

(b) God still seen as a large man with a beard and long white robes.

(c) A superhuman rather than a supernatural God; touchy and unpredictable; sometimes kind and loving but always to be feared.

(d) Jesus and God are frequently confused. Their names are interchangeable.

(e) Little grasp of Jesus as a real man; has the magical aura of God.

(f) Prayer is egocentric and materialistic; but an important and pleasurable experience.

(g) The Bible is taken as literal truth (including images and metaphors). It is a book of stories of long ago and far away and has nothing to do with today.

(h) "The religious" and the "real" world are separate; "the religious" is also separated from other types of experience.

Ideas of God

"He'd see(m) like a man with long hair with a cloak on and blue eyes. Jesus might be with him and they'd be sitting up in heaven."

"He'd have a shirt like, and a rag round his head, maybe with a stick. He'd be kind and he'd be praying."

"He's sitting in heaven in all his glory, on the throne, with angels around him, wearing a white satin robe with Saint John and Saint Peter on the left and right hand. There'd be people what's dead playing golden harps all around."

(*Religious Thinking from Children to Adolescence*, pp 89-90.)

3   *Sub-Religious Thought Stage II* (Late Juniors 9 to 11 years)

(a) God's external appearance less important, anthropomorphic views giving way to supernatural emphasis. But limiting physical ideas still persist, e.g. God speaks with a physical voice.

(b) A great deal of intellectual confusion, especially over the idea of God being everywhere and at one place at one particular time (i.e. transcendence).

(c) Dualisitic confusion unable to be resolved by view of God as "spirit" as this is outside the limits of concrete thinking.

(d) Awareness of conflict between "religious" ideas and the world of reality (e.g. the problem of miracles).

(N.B. Goldman links this stage, which he calls "Late Childhood" with the next stage, called "Pre-Adolescence", as he finds many characteristics similar to both groups. It would appear that for some children the years between 11 and 13 years are a sort of "incubation period" during which they gradually outgrow childish concepts. For others it is a time when childish concepts persist and become the cause of extreme confusion and often the rejection of religion follows from this. Thus, whereas some children move towards "Personal Religious Thought" between 11 and 13, for others it is a stage which might more accurately be seen as a continuation of "Sub-Religious Thought".)

Personal Religious Thought Stage I (Early Secondary 11 to 13 years)

(a) Persistence of dualism.
(b) Consciousness of the absence of God but a feeling that God should be active today.
(c) Still a tendency to think of God in heaven.
(d) Prayer is more altruistic and involves self-examination. A magical element still persists.
(e) Guilt-feelings arising from the idea of a God of vengeance rather than of love.
(f) More realistic view of Jesus; a normal boy who was rather serious-minded.
(g) Belief stronger than unbelief, but the beginning of real doubts.

Views of God

"I see a man with his arms out and a round thing over his head, shining. He'd be about 30 years old, with a beard and clad in white garments. I see him above me in the air."

"He'd be a holy person, living up in heaven and not on earth. He's very, very, old and wise."

"He'd be standing in the clouds, with lots of glory around."

"A wonderful man sitting on a throne of clouds with angles round him, and the sun glittering. A man who teaches what is true. He doesn't seem real because he's too good to be real."

"A piece of sky or something, maybe a cloud with a face on it. God is the sky."

(*Religious Thinking from Childood to Adolescence*, p 90.)

41

(These comments illustrate the difficulty of classifying children's religious thinking at this stage of their development. The last comment represents an attempt to move away from the limitations of anthropomorphism towards elementary symbolism—a feature of the next stage.)

5 *Personal Religious Thought Stage II* (Middle Secondary 13/14 years onwards)

    (a) God is unseen and unseeable.
    (b) Divine communication is mental, internal, subjective, "the voice of conscience".
    (c) Recognition of metaphorical and poetic truth. Symbols seen as symbols.
    (d) Interest in the mission of Jesus.
    (e) Jesus is seen as a good man, as a miracle-worker or as a "Saviour".
    (f) Consciousness of unanswered prayer.

Views of God

Using spiritual concepts
"You can't describe God because he can't be seen. There's just an empty space or spirit."
"God can look like an ordinary person but he can really look like anything and everything."
"God is a ghost-like person, not a clear shape, but a spirit."

Using symbolic concepts
"A loving man, knocking on the heart of a person."
"A shepherd dressed in white, with a sheep in his hands."
"A king sitting on a throne with Jesus beside him."

Using abstract concepts
"An idea or feeling of fatherliness."
"An idea of love."
"Light, because God is supposed to be a perfect being."
(*Religious Thinking from Childhood to Adolescence*, p 91.)

We have already considered Piaget's explanation for the existence of stages in the development of a child's thinking, but how can we account for the obvious difficulties that children have in developing useful religious concepts? Why, for example, is the period of Concrete Operations so long and the onset of Formal Operations so late in this field? What are the particular conceptual problems that religion presents? These are questions which have to be faced up to realistically because the answers will influence approach, content and methods of R.E.

Goldman's investigation is concerned basically with religious thinking as reflected in children's responses to selected Bible passages. In other words, he assumes that a child's ability or lack of ability in discerning *Biblical concepts* is indicative of his ability or lack of ability to form *religious concepts*. This is perhaps a questionable assumption, especially in the light of recent theological opinion—as mentioned in Chapter 2. Goldman seeks justification for his assumption by way of his definition of religion and religious thinking. He accepts William James' definition of religion as "the feelings, the acts and experiences of individual men . . . so far as they apprehend themselves to stand in relation to whatever they may consider the divine" but then goes on to say :

> This divine in our culture is interpreted in terms of deity, and more specifically in terms of the Christian concept of God as love, revealed most fully in the historic fact of the Incarnation. On this definition, religious thinking is thinking directed towards the nature of God, his relationships with men in history, his dealings with men today, his revelation of himself through the inspired literature of the Bible and through the person of Jesus Christ. It follows that the content of religious thinking will be concerned in our society with concepts involving these ideas.
>
> (*Religious Thinking from Childhood to Adolescence*, p 4.)

It is not unrealistic to argue that Goldman's investigation is not into the child's capacity to form religious concepts as much as into his capacity to grasp and interpret first century religious or theological ideas as expressed in and through the language and thought-forms of first century man. In other words, the research is not concerned with the child's ability to communicate his own "feelings, acts and experiences" which might be said to point to an appreciation of dimensions existing in life other than the materialistic ones (i.e. his own notion of religion); nor is it concerned with the question of whether or not children have such an appreciation and engage in this type of reflective thinking. Rather the research is interested only in determining how far and how accurately a child can make sense of a developed and highly complex *interpretation* of man's feelings, acts and experiences which expresses itself in mythological, metaphorical, poetic and occasionally historical categories. It is little wonder, then, that children encounter considerable difficulies in attempting this task.

Not surprisingly Goldman's findings point to the futility, let alone the danger, of attempting to teach fully-developed, formalised religious concepts couched in symbolic language to children before they have reached the stage of Formal Operations. This is what the Bible contains. Thus, if we present a child below, say, the age of 11 with the story of Moses and the burning bush his reliance on perceptual, concrete details (often the unimportant ones) and his inability to deal effectively with any form of expression other than the literal one, cause him to interpret it in crudely materialistic ways. Instead of his gaining an insight into the religious significance of the story—it symbolises an experience in which man is confronted with an awareness of "the numinous" or the "holy"—the child is given the impression that God is exactly as he is in the story. By using such a story or any other story requiring the application of sophisticated interpretative techniques which lie outside the capacity of the child, a teacher is actually reinforcing "childish" concepts rather than helping the child to move beyond them. Such teaching becomes a hindrance to education in religion as it only succeeds in retarding the development of intelligent and creative religious concepts.

Biblical teaching, then, not only makes unrealistic demands on the child but would appear to be a major determinant in causing the religious thinking of many children to remain at concrete operational level. Certainly the fact that the more intellectually gifted children generally pass from one stage to another at an earlier age than their fellows does suggest that intellectual capacity greatly assists development but there is a notable number of intelligent children who attain formal operational thought in all areas except in religion. It is unrealistic to seek an explanation in the notion that success in religious thinking demands possession of a special "religious" factor in the child's cognitive endowment—although K. E. Hyde has shown that the possession of "positive" or sympathetic attitudes to religion does help in this respect. Goldman's tests, as we have already seen, make demands on the purely cognitive skill of making sense of a number of archaic thought-forms. Those who were able to do this were considered to have achieved a higher level of religious understanding than those who could not. The answer to the problem of the intelligent child whose religious thinking remains at concrete operations would appear to be that of motivation (which is, of course, closely connected with attitudes—hence the value of Hyde's observation). If the religious teaching such a child receives between the ages of nine and 13 only serves to underline "concrete" concepts and so suggest that religion *is* as he then believes it to be—about an old man in the sky and so on—one can hardly expect him to continue to consider the subject worthy of his serious attention when he attains formal operational thinking in other areas. Goldman writes:

To say that the child will "grow out of his misunderstandings" is not an accurate statement, since all the evidence points to the fact that most children carry their misunderstandings through with them into early adolescence. They then find the crude ideas untenable, and because the alternative is not put before them or left until it is too late, they may then reject religion as intellectually untenable.

(*Religious Thinking from Childhood to Adolescence,* p 223.)

These findings, therefore, lend psychological support to the philosophical objections to R.E. being conceived as "teaching the Bible to children". They also indicate that the incorporation into R.E. of doctrinal or credal statements, especially in the Primary school, has the same retarding effect on children's religious thinking as does the use of the Bible because they too demand the application of interpretative techniques beyond the capacity of younger children. Religious teaching in schools has clearly been guilty for a long time of teaching the worst type of subject-matter for the worst possible reasons; it is not surprising therefore that few of our pupils leave school having received a good religious education. What do we have to do to alter this state of affairs?

What are the educational implications of this research for the teaching of religion in schools?

As mentioned earlier, Dr Goldman examines this question in his book, *Readiness for Religion,* and attempts to translate the implications into practical terms. His comments, observations and conclusions are most pertinent to our task and merit very careful examination and consideration. Any attempt to offer a summary of his recommendations is unlikely to do justice to them and so you are strongly advised to refer to his publications, especially Chapter 15 of *Religious Thinking from Childhood to Adolescence.*

It is important to recognise, however, that despite his view that very little biblical material is suitable for use with children before Secondary level and that its place needs to be taken by material designed to assist the development of religious concepts (i.e. "Life-themes" and "Religious-themes"), his approach to R.E. is one that falls within the category of "Neo-confessional". His choice of themes, excellent as many of them are, are designed to promote conceptual insight into Christianity rather than into Religion. Furthermore, the development of the themes, especially those given in the *Readiness for Religion Series* incorporates suggestions to the children (writing and saying prayers, not to mention closing their eyes!) which appear to indicate that he sees the process as leading both to insight *and* Christian commitment. Because of his view that

45

R.E. should be Christian and that religious truth is revealed "through the inspired literature of the Bible and through the person of Jesus Christ", his "developmental" schemes are primarily concerned with equipping the child experientially and intellectually, during the earlier stages of his development, with concepts and knowledge (e.g. life in Palestine) which will eventually enable him, when he reaches Formal Operations, to make greater sense of the Bible and its message. Two points may be made about this approach. Firstly, although he seeks to make the child's own experiences the starting-point of his themes and introduces a wide range of "across-subject" teaching to promote insight into different dimensions of the situations and concepts involved, the course which the theme's development takes often appears to be contrived and artificial because of Goldman's attempt to steer it towards some particular biblical idea or Christian practice. He gives the impression that an experience-based theme has no place in R.E. if it does not provide an opportunity for the teacher to introduce a "Christian punch-line". Secondly, his approach seems to imply, like his research, that R.E. should primarily be concerned with initiating the child into the traditional language and thought-forms of Christianity rather than with helping them to discern dimensions in their own "feelings, acts and experiences" which might be called "religious" and which can be expressed and communicated in terms far more relevant and meaningful to life in the 20th century. While accepting the need for children to be "infantile theologians" experimenting with ideas and concepts (p 5 *Religious Thinking From Childhood to Adolescence*) he would appear to believe that the eventual outcome of their "long period of apprenticeship" should be acceptance and use of traditional Christian formularies. Nothing could be less attuned to the demands of contemporary theology!

These comments should not be seen as an indictment of Goldman's recommendations or even of his practical suggestions but rather as a plea for their being broadened in both content and approach. Contemporary trends in theology, education and society provide guidelines to assist us with this task. Certainly in R.E. we can begin with the existential experiences of children whatever their age and assist them to explore and examine these at greater depth, because it is out of these experiences that "religious" concepts arise. We can also present *religion* to them in such ways as to bring out the meanings and values it has to the participants; an aspect of this will be concerned with helping children to acquire the necessary techniques for interpreting traditional religious language and symbols as used in different religions. But the predominant concern throughout this process will need to be that of providing children with an opportunity to build *conceptual bridges* between their own experiences and what they recognise to be the central concepts of religion. It is here that they can encounter the "implicit" side of religion and *understand it and express it in contemporary terms.* The latter might be said to constitute the desirable outcome of R.E.

On the basis of these observations we can identify a number of points which need to be taken into account when devising curricula for R.E. :

1 If the child's thinking is developmental so too must R.E. be developmental.

2 A developmental approach demands that the child's own experiences, needs and interests become the starting points for learning. Thus a child's first acquaintance with "religious" concepts should result from his being encouraged to look more deeply into his *own* feelings, acts and experiences and to express what he discovers in *everyday language.* This is a process which should begin in the Infant school and continue throughout the Junior and Secondary schools.

3 When presenting the formal, traditional concepts used in religion, both content and methods must take into account the different characteristics of each stage of the child's cognitive development if misunderstanding, "verbalism" and the reinforcement of crude and childish ideas are to be avoided. Subject-matter, drawn from the six dimensions of religion described earlier, should provide "stepping-stones" (rather than "stumbling-blocks") to the development of *mature* religious concepts and never the means by which crude and childish concepts are underlined and reinforced.

4 Every opportunity should be taken to *link* the children's own experiences with what they recognise to be the central concepts of religion. This is especially necessary in relation to the "implicit" or feeling side of religion and should result in greater understanding of religion *as a special way of looking at and talking about the experiences of living.* Although children should be helped to acquire the necessary techniques for interpreting religious language and symbols and encouraged to use such expressions, equal consideration should be given to finding and using contemporary or "secular" forms of expression more relevant to 20th century man.

5 The term "developmental" embraces social, emotional and physical dimensions as well as cognitive ones. Although intelligent intellectual grasp of formal religious concepts is rarely possible before 13/14 years of age, even very young children can *feel* (a kind of knowing) things which they are capable neither of articulating nor of fully understanding intellectually. This fact points to the great importance of the implicit or feel-

ing side of religion/experience becoming the core of R.E., especially with children aged between four and nine. We will need to accept, then, that in its early stages R.E. must be grounded in the child's emotional and social experiences and less concerned with purely cognitive development.

6 Although religion is a unique mode of thought and awareness possessing its own distinctive forms of communication and verification procedures, we must be prepared to see religion as inherent in *all* activities and subjects if we are to prevent the persistence of dualism in the child's thinking and encourage him to find "religious" dimensions in his own experience. This means that R.E. will need to include "across-subject" teaching and become part of "Integrated Studies" programmes.

Two questions which might be asked when preparing an R.E. curriculum unit

1 Am I teaching them something which will eventually be a stumbling-block to their development of an intelligent, creative and mature understanding of religious ideas?
2 Am I teaching them something which will be a stepping-stone in their development of the capacity to understand and think about religion intelligently?

In the following chapter we will attempt to draw these points together to form a basis for an approach to R.E. which might be considered to be educationally valid within a state system of education serving a pluralist, multi-racial and multi-cultural society.

Further reading

D. G. Boyle : *A Student's Guide to Piaget* (Pergamon, 1969).

J. S. Bruner : *The Process of Education* (Harvard Univ. Press, 1960).

J. S. Bruner : *Towards a Theory of Instruction* (Norton & Co., N.Y., 1966).

J. S. Bruner et al : *Studies in Cognitive Growth* (John Wiley & Sons, 1966).

R. J. Goldman : *Religious Thinking from Childhood to Adolescence* (R.K.P., 1964).

R. J. Goldman : *Readiness for Religion* (R.K.P., 1965).

P. G. Richmond : *An introduction to Piaget* (R.K.P., 1970).

E. Stones : *Learning and Teaching* (John Wiley & Sons, 1968).

Chapter 5

A Conceptual Framework for Religious Education in Schools

Part One: The Existential Approach

The approach to R.E. which has so far emerged from our consideration of aims and pupil characteristics may be described, briefly, as one which seeks to create in pupils certain capacities to understand and think about religion as a unique mode of thought and awareness; which takes as its starting-point the child's own existential experiences and which attempts to help children to build conceptual bridges between these and what they recognise to be the central concepts of religion—as presented in and through six inter-related and inter-dependent dimensions (i.e. experiential, mythological, ritual, social, ethical and doctrinal).

We need now to move towards formulating some kind of *structure* or *framework* within which this approach to R.E. may be presented. The framework will need to be conducive to the achievement of educational aims and objectives. It will need to make provision for the developmental nature of the child's thinking and for the use of the child's needs, interests and experiences as a basis for learning. It will need to allow for both specialist and non-specialist teachers of R.E. to operate within it at levels appropriate to their knowledge and expertise. Without such a framework it is impossible to translate our theoretical considerations of what might constitute an educationally valid approach to R.E. into practical terms.

It is important to recognise that such a framework is not a syllabus. Unlike a syllabus a framework does not dictate actual subject-matter but rather serves to indicate when and where certain *types* of content may appropriately be introduced, depending, of course, on the teacher's knowledge, expertise and objectives (see Chapter 7) and the particular needs, interests, experiences and abilities of his pupils. It is, then, the flexibility of the framework to accommodate the particular requirements of pupils and teachers and yet, at the same time to direct learning towards carefully defined and validated educational aims that makes it so much more preferable to a syllabus.

A CONCEPTUAL FRAMEWORK FOR R.E. IN SCHOOLS

RELIGIOUS UNDERSTANDING

Age	5	6	7	8	9	10	11	12	13	14	15	16
LEVEL 1 EXPERIENTIAL												
Using the child's feelings, acts and experiences as the basis for developing religious concepts.	Depth Themes				Symbol & Language Themes		Situation Themes					
LEVEL 2 DIMENSIONAL												
Presenting selected religious concepts by way of the six dimensions of religion.	Experiential, Mythological & Ritual material						Social & Ethical material			Doctrinal material		

50

Set out on p 50 is a framework which might be said to provide for the approach to R.E. which we have been considering. You will notice that the framework has two levels. Level 1 is entitled the *Existential Approach,* and Level 2, the *Dimensional Approach.* Ideally a teacher should ensure that these two approaches are used *in combination with each other* as they are complementary. Work undertaken at Level 1 provides the basis for understanding work at Level 2. Thus, although both levels are designed to promote *Religious Understanding* in their own way, they do this most effectively when used together. However, the non-specialist teacher of R.E. may not be able to introduce the richness and variety of material at Level 2 which the specialist should be able to introduce. Although this will impoverish the overall approach it will not totally impair it. It is Level 1 which contains the "core" of R.E. and so it is perfectly reasonable for the non-specialist to devote most of his time to work at this level. Thus, the framework makes provision for the limitations of the non-specialist teacher while allowing the specialist to make full use of his wider knowledge and expertise. In this chapter we will consider the rationale and content of Level 1—the *Existential Approach.*

Level One: The Existential Approach

We might begin our examination of the rationale underlying Level 1—the *Existential Approach*—by asking the question : "How have religious concepts come into being?" In Chapter 3 (p 24) it was suggested that mature religious concepts, as expressed in and through traditional religious symbols and language, are essentially the outcome of man's reflection on his own and other's life experiences. We will need to take a little time examining this suggestion in order to prevent possible misunderstandings.

On the surface the statement appears to imply a complete abandonment of the notion of "Revelation" and an assertion of man's capacity to perceive and understand, and even to create his own religious concepts. Carried to its logical conclusion it is an assertion of "Natural Theology"—a view that knowledge about God may be obtained by human reason alone. This is clearly not the place to begin a detailed discussion of the strengths and weaknesses of one theological position in relation to another—that of "Revealed Theology". The suggestion, however, may be viewed from another angle—namely, that religious concepts, even those which are traditionally regarded as "revealed", can only be understood when the "truth" to which they point is somehow *disclosed* in and through a man's own experiences. In other words, the *validity* (not necessarily the reasonableness) of a particular religious concept for an individual is not merely to be found in his knowledge that it is revealed in the Bible or in the unwritten traditions of the Church, but in his knowledge that what it points to "squares with" or "illuminates" his own experience and situation. Indeed, one may say the same about the phenomenon of religion; its validity for the individual lies in its ability to speak directly to him in his existential situation. (The work of Rudolph Bultmann and Paul Van Buren is concerned with more than "demythologising" Christianity or translating the Christian Gospel into secular terms; it is an attempt to grapple with the problem of whether in fact the Christian Gospel is *able* to speak directly to twentieth century man in his existential situation and whether what it says still has significance for him.)

If it is true that the *validation* of religious concepts depends to a considerable measure on *their* ability to illuminate man's situation and experience, then it is also true that a man's *understanding* of religious concepts is determined by *his* ability to relate them to his situation and experience. Thus, regardless of whichever theological position we may subscribe to—"Natural" or "Revealed" or a combination of both—we need to recognise that religious concepts only "come alive" when we are able to relate them, sometimes partially, sometimes completely, to our life experiences. And by "life experiences" we mean *all* experiences, all that results from being existent. It is because it points to the totality of man's experiences without dividing them into, say, "religious" and "secular", that the word *"existential"* is particularly useful in this context. Thus, when we speak of *The Existential Approach* to R.E. we are referring to an approach which focuses attention on the *whole* of the child's experiences, or, more precisely, which focuses the child's attention on the whole of his experiences, and uses these as the basis for forming religious concepts.

Let us look a little more closely at the theological and educational justification for the Existential Approach. In Chapter 1, p 6, a passage from Paul Tillich's sermon, "The Depth of Existence" was quoted. This passage contains the sentence, "He who knows about depth knows about God". Here Tillich is inviting us to plumb the depths of our "existential" experiences; to get below the surface of life and examine it from the inside, from a position of depth. This, according to Tillich, is not merely the starting-point of a religious quest for God, it is the completion of the quest itself—for "God is Depth". On this basis, the task of R.E. is to help children to "know about depth" by encouraging them to look into their own lives at depth, to explore their existential experiences deeply.

Different people invariably translate Tillich's statement in different ways—and that, perhaps, is no bad thing. Some see it as a deification of our deepest thoughts, our ultimate concern and so on, others as an attempt to create another more useful and relevant symbol for "God"—a symbol which each man fills out for himself in terms of those thoughts and feelings which he considers to be his profoundest and most meaningful. Some may find a similarity between Tillich's statement and one made by George Berkeley, the 18th century Irish divine; "My notion of God is obtained by reflecting on my soul, heightening its powers and removing its imperfections". Others may prefer to see it as reflecting the same brand of pantheism that characterises Wordsworth's "Lines on Tintern Abbey Re-visited" :

... And I have felt
A presence that disturbs me with the joy
Of elevated thoughts; a sense sublime
Of something far more deeply interfused,
Whose dwelling is the light of setting suns,
And the round ocean and the living air,
And the blue sky, and in the mind of man :
A motion and a spirit, that impels
All thinking things, all objects of all thought,
And rolls through all things . . .

And Tillich's view of God as "depth" may also be seen as a parallel to the teaching of Classical Hinduism with its emphasis on knowing God through knowing yourself. (The Upanishads teach that man's soul, "atman", and the world's soul, "paramatman" are one with Brahman; to "know" this is to escape from the Round of Births and attain Nirvana.) John A. T. Robinson in *Honest to God* (p 47) puts his view like this :

What Tillich is meaning by God is the exact opposite of any *deus ex machina,* a supernatural Being to whom one can turn away from the world and who can be relied upon to intervene from without. God is not "out there". He is in Bonhoeffer's words "the 'beyond' in the midst of our life", a depth of reality reached "not on the borders of life but at its centre", not by any flight of the alone to the alone, but, in Kierkegaard's fine phrase, by "a deeper immersion in existence". For the word "God" denotes the ultimate depth of all our being, the creative ground and meaning of all our existence.

We might say, then, that the "New Theology" is concerned to show that theological statements, in Robinson's words, "are not a description of "the highest Being" but an analysis of the depths of personal relationships—or, rather, an analysis of the depths

of *all* experience "interpreted by love". On this view, the theological significance of helping children to engage, at their own
levels, in analysis of their life experiences becomes immediately
apparent. And yet, even if we reject the "New Theology" and
continue to accept the view that theology is concerned with *describing* a "God up there" or a "God out there" and making statements about his relationships with man, the task of understanding
traditional religious concepts demands precisely the same sort of
reflective process on the part of the child. It is only by first helping him to deepen his understanding of his own experiences of love,
forgiveness, justice, care, sonship and so on, that he is able to
give meaning and significance to the traditional religious concepts
of God. The same is true of such traditional concepts as "awe",
"mystery" and "worship". It is far more likely that a child will
come to grasp the meaning and significance of awe, for example,
through his involvement in so-called "secular" experiences (e.g.
his first sight of the sea, a kitten, a new born child; meeting a pop
star or football star; hearing a piece of music or the sound of the
sea in a shell; looking at a painting or examining a copper sulphate
crystal) than if he is presented with the story of Moses and the burning bush or told about the Transfiguration. If we can help the
child to learn to look into his own existential experiences at depth
and then, at the appropriate time, bring religious concepts within
the ambit of these experiences, not only will we assist his development of mature, creative religious concepts but also give him the
opportunity of assessing their relevance or irrelevance to him.

(a) *Depth Themes*

To return to the diagram on p 50, it should be reasonably
clear from the foregoing discussion why *Depth Themes* form the
basis of the *Existential Approach*. These themes take as their subject matter or topic the child's immediate situation and experiences
and seek to provide him with an opportunity to examine them
more closely and discern new dimensions within them. In using
Depth Themes we are in effect saying to the child : "Look more
deeply into this familiar thing; do you see anything about it which
you haven't seen before?" Appendix One of this book contains a
number of examples of Depth Themes but it may be useful at this
point to clarify their special characteristics, especially in terms of
their purpose or intention.

First of all it will be apparent that Depth Themes have several
characteristics in common with the well-known "Life Themes"
usually associated with the name of Dr Ronald Goldman. For
example, the titles of Depth Themes—Homes and Families, People
who help us, Friends and Neighbours, Living in Groups, Things we

like to do, Today's Songs and so on—are not unlike those of Life Themes. Both incorporate "across-subject" teaching and both are concerned, in their own way, with assisting the growth of "religious" concepts by encouraging the child to explore and examine his own "secular" experiences.

We have seen earlier, however (p 45f), that the Life Theme, or rather, the way in which it is so often used, is open to a number of serious criticisms. Those who have pioneered its use in R.E. have tended towards a Confessional or Neo-Confessional outlook. Consequently they have felt that distinctly "religious" subject-matter, especially traditional Christian teaching, *must* be introduced into the theme at some point in its development—usually towards the end. Not only has this made the Life Theme educationally suspect in terms of its intention but it has proved to be extremely difficult to link traditional religious subject-matter with the child's secular experiences *within the context of a Life Theme* without the theme appearing to be artificial and contrived. Indeed, so tenuous have some of the links been between the traditional religious teaching and the "life" content that one suspects that many Life Themes have actually served to perpetuate the division in the child's mind between religion and life rather than unite these two areas.

Depth Themes attempt to overcome these difficulties and objections largely through the modified intention behind them. They, unlike Life Themes, are not designed to lead the child towards a particular religious position or to provide him with knowledge of traditional religious ideas or teaching. Rather they are designed to provide him with an opportunity to practise a particular *skill*—that of reflecting at depth on his own experiences. Accordingly, Depth Themes are purely "secular"; they do not make use of religious language nor do they necessarily incorporate distinctly "religious" subject-matter. An R.E. lesson using Depth Themes is not characterised, then, by its concern with a distinctive body of knowledge called "religion" but rather by its *intention* to explore and examine life through the child's own feelings, acts and experiences. To this end the "R.E. curriculum" is inevitably "integrated"; it draws on any subject-matter which can serve to illuminate and inform the child's experiences at depth.

We have already spent some time looking at the theological and educational justification for the Existential Approach, especially the view that it is from this reflective type of thinking that an awareness and understanding of religious concepts arises. It is important to note, however, that teaching by Depth Themes is a *planned* activity and involves *selection* on the part of the teacher. Although the *whole* of the child's existential experiences provide the starting-point for Depth Themes and also determine to a large extent the course of the Themes' development, in order to ensure that the child is actively engaged in *deepening* his insight into life and not continually "skating" over a number of different surfaces, the teacher needs to determine what might be called the "points of focus" within a theme.

In our earlier discussion of the nature of religious concepts we noted that their *validation* depends to a considerable extent on their ability to illuminate man's situation and experience and that a man's *understanding* of religious concepts is determined by his ability to relate them to his situation and experience. It is not unreasonable to infer from this that a crucial requirement in both processes—validation and understanding—is that a man possesses insight into himself. Without self-understanding or an awareness of personal identity there is very little likelihood of a man being able to make sense of his situation or his experience. The same, of course, is true of the child, except that for him self-understanding presents even greater difficulties.

The importance of the idea of "self" in the child's development is indicated by the number of psychologists who point to its establishment as the central task of infancy. The building up of a sense of self or of the ego is paralleled by awareness of the outside world. Once this boundary between "me" and "not me" is established the child embarks on the long process of developing a "self-image"—a sort of internal picture of what kind of person he is. Alongside this process, through introjecting traits from figures in his environment (good and bad), the child begins to form an "ego-ideal" or an idealised self-image. The ego-ideal provides the child with a positive set of values to be aimed at and also the means by which the whole perception of self may be modified. It is not only in his task of developing a realistic self-image and a desirable ego-ideal that the child needs help during childhood, but also in bringing about a rational and effective solution of possible conflicts between the two. This is especially so of the adolescent period when the child's identity, the whole perception of his self, is usually completely reorganised.

The teacher, therefore, needs to plan the development of a Depth Theme in such a way as to allow the child's attention to be focused at certain points on situations and experiences which are valuable in promoting a "disclosure of self" and in contributing to the child's development of a realistic self-image and a reasonable ego-ideal. For example, a theme on Homes and Families, irrespective of the age of the children, needs to be planned in such a way as to prompt individual children to reflect on their own identity within the family, how they actually are as well as how they feel they might be. It is this type of reflective thinking which ultimately can lead to what are often called the "frontier-questions" of life : Who am I? What is man? How am I related to others and to the rest of the natural world? What is the purpose of life? and so on. Thus, although Depth Themes involve no specifically "religious" subject-matter, they do prompt the child to begin to form in his mind those questions which are central to religion or religious thinking.

As well as focusing the child's attention on situations which promote a "disclosure of self", Depth Themes also need to be planned in such a way as to foster the child's insight into other people—or to promote a "disclosure of others". In many cases the same situation serves to promote both kinds of disclosure, but especially valuable are situations which illustrate the very wide range of different feelings and attitudes that others have. The understanding that results from this forms the basis for a third type of disclosure—a disclosure of what constitutes a distinctly human relationship between "self" and "others", and this needs to be yet another point of focus in a Depth Theme.

Using Depth Themes, then, in R.E. does not mean merely exploring, in an arbitrary way, anything and everything which might happen to appeal to the child's needs and interests or which is consistent with his experiences. Rather the use of Depth Themes implies a *planned educational process* which seeks to use the child's needs, interests and experiences as a basis for the achievement of certain distinct educational aims. These are to provide the child with an opportunity to :

1 practise the skill of reflecting on his own experiences at depth.
2 develop insight into himself and his feelings.
3 develop insight into other people and their feelings.
4 develop insight into what constitutes a distinctly human relationship between self and others.

These aims, it may be argued, are worthwhile or valuable in their own right. Indeed those who are familiar with John Wilson's work in Moral Education (See J. Wilson et al *Introduction to Moral Education,* Penguin, 1967) will see a close similarity between them and at least two of the six "moral components" which he believes should be present in a morally-educated person. Wilson's EMP (the ability to have insight into other people's feelings and into one's own feelings) approximates to aims one, two and three, and his PHIL (the attitude that the feelings and needs of other people are equally important with one's own) might be taken as the attitude which should result from an understanding of what constitutes a distinctly human relationship (Aim four). That Moral Education and at least one aspect of Religious Education (the use of Depth Themes) share a common basis and are able to use identical subject-matter should be a source of relief rather than of concern, but it is important to note that in R.E. the value of Depth

Theme is not only to be seen in its ability to foster certain personal qualities which contribute to the process of becoming morally educated but *in laying the foundations for an understanding of religious concepts.*

If in using Depth Themes a child can be helped to achieve these four aims we can say that he has attained a new perspective from which to view life—a perspective of *depth.* It is within this perspective, as Tillich has indicated, that religious or theological concepts cohere. We have already noted that Depth Themes ultimately can prompt the "frontier-question" of life to be asked; they also provide the "raw material" from which religious concepts are made. For example, a Depth Theme in the Junior school on "Friends and Friendship" which provides children with an opportunity to look below the surface of their own experiences of friendship and to talk about their friendships, may involve them in the same type of deep experiences which underlie the Christian concepts of discipleship, forgiveness, self-sacrifice and salvation—experiences which these concepts are designed to point to and illuminate.

In the past we have persistently tried to *talk* about these Christian concepts without ever attempting to arouse in our pupils an awareness of the deep experiences underlying them. It is little wonder that for the vast majority of pupils such talk has been meaningless. Now we must be prepared to reverse the process. We must begin by getting children to look more closely at their own familiar experiences and then encourage them to talk about what they discover in their own words. We must not be disturbed if this process appears to be a purely "secular" one. If they are learning to think at depth, seeing new dimensions in their experiences and forging out for themselves both meaning and purpose in what they encounter and what they do, then the activity in which they are engaging is also theological. Not only is it equipping them with insight and understanding which they can eventually bring to bear on traditional religious concepts, but it is actually involving them in the crucial task of expressing "religious" ideas in terms which are meaningful and relevant to 20th century secular man.

From these observations it should be reasonably clear why, as the diagram on p 50 suggests, it is both possible and desirable for Depth Themes to form the basis for work in R.E. in the Infant, Junior and Secondary school. It is possible because a theme, unlike traditional Biblical material, can easily be adapted to the different developmental levels of children. In other words, the *depth* at which a Depth Theme is explored is determined by what we called, in Chapter 4, "pupil characteristics". It is desirable because children of all ages need to have an opportunity to practise the skill of reflecting on their experiences, for the process of gaining insight into self, others and the relationship between them is progressive and cumulative. We need to remember, then, that whatever the age of the children, the choice of theme needs to be made on the basis of their present experiences.

With regard to the choice of theme, it is fairly common to find that children will suggest themes themselves, either directly in discussion or indirectly through what the teacher knows they happen to find interesting. This raises a practical consideration. Events which happen in school, at home, in the local community or in a national or international context often arouse interest and excitement in children. The teacher who is able to channel this into an appropriate Depth Theme will find that really active participation on the part of the children will follow. It is important, however, for the teacher to be able to assess in advance the possibilities of a particular theme—whether it has potential for interesting and relevant development or whether it is likely to be short-lived in terms of interest and value. It is also necessary when deciding on a theme for the teacher to be clear in his own mind about the course of its development. Not only should he be conscious of the purposes for using a Depth Theme (see aims on p 57) but also he should select in advance the particular *concepts* which he believes should emerge in the course of its development. We will see in Chapter 7 that the planning of a Depth Theme, like any educational process, needs to begin with the careful identification of Aims and Objectives.

Further reading

Religion
R. Bultmann: *Jesus Christ and Mythology* (SCM Press, 1960).
D. Bonhoeffer: *Letters and Papers from Prison* (Collins Fontana, 1959).
P. Tillich: *The Shaking of the Foundations* (Penguin, 1962) (especially "The Depth of Existence").
P. Tillich: *The Courage to Be* (Collins Fontana, 1962).

Education and Religion
J. W. D. Smith: *Religious Education in a Secular Setting* (SCM Press, 1969).

(b) *Symbol and Language Themes*

It might be said that Depth Themes, with their avoidance of traditional religious language, represent an attempt to "demythologise" basically "religious" ideas into "secular terms". This illustrates how the *Existential Approach* to R.E. is consistent with a major concern of modern theology—namely, to re-define religious concepts in ways which bring them into line with the thought-forms, language and experiences of modern man. And yet Depth Themes are only the beginning of this process; they certainly cannot be said to bring children into contact with the whole of "Religious Understanding". Rather they seek to give them an insight into the type of thinking that leads to Religious Understanding. It is for this reason that it is useful to see Depth Themes as providing children with an opportunity to practise a *skill*—that of reflecting on their own experiences at depth.

As we have seen, however, reflective thinking has the effect of bringing certain ideas and concepts into sharper focus and prompting the expression or communication of these in what might be regarded as appropriate language. We might define "appropriate language" in this context as language which has the power to "disclose" to others what we know or what we have sensed or felt to be true. Thus, work on Depth Themes often has the side-effect of leading children to an awareness of the importance and difficulty of communicating their ideas, thoughts and feelings and then involving them in a search for appropriate language through which this may be achieved. This concern with language and communication is, of course, valuable in its own right, but even more important is the possibility that it can become the means by which children may be initiated into Religion as a "unique mode of thought and awareness".

In the section on "Educational Change" in Chapter 1 we noted briefly the view (associated with Professors R. S. Peters and P. H. Hirst) that "Knowledge" or "Thought" may be divided into different "modes" or "forms" each with its own distinctive "structure", its own set of unique concepts and principles, its own symbolic means of communication and its own peculiar forms of "proof" or "verification". Thus when we speak of "Forms of Understanding" we are recognising the existence of Mathematical, Scientific, Historical, Ethical, Aesthetic, Religious Understanding and so on. The school curriculum needs to be designed so as to ensure that one of the outcomes of the educational process is that pupils can find their way about each Form, can recognise its special characteristics and also its special limitations. Another way of putting this would be by suggesting that education should help children to become aware of the existence of "different kinds of truth" each with its own basis (either objective or subjective or a mixture of the two), its own way of expressing its truth and its own way of verifying its claims. The task of verification is a difficult one, especially in religion, but education should at least be able to ensure that pupils when faced with the task of verifying the "truth" of something, recognise the importance of determining the "form" to which it belongs and then asking questions *appropriate to that form*. Perhaps one of the most obvious signs of the failure of religious teaching in schools is the frequency with which pupils in the senior part of the secondary school ask the "wrong" type of questions about religion—questions which demonstrate that they have not grasped how, say, religious thinking differs from scientific or historical thinking. Of course the fault does not rest entirely with teachers of religion; few teachers of mathematics, science, history and so on, give time in their lessons to examining the philosophical basis of these forms with their pupils.

It might be profitable at this point for you to consider the following statements, asking three questions of each one; To which form does it belong? What does it mean? How can it be shown to be true?

1 $2+2=4$.
2 Every body stays at rest unless an external force acts upon it.
3 1066 was the year of the battle of Hastings.
4 It is always wrong to take something that does not belong to you.
5 Beethoven's music is great.
6 All you need is love.
7 Jesus is the Way, the Truth and the Life.

A detailed analysis of these statements is inappropriate within the plan of this book, but several points need to be made, especially about the last statement, if the practical approaches to R.E. suggested later in this section are to be understood. Firstly, the statements should serve to indicate the existence of Forms whose claims to truth are based on their appeal to certain observable, cognitive, objective or positive facts and their relations (e.g. 1, 2 and 3), and the existence of Forms whose claims to truth are based more on their appeal to certain types of experience on the part of the individual which in some sense disclose "truth-for-him" (e.g. 4, 5, 6 and 7). The task of verifying ethical, aesthetic and religious statements is complicated, then, by the fact that these involve a value-judgment —a judgment which is grounded in a personal experience which is believed to be universally illuminating. Thus, whereas verification of statements 1, 2 and 3 will consist of examining the objective data, in the other statements it will consist of examining the experience which, it is claimed, gives validity to the assertion and then going on to see if, *in the light of the experience,* the assertion has any meaning. A further step is to consider whether something which is personally illuminating can ever become the basis for an assertion of "universal" truth. It is useful, therefore, when considering different Forms of Understanding or different kinds of truth, to point to the different types of verification procedure involved by speaking of some expressing a "truth-for-all" and others a "truth-for-me". Religious statements belong to the second category.

Let us look for a moment at the statement, "Jesus is the Way, the Truth and the Life". Unlike the first six statements, the meaning of this one is not at all clear. How can we say that it is "true" or "untrue" if we are not sure what it means? The actual words are simple enough—"way", "truth" and "life" are words that we use in our normal, everyday conversations—it is how they have been linked together and related to the proper noun "Jesus" that causes us difficulty. Perhaps it would be easier to understand this statement if we expanded it a little. For example, if it said, "Jesus provides us with the way to God, with the truth about God and with Eternal Life if we believe in Him", then we could make much more sense of it. Or could we? Given more knowledge about what Jesus said and did we might be able to satisfy ourselves that this is a sort of short-hand version of his teaching and in many respects is a fair enough summary of it. In this sense we might assent to its truth. Yet in doing this we have changed both the meaning and intention of the original statement. It is rather like altering it to read, "Jesus said he was the Way . . ." or "Jesus believed that he was the Way . . .". Here we have made it into an historical statement open to historical verification procedures; but the statement claims to be more than historical, it claims to express "Religious Truth". What, then, must we do to make sense of this statement?

Perhaps to begin with we should concentrate on the person making the statement. For one thing the statement tells us as much if not more about the person than it does about Jesus because it is a statement of his belief. In order to be able to make the statement the person would have to have a personal belief that what Jesus said was true or "truth". This belief would not be merely an unconfirmed conjecture such as would be the case if he had said, "I believe that I'm catching a cold"; rather it would be an actual acceptance of the truth of Jesus's claims as if they were "facts". What is the basis of this belief which is strong enough to count as a fact? It may well be an experience in which the "truth" of Jesus's claims "came alive" for him. Although it will be difficult to define the nature of this experience we can note that in some sense it prompted a commitment on his behalf. Indeed the language he uses, although familiar as everyday vocabulary, is the *language of commitment* or, in more traditional terms, the *language of faith*. As such its behaviour is logically odd. How then, does religious language differ from other types of language? In what sense is it "peculiar"?

Those who are familiar with the work of such philosophers as A.

Flew, A. MacIntyre, R. M. Hare, I. Crombie, R. B. Braithwaite, I. T. Ramsey, J. Hick, J. Macquarrie et al, on the nature of religious assertions and language will be aware of the increasing importance being attached to this complex and difficult subject within both philosophy and theology. Consequently it is a subject which the teacher of religion cannot afford to neglect. A number of books have been listed at the end of this chapter which will help to augment the very brief and over-simplified account of the nature of religious language and symbolism which follows. This account draws heavily on the thinking of Dr I. T. Ramsey.

To begin with we must note something rather confusing about the way in which language is used in religion—especially within historic Judaism and Christianity. On the surface, religious assertions look very similar to ordinary factual assertions. For example, "Our father is in the country" and "Our Father is in heaven" both look like descriptive or factual statements which, on the basis of their grammatical similarity, could be verified in the same way. The same could be said of the statements, "Jack rose from the bed" and "Jesus rose from the dead"; we could easily assume that both are using language in a descriptive or observational way characteristic of historical statements. The same point may be illustrated by reference to the Apostles' Creed. Here we find the factual, historical assertion that Jesus "suffered under Pontius Pilate, was crucified, dead and buried" linked in the same sentence with "He descended into hell; The third day he rose again from the dead, He ascended into heaven, And sitteth on the right hand of God the Father Almighty; From thence he shall come to judge the quick and the dead". These latter phrases may appear to be as descriptive, historical and "factual" as the former and yet, unlike the former, their content is almost entirely mythological or symbolic—some would say entirely so. This does not mean that we should dismiss them as worthless fiction but rather that we should look carefully for the truth that such language seeks to express. Myth and symbol in this context becomes the language of commitment and faith and that means that the significance and validity of such statements is not to be sought in how far they *describe* an actual state of affairs but how successful they are in pointing us to that experience in which the "truth" about Jesus "came alive", not just for a single individual but, in this case, for a community—the Christian Church.

Let us develop this final point about language being used to evoke in us a sense of someone else's experience by using an analogy—itself a way of "pointing us" to a truth without actually describing it. Let us imagine that we are trying to teach someone how to calculate the area of a circle. We introduce them to the symbol pi as representing the ratio of the circumference of a circle to its diameter and we tell them that pi=3.14159; we show them how to calculate the radius and we explain what is meant by "squaring" a number and so on. In other words, we give them the necessary information and then show them how to do the calculation. Even after going over the steps a number of times the person may still fail to understand. If we try again our efforts may this time be rewarded by the person saying something like, "Oh! Yes! The penny has just dropped!" or "Oh! Yes! The light has dawned! I see it now!" Now experience has taught us how to interpret these exclamations. We don't start looking round for dropping pennies and dawning lights, instead we understand the statements as "signals" that the person has understood the principle and is now able to do the calculation. Suddenly things have become clear for him, or, in other words, truth has been *disclosed* to him. In short, we have witnessed what I. T. Ramsey has called "a disclosure situation". The words that the person uses are not *descriptions* of what he understands, even though his language appears to be descriptive. Had he wanted to have described what he has suddenly understood he would have started talking in terms of what you do with pi, the radius and so on. Instead he has chosen to use an entirely different set of words which have the effect of pointing us to the disclosure of truth that has occurred—words which seeks to evoke in us an appreciation of what he has just experienced.

Now this is precisely how a great deal of religious language behaves. If a man says "I saw that I was a sinner who needed to be washed in the Blood of the Lamb" or "I have seen the Risen Christ" or "I have stood at the foot of the Cross", then just as we didn't start looking around for dropping pennies and dawning lights so we mustn't start looking for Lamb's Blood, Resurrection appearances and Crosses. Although in appearance the language is descriptive the man is using it in an evocative, poetic, metaphorical and dramatic sense. He is in effect saying, "Don't attempt to tie the meaning of what I am trying to say to the literal meaning of the words that I am using—they are inadequate. There are no words that I can use to *describe* what I know to be true; these words I hope will evoke some feeling in you of the experiences that I've had. Behind the words lies my consciousness of a new dimension in my life which has caused me to see things from a different perspective—that is what I am trying to point you to". It is, then, the experience that the man has had which fills out the words for him and gives them meaning. Suddenly he can use the traditional language of religious belief with insight and meaning. In more traditional terms, his experience of transcendence, of the numinous or, more symbolically, of the "presence of God" has provided the "currency" of religious language with a "cash" value. For others, however, these traditional words may still be meaningless. This will certainly be the case if they are mistakenly regarded as descriptions of observable, objective "facts" of the same kind as those providing the data of science and history. But even if the words are seen for what they are—evocative, poetic, metaphorical, dramatic—and we recognise that their appeal is to the totality of man's experiences and not merely to his intellect, they may not have the power to evoke in others a "disclosure" of the truth to which they point. Thus, even if we are aware of the peculiar character of religious language and make an effort to see what it attempts to do and how it attempts to do it, for many of us much of it has become sterile and unable to point us to the truth which the religious man calls "God". Besides, 20th century man is largely reluctant to express his awareness of "transcendent experiences" in religious categories; he prefers to see them as falling within the category of aesthetics or ethics, or more popularly, psychology. If we add to this the fact that descriptive, scientific or observational language is the norm for 20th century man, we can perhaps appreciate why the task of understanding such a statement as "Jesus is the Way, the Truth and the Life" presents us with so many difficulties. Even greater difficulties, however, are presented by the word "God" and it is to an examination of the behaviour of this word that we must now turn.

A recurring theme in this book is the view that insight into religious concepts arises from the process of reflecting at depth on our own life experiences and those of others. In a moment we will consider how human experiences provide us with "models" which, when suitably qualified, enable us to engage in what J. Macquarrie has called "God-Talk", but let us first ask if there is a word which we use in everyday conversation whose logical behaviour might provide us with a guide to the logical behaviour of the word "God" in religious assertions. We have seen that an important aim of Depth Themes is to promote insight into self or to bring about "self-disclosure". A signal that "self-disclosure" has occurred is when children working on Depth Themes begin to translate third-person assertions ("John cares about his family" and so on) into first-person assertions ("I care about my family" and so on). Here something which is objectively revealing (i.e. talk about John and his family) has the effect of disclosing a "truth-for-me" (i.e. how I stand in relation to my family) and a "truth-about-me" (i.e. how I actually am as a person). The use of the personal pronoun "I" in this context has a very special significance. It signals that a disclosure of truth has occurred; it points to the subjectivity of the experience as providing the ground for the significance, meaning and "truth" of the assertion, and it indicates that a personal response and commitment has been made to the "truth" that has been disclosed. Thus the "I" in the sentence "I care about my family" acts as a *reference-point* against which we are to understand and talk about what the person is asserting. For example, it tells us to understand the assertion in the light of the person's commitment to what he has "seen" to be the truth for him. It also reminds us that should we choose to question the person about his assertion by asking "Why do you care about your family?", whatever explanations he may give his ultimate causal explanation may legitimately be one which points directly to his subjectivity—"Because I'm I". This tautology marks the limits of our enquiries; we cannot ask, 'But why are you *you*?" We are confronted by a mystery and all our talk about the person, all our attempts to describe him, although pointing to this, can never actually describe or define it. We have to accept that no number of verifiable criteria is ever adequate as an account of what another person knows to be himself.

I. T. Ramsey has argued that a useful parallel exists between the way in which "I" behaves in those contexts we have just been considering and the way in which "God" behaves in religious assertions. Just as disclosures occur which promote insight into "self" so too do disclosures occur on a cosmic scale which promote insight into the Universe and into life itself. Ramsey contends that in "cosmic disclosures" . . . "the Universe comes alive and existence takes on depth or another dimension". He writes :

> Such situations can occur on countless occasions of the most varied kind—by a fireside, or on a country walk; on a windswept moor, or in the crowds at Charing Cross; while reading the Bible, or attending Mass—there is no situation which cannot in principle give rise to a cosmic disclosure. . . . Now because of the cosmic character of such a disclosure, because of its all-embracing range, because in it the whole Universe confronts us, I think we are entitled to speak of there being a single individuation expressing itself in each and all of these disclosures. . . . I would claim that it is quite clear that cosmic disclosures are ontologically privileged in so far as they disclose that which confronts us as a basic "given", that which is set over against ourselves in every situation of this kind, that which individuates the Universe.
>
> (I. T. Ramsey (edit.), *Words about God,* SCM Press Ltd., 1971, p 211.)

As in our earlier example of "self-disclosure", in a "cosmic-disclosure" certain events combine in and through which a person is able to discern "truth"—but not merely truth about himself but what he feels to be truth about the Universe and about existence. This discernment results in a commitment whereby what is "seen" becomes so important that it determines all subsequent seeing. The "truth", to use Tillich's phrase, becomes "Ultimate Concern"—it brings about a changed perspective. It is within this type of context that the use of the word "God" becomes appropriate as a *reference-point* against which to understand and talk about the perspective which follows from the disclosure. To use the word "God" is not, then, to *describe* something which exists in a localised sense—like a chair, an orange or a car—*rather it is to confine discussion to a perspective of commitment and mystery*. The word "God" acts in this way because, contends Ramsey, it functions like the tautology "I'm I". Just as "I'm I" confronts us with a mystery which can be pointed to but never completely defined, so too does the word "God". At the same time it is expressive of the *kind* of commitment with which a person responds when he is confronted by a cosmic disclosure—a "religious" commitment.

The word "God", then, organises or co-ordinates other religious language within a framework of significance. To put it another way, all religious language serves to illuminate that perspective of commitment and mystery of which the word "God" is an expression. This is not to say that such language is ever adequate to actually describe and define that mystery but that its function—in spite of its descriptive appearance—is to point us towards it or evoke some sense of it within us. Thus, religious language fulfils its function when it is able to point us to that mystery so effectively that the language itself generates a disclosure in which we discern the mystery, respond to it with commitment and express our discernment and commitment by using the word "God". It does this by taking the language of everyday experience—especially those words we use to express concepts of special human significance such as love, forgiveness, protection, friendship, fatherhood and so on—and lifting it, by the use of certain qualifying words like "Infinitely" and "Eternal", beyond the limitations of human situations to point to the mystery and transcendence which is characteristic of religious truth. In short, it is by so qualifying observational language used of distinctively *personal* situations that we are able to generate not one but a series of disclosures, each serving to expand and deepen our discernment of the mystery that a religious man calls "God". At the same time we can speak of God in terms of the language derived from what Ramsey has called "disclosure models". In so doing, however, we should remember that the words are not to be taken as "descriptions" but as ways of evoking a discernment of mystery. In this sense theological language has a logical kinship with the language of poetry.

Although no direct reference has so far been made to the place and use of symbols and symbolism in religion, almost everything that has been said about language is just as applicable to symbols. Indeed, instead of saying that religious language is evocative, poetic, metaphorical and dramatic we could have simply said that religious language is symbolic. Like religious language, symbols point to something else beyond themselves. In other words, they too are designed to evoke a "disclosure" of truth by acting as signposts to levels of reality which cannot be reached in any other way. Without such symbols certain kinds of truth (especially religious truth) cannot be disclosed or even talked about and it is this which leads to the view, held by Tillich, that a symbol participates in the reality to which it points. He writes :

Whatever we say about that which concerns us ultimately, whether or not we call it God, has a symbolic meaning. It points beyond itself while participating in that to which it points. In no other way can faith express itself adequately. The language of faith is the language of symbols.
(Paul Tillich, *Dynamics of Faith*, Harper and Row, Inc., New York, p 45.)

Tillich's notion of participation would appear to be a product of his acceptance of the basically Jungian view that symbols grow out of the individual or collective unconscious and, as such, have a life and power of their own. Certainly religions throughout the world do make use of a number of identical symbols in their expression of faith but does this necessarily mean that they cannot be replaced by new ones—ones more directly relevant to the thought-forms of modern man? We have only to look at the arts to see how composers, artists and dramatists are constantly seeking to evolve new ways of expressing ideas. And as ideas themselves change so too must symbols and images.

The function of a symbol is to deflect attention away from itself to the reality to which it points. If a symbol is only serving to deflect attention away from the reality and to focus it upon itself, then it is no longer fulfilling its function. Is not this precisely what some of the traditional symbols in religion actually do? (e.g. the Ascension). Instead of "disclosing" truth they hide it; we become all too aware of the symbol without perceiving the reality that it is seeking to express. Thus, not only do we need to learn how symbols function and how to make use of them, we also need to set ourselves the task of finding and using ones which are more serviceable in our own situation. The need for this becomes even more apparent when we consider that the vast majority of symbols, images and models used by the Christian faith grew out of the life and times of people living 2,000 years ago—people whose language and thought-forms were radically different from our own. We can go so far in our attempts to place ourselves in their shoes and use their symbols drawn from their national institutions and agrarian way of life, but this can never totally compensate for the need for living symbols drawn from our own experiences. The same is true of the "framework" in which a religion such as Christianity exists. Is it realistic to expect such a framework, fashioned on the basis of a three-decker universe, to continue to provide a relevant means of communication in an age in which the universe is known to be infinite? Religion like science and the arts is engaged in an evolutionary process—and that affects its modes of expression and communication as much as the ideas and concepts underlying it.

What are the implications of these observations about religious language and symbolism for the teaching of religion in schools?

Given that the aim of R.E. is "to create in pupils certain capacities to understand and think about religion as a unique mode of thought and awareness", it is obvious that very careful consideration needs to be given to ways in which children can be helped towards an appreciation of "Religious Undersanding" as compared with other Forms of Understanding. It may well be the case, as indicated in our earlier discussion, that by focusing their attention on the different uses of language employed by different Forms children may be led to a more intelligent awareness of the type of thinking characteristic of each Form. Certainly in R.E. very little attention is normally given to the peculiar nature of religious language and this could be one of the reasons why children display such limited insight into the nature of religion itself.

Depth Themes, as we have seen, go some way towards providing children with insight into the type of thinking that leads to Religious Understanding and also help to promote the development of concepts which underlie religious thinking. They do not, however, make use of traditional religious language but encourage children to express ideas in secular terms. What would appear to be necessary is the introduction of a further type of teaching scheme which, while capitalising on the insights provided by Depth Themes, brings children into contact with traditional religious language and helps them to learn how to use it. *Symbol* and *Language Themes* attempt to provide such a scheme and you will see from the diagram on p 50 that these themes are introduced in the middle years of the Junior school and continue, parallel with Depth Themes, through both the Junior and Secondary school.

Before trying to indicate the special characteristics of Symbol and Language Themes it is necessary to make some comments about their relationship with Depth Themes because it is important that we do not make too rigid a distinction between the two. For one thing the two types of theme complement each other; indeed it is frequently the case that a Symbol and Language Theme grows out of a Depth Theme. For example, a Depth Theme on "Things we like to make" undertaken by nine or ten-year-old children may be channelled into a Symbol and Language Theme on "Creation". In this way children may be helped to fill out the word "creation" with those insights they have gained through the Depth Theme—insights into the concepts of purpose, planning, care, pride, perseverance, awe, wonder, joy, celebration, giving, hope and love. Where this close, direct relationship between Depth and Symbol and Language Themes can be achieved we are encouraging children to use—initially at a very elementary level—religious language and symbolism for the expression of their own ideas and experiences. This has the effect of familiarising them with religious vocabulary in a practical way and also making it possible for them to see their own experiences reflected in religious ideas. Further examples of Symbol and Language Themes which can grow out of Depth Themes are :— "Fatherhood" and "Sonship" from a Depth Theme on "Homes and Families"; "Salvation" from a theme on "Help"; "Faith" from a theme on "Trust"; "Sacrifice" from a theme on "Gifts and Giving"; "Discipleship" from a theme on "Friendship"; "Spirit" from a theme on "Power" and so on. With children aged 12, 13 or 14 a Depth Theme on "Living in Groups" might very well lead first to a Symbol and Language Theme on "Unity in Community" and then to a theme on the Christian symbol of "The Holy Trinity".

There are occasions, however, when Symbol and Language Themes may be used independently of Depth Themes, although it will always be possible to see links between them in terms of the understanding that each seeks to foster. For example, one of the aims of Symbol and Language Themes is to promote understanding of the nature and function of symbols and the ability to use them. Accordingly, with a class of nine or ten-year-old children a series of lessons might be devoted to exploring "Signs and Symbols" commonly used in everyday life. The theme could consist of examining road and traffic signs, signs used in advertising, flags and emblems, badges and crests, number systems, mathematical symbols, alphabets (including cuneiform), codes, their own names and nicknames as symbols, signs of the zodiac and so on. (See Books 1-4 of *Symbols* by Norman J. Bull in the *Readiness for Religion* series for a wealth of information on this subject.) A natural progression would be to look at and draw the symbols adopted by different religions (e.g. Christianity the cross; Judaism the Star of David; Jainism the swastika; Hinduism the sacred word OM; Buddhism the eight-spoked wheel; Sikhism the warrior's sword and bracelet; Islam the star and crescent moon; Shintoism the temple gateway and so on) and write a quotation from one of their Sacred Scriptures beneath the symbol. (See *A Book of World Religions* by E. G.

Parrinder for both symbols and quotations.) Symbolism characteristic of a particular religion could then be examined; for example, the "Five K's" of Sikhism. This concern with symbolism at a very physical level could be paralled by work on symbols such as fire, fountain, tree and so on, in dance drama which, in turn, might lead to the symbolic interpretation of more abstract ideas—such as fear, loneliness, joy, awe, unity and so on. Art and music could provide for similar types of exploration into the nature of symbolism. Work of this kind, beginning in the middle years of the Junior school, should help to lay the foundations upon which an understanding of more complex religious symbolism may rest.

Provided that we do not interpret the word "theme" in its narrowest sense a number of other lines of approach to the task of initiating children into an understanding of religious language and symbolism may be developed under the heading of *Symbol and Language Themes*. One of these is to concentrate on the *context* out of which the traditional symbols and language of a religion have grown—namely the life, customs and beliefs of the adherents to different Faiths. For example, the enormous significance which "water" has in such faiths as Hinduism, Islam, Judaism, and Christianity, as a symbol of life, of spiritual cleansing, of renewal and rebirth and even of a way of talking about God, derives in large measure from the heightened sense of importance given to it in countries where its supply is limited and hardship and effort is involved in obtaining it. We can hardly expect a child in Britain to appreciate how it is that the Psalmist can talk of God as "The fountain of living water" if he has no knowledge of the temperamental behaviour of the former and latter rains in the south and east of Palestine or of the custom of giving the name of "living water" to those springs which do not dry up when the rains fail altogether. Neither can we expect him to make much sense of Jesus's offer of "living water" to the woman in John 4 : 7-15 without such knowledge. The success of eventually helping him to see such statements in their figurative sense as "models" which point us to the mystery and transcendence of God and the work and significance of Christ is very largely dependent upon how well we first equip him with this type of background knowledge. But we should always be careful when dealing with this type of background work that our aim—of providing insight into those aspects of a people's life which give strength and meaning to their religious symbols and language—is kept constantly in mind, because it is this which acts as the criterion by which we select material to be used in our lessons. If we forget this there is a danger, when planning schemes and lessons, of allowing the background material to become an end in itself so that under such headings as "Life in Palestine" we slip back into the traditional fare of "R.K."—a

71

potted history of the Jews, maps of Palestine, matchbox models of Palestinian houses, drawings of camels and so on. Widening the perspective to include background studies of countries and peoples outside the Judaeo-Christian tradition can not only offset this danger but also help to place religious symbolism in a universal setting.

A particularly fertile source for work on symbolism is provided by religious feasts, festivals and ceremonies. The concrete form which religious ritual takes, together with its evocation of a sense of mystery and drama, makes it especially appropriate for use with children from about the age of five or six onwards although any attempt to help children towards an understanding of its symbolic significance should be left until they have reached the age of nine or ten. A religious festival is really "dramatised theology"; religious ideas are concentrated into, and expressed through, a series of actions which, like religious statements, are concerned to symbolise or point to religious truth. With children in the final years of the Junior school lessons on feasts and festivals should be designed to acquaint them with the actions themselves and with ceremonial objects. In the secondary school greater attention should be given to *why* people engage in these ceremonies and *what* they signify. Occasionally it is useful to show there is a parallel between festivals of different religions. For example, the Jewish "Bar Mitzvah" and the Hindu "Sacred Thread Ceremony" could be presented together and these followed by an examination of the Christian ceremonies of baptism and confirmation. The Jewish feast of Hannukah, the Hindu feast of Diwali and the Christian feast of Candlemas may all be described as "Festivals of Light". There is also a parallel between the Jewish Feast of Passover (itself very rich in symbolism) and the Islamic "Great Feast" which ends the month of Ramadan, as well as with the Christian Last Supper. With children of 12 or 13 an examination of the Holy Week Liturgy, especially the ceremonies of Maundy Thursday, Good Friday, Holy Saturday and Easter Day, can provide them with very vivid insight into the distinctive theology of Christianity. (These examples illustrate how the Existential Approach links with the Dimensional Approach which will be explained in Chapter 6.)

In conclusion one or two observations may be made about the contribution that Symbol and Language Themes can make to the task of helping children to gain insight into the peculiar nature of religious language. As we have seen, religious language is dramatic, evocative, poetic and metaphorical; it makes use of myths and mythological language, analogies and models and symbols and images. In comparison with language of this type, its use of straightforward, descriptive, observational or "factual" language, despite appearances to the contrary, is very limited. Research has shown that when children are presented with evocative or metaphorical religious language they tend to impose upon it a factual or literal interpretation. Awareness of this fact has led to a belief among R.E. teachers and those responsible for planning Agreed Syllabuses that lessons should concentrate on those parts of the Bible which appear to be "factual" or descriptive and that the mythological, metaphorical and poetic elements should be carefully avoided. Accordingly the vast majority of pupils follow syllabuses which are heavily weighted towards "Lives"—"The Lives of the Prophets", "The Life of Jesus" and "The Life of Saint Paul". This type of syllabus with its emphasis on the Synoptic Gospels and Saint Paul's Journeys may prevent children from literalism to some extent but at the same time it actually prevents them from coming into contact with distinctively religious thinking and language. In short, this type of syllabus only serves to promote Historical Understanding; it does very little to promote Religious Understanding. By avoiding mythological, metaphorical and poetic elements it fails to present children with that which makes Religion into a "unique mode of thought and awareness". It is little wonder that pupils who have followed this type of syllabus display such limited awareness of the nature of religion when they leave school. One answer to this problem would appear to be that of trying to educate children in the use of evocative language rather than judiciously excluding all traces of such language from the syllabus. Certainly, we cannot afford to ignore the fact that children experience considerable difficulties in dealing with abstract ideas before the onset of Formal Operations at about 11 or 12, and yet this does not prevent teachers from encouraging even very young children to engage in "Creative Writing" and poetry writing in their English lessons—and often with very good results. A step in the right direction would be achieved if in R.E. children were encouraged to see that the Bible writers (and the writers of other Sacred Scriptures) also enjoyed "Creative Writing" and were just as given to poetic licence in their accounts of exciting happenings and experiences as the children are themselves. The Psalms are full of this type of writing and much of the Old Testament only begins to come alive when we stop asking questions about historicity and learn to enter into the spirit of the language and sense the writer's exhilaration in his faith in God. For example, a teacher choosing to deal with the Crossing of the Red Sea with Late Juniors is more likely to promote insight into religion and religious belief by spending time reading, discussing and acting out "The Song of Moses" in Exodus Chapter 15 and then encouraging the children to write poems in the same vein, than by reading the prose account in Chapter 14 and then offering them a selection of "scientific explanations" of how the dividing of the sea could have come about. The same is true of

73

the myths of Genesis. If instead of excluding the Creation Myths we seek to communicate in our presentation of them a sense of their dramatic grandeur and their association with the liturgical life of Israel, then we are likely to prevent the sort of misconceptions normally associated with this part of the Bible.

The task of educating children towards an appreciation of the nature of religious language requires us, then, to acquaint them with evocative language being used within the context of religion. This means being open to the possibility of using a wider variety of types of writing in our lessons—writings which have a strong dramatic or poetic element such as may be found in the Psalms (see Psalm 65), the Prophets (see Isaiah 6) and in the apocalyptic writings of both the Old and New Testaments. The use of writings outside the Judaeo-Christian tradition can do much to foster this type of appreciation. World Creation Myths (e.g. Babylonian, Sumerian, Hindu, Shinto and so on), Epics (e.g. The Epic of Gilgamesh, parts of the Hindu Mahabharata and Ramayana (especially the Bhagavad-Gita), Hymns (e.g. from the Rig-Veda, Qur'an and the Guru Granth) and Liturgies all provide children with an opportunity to understand how religious language is the language of commitment and faith and how it seeks to evoke a sense of the mystery which the religious man calls "God". The pupil who is able to appreciate this is well on the way to being able to find his way about Religion as a Form of Understanding.

Work of this nature also provides an opportunity for the teacher to focus attention on the behaviour of the word "God" in religious discourse. A useful exercise for use with pupils of 12 or 13 is that of examining the different names given to God in the religions of the world and the multitude of images and models used to make talk about him possible. The Bible, the Vedas and "The Ninety-Nine Beautiful Names of God" of the Islamic faith are a very rich source of material for this work. At all times, however, it is important that children are helped to understand how the images and models are drawn from the world of man's experiences and that it is this which gives them validity as currency for God-talk. Furthermore, they should be shown how each image—father, shepherd, judge, king, and so on—highlights a different facet of deity and how it is very necessary for there to be a multiplicity of images and models if language about God is ever to evoke a "disclosure" of its subject matter. With children in the final year of the Secondary school and in the sixth form an approach may be made, at an elementary level, to the type of philosophical analysis of statements with which this section began. How successfully they are able to differentiate between different types of truth and apply appropriate verification procedures to them will depend, however, on how far they have achieved the sort of understanding that Symbol and Language Themes are designed to promote.

The aims of Symbol and Language Themes may be summarised as follows :
To initiate children into Religion as a unique mode of thought and awareness by providing them with an opportunity to :

1   express their own ideas, thoughts and feelings in appropriate symbols and language;
2   recognise the special characteristics of religious language and symbolism by :
    (a) acquainting them with language which is evocative, poetic, metaphorical and dramatic (firstly within a secular context and then within a religious context) and educating them in its use;
    (b) acquainting them with the context (country, life and customs) out of which the traditional language and symbols of religion have grown;
    (c) acquainting them with the feasts, festivals, ceremonies, ritual and myths of religion as symbolic expressions of the faith of adherents;

A number of examples of Symbol and Language Themes are given in Chapter 7 and Appendix One.

Further reading

G. Aulén : *The Drama and the Symbols* (SPCK, 1970).
T. Fawcett : *The Symbolic Language of Religion* (SCM Press, 1970).
F. Ferré : *Language, Logic and God* (Eyre & Spottiswoode, 1962).
J. Hick : *Philosophy of Religion* (Prentice-Hall Inc., 1963).
A. Jeffner : *The Study of Religious Language* (SCM Press, 1972).
J. Macquarrie : *God-Talk* (SCM Press, 1967).
I. T. Ramsey : *Religious Language* (SCM Press, 1957).
I. T. Ramsey : *Models and Mystery* (OUP, 1964).
I. T. Ramsey : *Christian Discourse* (OUP, 1965).
P. Van Buren : *The Edges of Language* (SCM Press, 1972).

(c) *Situation Themes*

On p 57 we noted that the use of Depth Themes can not only serve to lay the foundations for an understanding of religious concepts but also foster certain qualities which contribute to the process of becoming morally educated. Thus, at least in one respect (the use of Depth Themes) Religious Education, we suggested, can share a common basis and identical subject-matter with Moral Education. In this section we will examine the possibility of extending the common ground between R.E. and M.E. even further while still ensuring that the work contributes positively to the development of Religious Understanding as well as fostering moral insight. This latter point is important. R.E., as we argued in Chapter 3, can only retain its place in the state school curriculum if it can be shown to be educationally valid in its own right and not merely because it may be used as a means of moral education. Thus, in suggesting areas in which R.E. and M.E. may be said to share a common basis we are not seeking to transform R.E. into M.E., nor are we implying that M.E. cannot exist in its own right as a subject which is distinct from R.E. Rather we are seeking to find a means by which a teacher can educate his pupils in Religion and Morals at the same time, with the same subject-matter but in a way which allows for their distinctively different rationales to be recognised and appreciated.

Of all aspects of human behaviour studied by psychologists, two which present particular difficulties are those dealing with attitudes and moral conduct. Adult human beings normally display considerable resistance to changing or modifying their attitudes largely because these dispositions, learned from others during childhood and adolescence often by conditioning, act as defence-mechanisms against those forces and fears which threaten their feeling of security and well-being. Closely connected with the emotional life of a person, attitudes quickly acquire an autonomy which makes them, at least initially, resistant to rationality. Thus, although a person may be able to argue cogently and forcefully against colour prejudice he may not be able to overcome his own feelings of prejudice if his attitudes are inclined towards it. A similar situation exists in relation to moral conduct, although possibly for different reasons. Studies have shown that there is no guarantee that a person who displays a capacity for making perceptive moral judgments will automatically modify his conduct in the light of the judgments that he makes. Indeed it has been shown that conduct varies from one situation to another even though both present the same moral problem. In this latter case there are grounds for believing that the reason for variability in moral conduct is to be found in the different influences exerted upon the individual by others in different situations (such as peer group pressure, parental or teacher expectations, threat of disapproval or punishment, and so on) rather than in a modification of attitude—although this cannot be excluded as a possibility.

These observations, brief and over-simplified as they are, serve to illustrate something of the complexity of the problem that moral education presents to the teacher. While recognising that attitudes are of decisive importance in determining both moral perception and conduct, he is aware of the special difficulties that their modification presents. Furthermore he is conscious of possible ethical objections to a teacher engaging in a programme of work which is intentionally designed to bring about changes in his pupils' attitudes. The fact that all teaching is directed towards "behaviour modification"—more commonly called "learning"—does not seem to inhibit some from regarding such work in moral education as an ethical exception. This means that special care must be paid to methodology. Even though most attitudes may be regarded as "conditioned responses" which can only be modified by the substitution of different, more acceptable "conditioned responses", such a process, it is frequently argued, can have no place in the educational system of a democracy. To speak, then, of the aims of moral education in terms of "inculcating favourable attitudes to . . ." is to invite both criticism and censure although in actual fact little headway is likely to be made in helping pupils to translate their moral judgments into moral patterns of conduct if such an aim is avoided.

Given these difficulties and limitations, what can a teacher do to promote the development of attitudes which will make a positive and useful contribution to his pupils' moral development? In an earlier section (pp 56-57) we spoke of the teacher's contribution to the child's development of a realistic self-image and a reasonable ego-ideal. Special reference was made to the way in which the child introjects traits from figures in his environment. Here we should note that what a child introjects is not so much what we say to him but how we actually feel about things—our attitudes, in other words—and the process is greatly facilitated when the child is able to identify or empathise with us. The process is, of course, a continuous one in the sense that a child usually experiences contact with a wide range of people displaying a variety of feelings and attitudes. Inevitably he quickly discovers that the attitudes of one person (and, subsequently, their behaviour) differ from those of another and that he himself is often required to discriminate between such conflicts and determine his own position. Thus, an adolescent may resolve a conflict between those attitudes held by his parents and those held by his peers by choosing to adopt the latter and so ensure approval amongst those whose friendship he is anxious to secure. Influential as this criterion is it cannot be said to provide a very satisfactory solution to problems of value conflict—indeed its application may only serve to intensify the conflict in some contexts. Thus the need arises for the individual to devise and adopt certain principles which may be applied both to circumstances in which there is a conflict in attitudes and where some decision about conduct is required. It is important to note, however, that without help, encouragement and practice there can be no real certainty that an individual will be able to recognise these circumstances nor can we be sure that he will possess sufficient resolution or will to translate principle into practice.

What does this mean in practical terms? Firstly that schools need to think very seriously about the crucial role that they play in providing children with opportunities to introject attitudes and values. Especially influential in this respect is a school's social climate. Of the many forces which combine to create a social climate two may be selected as having overwhelming significance; the educational aims that a school accepts and tries to implement and the sort of relationships which exist between members of the school. In both of these the influence of the Head is paramount. If he or she is the sort of person who has an equal respect for academic excellence and persons, or, in sociological terms, who makes an effort to balance "instrumental" (i.e. administrative) and "expressive" (i.e. concern for individuals and their problems) roles, this type of concern will be felt by both staff and pupils and will influence the sort of relationships which exist between them. It is within a climate of mutual respect and trust in the integrity and sincerity of others that the sort of attitudes and values of most worth to a child's moral development are most easily introjected. And what is true for a school is, of course, also true for a classroom. Within such a social climate the adage that morals or values are "caught rather than taught" is shown to have more than a grain of truth.

Secondly, even if a school's social climate, its ways of encouraging respect for the feelings of others and its choice of procedures for determining rules and solving internal problems and disagreements are all conducive to the development of a moral outlook in the pupils, there is still a need for teachers to underline and extend this by a positive teaching programme specifically designed to foster worthwhile attitudes and values. For children in the Junior school, Depth Themes, with their aims of promoting insight into self, others and the sort of relationship that is required between the two, may be said to fulfil this need adequately; but for children in the secondary school whose capacities for moral judgments are greater and whose social experiences are beginning to take on new and more complex dimensions, Depth Themes need to be augmented by a further scheme which makes special provision for these changes. *Situation Themes* attempt to provide a basis for such a scheme. As indicated in the diagram on p 50, it is suggested that Situation Themes are introduced in the first or second year of the Secondary school, parallel to Depth Themes and Symbol and Language Themes, and continue until the fifth year. Once again we need to note that a rigid distinction should not be made between these three types of theme; Situation Themes may grow naturally out of both Depth and Symbol and Language Themes as all three are designed to contribute to the fulfilment of the wider aims of the *Existential Approach*.

Situation Themes, as their title suggests, provide children with an opportunity to explore, examine and discuss situations which call for some sort of moral choice or judgment to be made, either about the situation itself or about the actions of people involved in the situation. The situations chosen for this work should preferably be ones which children are likely to encounter in real life or, failing this, ones which are potentially analogous to them. By encouraging them to analyse such situations carefully, especially in terms of the likely consequences of certain actions and decisions, and to use the undertanding which this provides to formulate their own points of view, children can be helped to become more perceptive of situations in which moral choices are required and more sensitive to the complex dimensions which they involve. A further step is to encourage pupils to see the need for their specific observations and views to be generalised into principles which might provide useful guidelines for decision-making in these and other contexts. This quickly raises the question of what sort of criteria they should use when determining principles—a question which cannot be answered without reference to attitudes and values.

In many respects earlier work on Depth Themes will have already provided some insight into the needs, feelings and interests of others and the importance of acting in ways which take account of them. The task of the Situation Theme is to extend this insight by presenting examples of persons acting and behaving in accordance with the beliefs and values that they happen to hold about themselves and about others. Thus, the child is placed in a position where he can perceive the crucial connection which exists between the sort of beliefs and values that a man holds, the attitudes that he displays and the actions and behaviour that he adopts. Furthermore, if care is taken to ensure that persons are presented as realistically as possible with opportunity for real discernment of character to occur, children may very well introject the attitudes they exemplify.

An excellent example of material which encourages children to empathise with the characters in an imaginative range of real-life situations is "The Hopwood Family", first broadcast on Radio 4 in 1968 as interludes in the BBC series for secondary school assembly, "An Act of Worship", and still continuing in the BBC broadcasts for schools. In a sleeve note for the LP record of the same name (BBC RESR 9), Ralph Rolls, who designs and edits the series, writes :

As I felt it important to create characters whose predicaments young people could share and appreciate, the young Hopwoods represent a spread of the experience of young people of secondary school age. Nick is in his first year at secondary school, Peter is approaching school leaving age, and Janet has just started work. . . . My brief to Robert Lamb (who writes the series) was clear. The episodes in the life of the Hopwood Family must not contain any pre-selected moral conclusion. The situations from life must be clearly presented and the quality of the writing and presentation must attract the listener to associate and sympathise in his imagination. When these episodes appear in the "Act of Worship" I always invite the listeners to think what they would do if they were in the situation we present.

The teacher, however, is not dependent upon specially written material such as this for the content of Situation Themes. As well as drawing upon the real-life experiences of his own pupils or encouraging them to devise their own situations for discussion, he has all the wealth of literature, theatre and cinema at his disposal—not to mention the sports and "pop" culture of the young people themselves. When selecting material from these sources, though, it is essential that equal consideration is given to situation and character. This does not mean that all the characters should be paragons of virtue but that they should be well-defined, real and convincing. It is very unlikely that children will be able to identify with anyone who does not appear to be made of flesh and blood, who does not live in the real world and is not subject to the same temptations, feelings and aspirations as they are themselves. Without this identification there is very little possibility of their introjecting any of the attitudes displayed—something which is a major aim of Situation Themes. It is also helpful if work of this nature is not restricted to the R.E. or M.E. period but features also in other subjects. Integrated Studies provide a useful context for examining the wider social implications of actions and some English courses lend themselves to exploring situations involving moral dimensions. One such course is "New English" written by Alan Durband and published by Hutchinson. Each of the four volumes cover one year's work and contain suggestions for comprehension, practical work, criticism, creative writing, oral English and language development. In the sections entitled "Oral English" the author offers a wealth of situations involving carefully defined characters and prompts children to discuss these and come to a personal decision about what they would do in the circumstances. As well as fostering their capacity to express themselves clearly this work makes, therefore, a valuable contribution to their moral awareness. The Schools Council Nuffield Humanities Curriculum Project, especially "Relations Between the Sexes", "The Family" and "People at Work", is also a rich source of subject-matter for Situation Themes.

Special reference may be made at this juncture to the materials currently being produced by the Schools Council Moral Education Curriculum Project under the direction of Peter McPhail. These materials, which Longmans are publishing under the title "Life-line", form a comprehensive approach to moral and social education in the secondary school which promises to be one of the most exciting and valuable contributions to this field yet devised. As will be seen from the brief summary of the materials which follows, situations once again form the basis of the approach.

In Other People's Shoes: three sets of cards presenting situations as starting points for pupils. These are entitled "Sensitivity", "Consequences" and "Points of View".
Proving the Rule: five short books centring around situations involving the character of Paul and his relationships with his family, friends and society.
What Would You Have Done?: six 16-page booklets each considering a topic (commitment, persecution, compassion, addiction, disaster, prejudice) by taking a true situation as a basis for further work.

The rationale which underlines the approach and which is very similar to the one that we have been considering in this section is explained in *Moral Education in the Secondary School* by McPhail, Chapman and Ungoed-Thomas (Longmans, 1972).

We have already had occasion to refer to the work of John Wilson in Moral Education (p 57), especially to his suggestion that being morally educated is a complex concept involving six components. Depth Themes, we suggested, contribute to the development of some of these components; for example, EMP—the ability to have insight into one's own feelings and into other people's feelings—and PHIL —the attitude that the feelings and needs of other people are equally important with one's own. From what has been said about Situation Themes it may be argued that these may also contribute to the development of several of the components that Wilson has identified. For example, careful analysis of situations in the ways which we have suggested should foster DIK—the ability to form principles of behaviour in relation to other people's needs—and PHRON—the ability to form principles of behaviour in relation to one's own needs—as well as promoting sensitivity to those situations which require a moral decision—KRAT 1. And providing that the teacher ensures that work on situations is accompanied by the giving of information about topics in question (e.g. what the law of the country requires; regulations relating to employment; sex and so on) Situation Themes should extend GIG 1—the possession of enough factual information to be able to predict the consequences of one's actions. (GIG 2—the ability to communicate one's thoughts and feelings to other people—is covered by Symbol and Language Themes.) This means that the only component whose development is not specifically catered for by the *Existential Approach* is KRAT 2—the resolution to act in accordance with one's principles—and we have already expressed reservations about the possibility of meeting this except by way of the development of the other components.

But in what sense can we say that work of this nature contributes to the development of Religious Understanding as well as fostering moral insight? Can Situation Themes, as defined in this section, play a part in the process of initiating pupils into Religion as a unique mode of thought and awareness? No matter how we choose to try and answer these questions we need to recognise that behind them lies a very much larger question, namely, "Is there a logical connection between Morals and Religion?" The particular standpoint and conclusions that we adopt in relation to this question will, of course, be reflected in the sort of answers we give to the others. Unfortunately a careful analysis of so complex a question is clearly outside the plan of this book. This means that the points which follow should be seen as indications of *some* of the ways in which Situation Themes can provide a link between M.E. and R.E.

We have already stressed the crucial role that attitudes play in determining both moral perception and conduct. In an important book entitled *Education in Religion and the Emotions* (Heinemann, 1971) John Wilson points us to the emotions that underlie attitudes and reminds us of the importance to moral education of helping pupils to become more "reasonable" in this field. He also points us to an "arena" or "topic-area" in which all the most important emotions—love, hate, fear, guilt, anger, pity, forgiveness and so on—are considered and dealt with in one way or another, namely, Religion. Indeed, he observes that "religion can be regarded from one viewpoint as an institutionalisation of these emotions" (p 164). Furthermore some emotions—awe, reverence and worship—although perhaps not unique in religion are so central to it that they could be designated *"particularly* characteristic of the religious attitude" (p 42). Here then is an argument for a connection between Moral and Religious Education—in the use of religion as a means of presenting the spectrum of human emotions and so contributing to the education of children's emotions which we have already acknowledged to be of central importance to their moral development. Wilson, however, goes further. Although he concurs with the view that R.E. is "fundamentally concerned with the education of attitudes" he is anxious that R.E. should also be concerned with :

. . . educating children *in* religion; . . . that is, helping them to become more reasonable (i.e. to develop their moral components EMP, GIG and so on) in respect of those emotions and attitudes that are central to religion, so that they may more reasonably make or not make their own religious commitments, and assess those of other people (p 161).

Chapter 11 develops the implications of this view and this chapter, like the entire book, has a very great deal to offer to R.E. teachers, although, as the author warns in the preface, they may find some of the book rather heavy going.

Wilson's comments provide us with some guidelines for our own thinking about the ways in which Situation Themes may be used to promote insight into Religion—although we recognise that he may not necessarily agree with our interpretation or with our conclusions. Firstly, our choice of situations for examination can include ones which confront children with persons taking a particular line of action or adopting a particular attitude because of the *religious* beliefs that they happen to embrace. In Chapter 2 of this book we spent some time emphasising the importance of presenting religion in such ways as "to bring out the meanings and values to the participants" or, more simply, to help children to appreciate what it "feels" like to worship a particular god or believe in a particular religion. Situation Themes can meet this need by pointing children beyond actions and attitudes to the beliefs that underlie them—beliefs which reflect a particular type of response to distinctive emotional experiences. Here, then, is an opportunity for children to gain insight into a fundamental characteristic of Religion and religious belief and, at the same time, to examine how some people respond to those emotions and feelings which are also part of their own experiences. Here too is a chance for them to witness how, for some people, religious belief provides them with the resolution to act in accordance with certain principles (KRAT 2). It is important to note, however, that our aim in this respect is not necessarily to promote "religious attitudes" in children but rather to help them to understand the nature of religious attitudes so that they are in a position to assess religious claims more reasonably. Unless they are able to do this we are unlikely to succeed in our overall aim of helping them to find their way about Religion as a Form of Understanding. Similarly, in confronting them with "religious" responses to feelings of love, hate, fear, guilt, awe and so on —we are not seeking to lead children towards an acceptance of such responses as their own (although, of course, this may happen) but rather to encourage them to accept or admit to their *own* experiences of such feelings and come to some conclusions about the sort of responses *they* might reasonably adopt towards them.

The main aims of Situation Themes may, then, be summarised as follows :

1 To promote moral insight and development by providing an opportunity for children to :
   (a) explore, examine and discuss situations which call for a moral choice or judgment to be made about the situation or/and about the attitudes and actions of persons involved in it;
   (b) learn how to assess situations in terms of the consequences of attitudes and actions;
   (c) perceive the need for principles which can provide guide-lines for moral decision-making;
   (d) formulate principles which can provide guide-lines for moral decision-making;
   (e) perceive the connection between beliefs, values, attitudes and behaviour;
   (f) introject attitudes and values through identifying with characters displaying moral sensitivity;
   (g) accept or admit to their own emotional experiences and come to some conclusions about the sort of responses they might reasonably adopt towards them.
2 To initiate children into Religion as a unique mode of thought and awareness by providing them with an opportunity to :
   (a) explore, examine and discuss situations in which a religious belief is seen to provide the rationale underlying a person's attitudes, values and actions;
   (b) recognise that religious beliefs and attitudes reflect a particular type of response to certain emotional experiences;
   (c) gain insight into the "implicit" or feeling side of religion by examining the ways in which it deals with emotions, especially those particularly characteristic of the religious attitude, that is, awe, reverence and worship.

A number of examples of Situation Themes are given in Chapter 7 and Appendix One and some suggestions for methods of presenting them in Chapter 8.

Further reading

Psychology
M. Argyle : *The Psychology of Interpersonal Behaviour* (Penguin, 1967).
M. Argyle : *Religious Behaviour* (RKP, 1958).
M. Argyle : *Social Interaction* (Methuen, 1969).
J. A. C. Brown : *Freud and the Post-Freudians* (Penguin, 1958).

J. Brown : *Social Psychology* (Free Press, 1965).

D. Graham : *Moral Learning and Development: Theory and Research* (Batsford, 1972).

J. D. Halloran : *Attitude Formation and Change* (Leicester U.P., 1967).

A. W. Kay : *Moral Development* (Allen & Unwin, 1968).

L. Kohlberg : *Stages in the Development of Moral Thought and Action* (Holt, Rinehart & Winston, 1969).

R. D. Laing : *The Politics of Experience* (Penguin, 1967).

J. Piaget : *The Moral Judgment of the Child* (RKP, 1932).

N. & S. Williams : *The Moral Development of Children* (Macmillan, 1970).

D. Wright : *The Psychology of Moral Behaviour* (Penguin, 1971).

Ethics

R. F. Atkinson : *Conduct: an Introduction to Moral Philosophy* (Macmillan, Basic Books in Education, 1969).

R. W. Beardsmore : *Moral Reasoning* (RKP, 1969).

J. Fletcher : *Situation Ethics* (SCM Press, 1966).

J. Fletcher : *Moral Responsibility* (SCM Press, 1967).

M. Keeling : *Morals in a Free Society* (SCM Press, 1967).

J. D. Mabbott : *An Introduction to Ethics* (Univ. Paperbacks, 1961).

A. C. MacIntyre : *A Short History of Ethics* (Macmillan, 1968).

J. A. T. Robinson : *Christian Freedom in a Permissive Society* (SCM Press, 1970).

J. Wilson : *Moral Thinking* (A guide for students) (Heinemann, Concept Books, 1970).

Moral Education

P. R. May : *Moral Education in School* (Methuen, 1971).

P. McPhail et al : *Moral Education in the Secondary School* (Longmans, 1972).

J. Wilson *et al* : *Introduction to Moral Education* (Penguin, 1967).

J. Wilson : *Education in Religion and the Emotions* (Heinemann, 1971).

The Journal of Moral Education (Pemberton Publishing Co. Ltd).

In this chapter we have tried to show how the *Existential Approach* to R.E. is formed from the progressive combination of three types of theme—Depth Themes, Symbol and Language Themes and Situation Themes. All three types of theme seek to help children to discern and examine those dimensions in their own "existential" experiences which contribute to an understanding of religious concepts. Two of the themes—Depth and Situation Themes—encourage them to express and communicate their awareness of these dimensions in contemporary, "secular" terms while the other —Symbol and Language Themes—helps them to gradually acquire the necessary techniques for interpreting traditional religious language and symbols and gives them practice in using them. In this way the *Existential Approach* attempts to provide children with an opportunity to build "conceptual bridges" between their own experiences and the traditional concepts of religion—bridges which we hope will not only lead them towards a clearer perception of Religion as a Form of Understanding but also to a position where they can begin to assess for themselves its relevance or irrelevance as a special way of looking at and talking about the experiences of living.

Inevitably the reaction of some teachers and student-teachers to the approach we have outlined will be one of apprehension and scepticism. Some will, for example, find it difficult to reconcile its strong secular flavour with the notion of "religious teaching". Some will be hostile to the way that it apparently jettisons much of the traditional content of R.E. "Where," they will ask, "are we to include such things as the history of the Jews, the life of Jesus, the parables, the miracles, Saint Paul's journeys and so on?" Some will call in question the theological and educational premises upon which the approach rests, and some will query the choice of titles given to the themes—and why "themes" anyway? Some, we hope, however, will want to ask the really important question—"Does it work?"

To take this last question first, may we ask if the sort of R.E. which the vast majority of pupils in this country are receiving at the moment "works"? Do our pupils leave school theologically literate, willing and able to discuss religious ideas in an informed and coherent manner? If we could answer these questions with an assured "Yes" then there would be no need for a re-appraisal of R.E. nor, of course, for anyone to propose alternative lines of approach. Unfortunately, the only assured response that many teachers are able to give to these questions is a categorical "No" and when a subject is in that sort of position any change has to be for the better. The one that has been proposed in this chapter is not likely to be the answer; indeed, it doesn't claim to be. There is, however, more logic in risking failure with a different approach than continuing with an approach which we know has already failed. And when it comes to evaluation it is worthwhile reminding ourselves that any teaching approach is only as good (or bad) as the teacher using it.

In reply to the other points, one can only express the hope that

in setting out the approach in this chapter we have devoted sufficient time to an examination of its rationale for the reasons for
its "secular flavour" and apparent exclusion of much of the traditional content of R.E. to be understood if not accepted. There is,
however, one further consideration to be borne in mind. In our
increasingly secular and pluralist society we must not lose sight of
the importance of providing an approach to R.E. which meets
the needs of teachers as well as the needs of children. The number
of teachers and student-teachers who profess commitment to the
Christian faith and express willingness to accept and participate
in teaching traditional R.E. is diminishing. And yet these teachers
still find R.E. on their teaching timetable. Thus, one of the advantages of the Existential Approach is that it offers a possibility for
the teacher who is an atheist or an agnostic to engage in R.E. and
actively extend his pupils' awareness of religious concepts without
assaulting his own conscience. This is something which cannot be
claimed for the content and approach of traditional R.E.

Because of its concern with promoting concept formation, we suggested at the beginning of this chapter that work undertaken within
Existential Approach might be said to constitute the "core" of
R.E. For this reason and those that we have just given, we believe
that it is an approach which is suited to the needs of the non-
specialist teacher—although this is not to imply that it will not be
used by the specialist R.E. teacher. In our discussion of its rationale
we have indicated some of the ways in which traditional religious
content may be introduced into Symbol and Language Themes and
Situation Themes, provided, of course, that this content contributes to the achievement of the aims of these themes. Further suggestions along these lines are given in Chapter 7 and Appendix One.
It is envisaged that in College of Education "Professional R.E."
courses for non-specialist teachers the majority of time might be
spent acquainting students with the rationale underlying the Existential Approach and giving help in the choice of subject-matter, including traditional religious content, which might appropriately
be used at the different stages within it. It is important to note,
however, that although the *Existential Approach* seeks to provide
a basis for R.E. throughout both primary and secondary schools
and thus may be used on its own, it is likely to be more effective
when used in conjunction with the *Dimensional Approach*—Level 2
of our Conceptual Framework for R.E. It is to a consideration of
this approach and its relationship to the *Existential Approach* that
we now turn.

Chapter 6

A Conceptual Framework for Religious Education in Schools

Part Two : The Dimensional Approach

Introduction : A further comment on the Schools Council Working Paper No. 36, Religious Education in Secondary Schools

In Chapter 3 of this book we spent some time examining and commenting on the "phenomenological" or "undogmatic" approach to R.E. as outlined in the Schools Council Working Paper No. 36. It is important that we should acknowledge the fact that this approach, as far as schools are concerned, represents a strikingly new development in the teaching of religion. Indeed, it is so new that, at the time of writing, members of the Lancaster Project are still engaged in the process of examining ways in which it may be implemented in secondary schools. Their intention is to eventually recommend and illustrate by way of specimen teaching units, an approach to R.E. in the 11 to 16 age group which is consonant with the approach to any other subject of study.

Under the aegis of the Project over 100 teachers representing "a wide cross-section, not only of the different types of schools, County, Voluntary and Independent, but also the varied religious standpoints, Catholic and Protestant, Anglican and Free Church, Conservative and Liberal . . . and also several representatives of non-Christian faiths" are currently working in groups and sub-groups devising a large number of experimental "Units of Work". The Working Paper states :

> These will be first tried out by their authors with their own classes, and then, after revision, by a number of other teachers. The results will be carefully evaluated at both stages, and the Units which seem best to illustrate the theoretical basis will be made available generally. (p 83.)

Given the wide range of experience and expertise represented among members of the Project and the resources at their disposal, it may be confidently predicted that their efforts will undoubtedly result in proposals which, if implemented, will set R.E. on the sound educational footing that it has been needing for so long.

The success of any educational innovation, however, is determined to a considerable extent by the willingness of teachers to recognise the value and importance of what is recommended and to be educated in its use. Aware of this fact, the Working Paper speaks realistically of the "enormous demands" that this new approach makes "on the breadth of outlook and learning, the maturity of thought and the sheer professional expertise of the teacher" and acknowledges that "the success of this development will depend upon how far the Colleges of Education and the Universities are able to produce teachers with the right sort of education to undertake it" (p 77). Certainly one hopes very much that with the publication of the Project's final recommendations and materials both Colleges and Universities will revise their courses along lines consonant with the approach, and, in addition, make provision for serving teachers to become acquainted with its new demands. But, as we noted earlier, (pp 32-33) when considering courses it is important to make a distinction between the needs of the specialist teacher of R.E. and those of the non-specialist. Although one must not attempt to anticipate let alone pre-judge the final recommendations of the Project, the Working Paper, concerned as it is with secondary schools, does appear to imply, especially in the section entitled "Implications for Teacher Training", that its proposals will have the specialist rather than the non-specialist teacher in mind. If this is the case several points may be made.

Firstly, the recently published BCC Report (*The Recruitment, Employment and Training of Teachers of Religious Education,* 1971) shows very clearly that not only is there a great deficiency of specialist teachers of R.E. in secondary schools ("63.1 per cent of R.E. on average in all secondary schools is given by teachers 'who have not studied the subject' compared with 19.1 per cent for History and 36.1 per cent for what is often regarded as *the* shortage subject, mathematics", BCC Report, p 9) but that the limited number of students currently entering Colleges and Universities with the intention of specialising in R.E. is unlikely to bring about an improvement in the position in the foreseeable future. (The percentage of post-graduates training for R.E. in 1969 was 1.3 per cent compared with approximately 60 per cent of women and 43 per cent of men taking Arts subjects.) The number of specialists in the primary school is, of course, proportionally very much worse. This means that if we take primary and secondary schools together the number of children who are taught R.E. by a specialist (i.e. someone who has followed a three- or four-year "main" course in Religious Studies) is considerably less than the number who are taught the subject by a non-specialist (i.e. someone who has followed, *at best,* a one-year "professional" course in R.E.). Thus, even though we may be justified in setting our sights on increasing the number of specialist teachers and equipping them with greater expertise in the subject, at least equal consideration must be given to their non-specialist counterparts in the meantime. We may ask, then, if it is realistic to suppose that tutors will be able to "produce teachers with the right sort of education" to undertake R.E. based on this approach if their students are not specialising in R.E. and if the total time allocation for a one-year "professional" course amounts only to a mere 30 hours? (In some Colleges students receive only ten hours of "professional" R.E. in their three-year course!) To speak, as the Working Paper does on p 80, of the chief function of tutors being "to teach their apprentices the skills of disciplined enquiry" by learning "to give students one corner of a topic and refusing to go on to the next until from the one they have discovered the other three corners" is to hold up an educational ideal which many tutors applaud and already practice within their "main" course—courses which normally have a time allocation of six hours per week for three or four years. Few, however, would be prepared to attempt to realise the same ideal within a "professional" course twenty times shorter in length than a "main" course and often attended by students whose interest in the subject is minimal!

But, it may be argued, the Project is concerned with secondary schools and the points suggested here are more applicable to the primary schools. It is true that most "professional" R.E. courses in Colleges are attended by students who intend to teach in primary schools. But to admit to this is not to solve the problem—indeed it is to make it even more acute. If the "phenomenological" approach to R.E. is acknowledged to be one which sets the subject upon a sound educational footing then it follows that it should become the basis for R.E. throughout both secondary *and* primary schools. The Working Paper in its discussion of the importance of presenting more than one religious viewpoint and encouraging objectivity of judgment, concurs with this view when, from suggesting that "A Christian child can be a Jew for a day or an hour by witnessing a sacred festival or by acting out a part in an imagined ritual occasion", it goes on to state:

Objectivity is thus possible for pupils of all ages and all degrees of intellectual maturity. The same fundamental principle of self-transcending awareness governs at all intellectual levels. The difference in treatment between work with young children and that with more mature pupils is not the degree of objectivity that is possible but the degree of abstraction that can be employed in the consideration of alternative interpretations (p 20).

Thus, not only do we see the need for implementing the phenomenological approach to R.E. in the primary schools, we also see that it is at this level that it makes the greatest demands on the teacher's expertise. In addition to possessing a thorough insight into the nature of religion and religious belief and knowledge of the ways in which this receives expression in the various faiths, a primary school teacher needs to be especially sensitive to the problems of communicating religious awareness to children who have not yet reached the stage of abstract conceptual thought. This is clearly the job of a specialist and yet many students who leave College and enter the primary schools do so after receiving a "training" in R.E. of a mere 30 hours duration! The dilemma facing the Colleges is obvious. They see the need, we hope, for introducing the phenomenological approach to R.E. into schools and recognise the "enormous demands" that this approach makes on the teacher's expertise. At the same time they are aware that the vast majority of primary school teachers will undertake R.E. in the schools to which they are appointed and yet they can only offer these students a "professional" course of approximately one hour per week in their first year in College. Fortunately some Colleges, especially Voluntary Colleges, have been able to increase the time allocation to "professional" R.E. as a result of dispensing with a second "main" subject, but over-reliance on possibilities of extending courses is an unrealistic approach to the problem—too many other subject departments are anxious to press their claims for more time. It would appear then that we have to ask the question : "Given that Colleges are unlikely to be able to make more time available to "professional" courses, is it possible to educate non-specialist teachers in the phenomenological approach to R.E.?"

A definitive answer to this question cannot be given until considerably more work has been done on the approach, especially in adapting it for use at the primary level. Clearly its future lies in the expert hands of members of the Lancaster Project and in the sort of reception which schools, Colleges, Universities and Local Authorities give to their final recommendations. It is important to note, however, that developments in R.E. are dependent upon developments in Religious Studies and Theology generally. In Chapter 2 and following our discussion of the work of Piaget in Chapter 4, we emphasised the need for children to be taught the "structure" of a subject—the complex relationship of facts to concepts and concepts to principles—rather than an assortment of unrelated facts and pieces of information. We saw, however, that the primary task of identifying the "key-concepts" and the "structure" of a subject lies outside the competence of most teachers and that they are dependent here upon the work of acknowledged experts in the subject-field—University professors and their staffs. We expressed regret that in many academic fields, including theology, little thought and work has been devoted to this crucial task. It would appear, though, that work in the Religious Studies Department of Lancaster University under the direction of Professor Ninian Smart, has a very direct bearing on this task. One hopes, therefore, that the reference on p 80 of the Working Paper to College tutors choosing the "representative ideas" of a subject in their work with students, may be taken to imply that we may look forward to receiving eventually an outline of the key-concepts and structure of religion and of some of the different faiths of which it is composed together with examples of subject-matter which best illustrate these. Educationists will then be in a position to determine ways in which it is possible to relate this subject-matter and methods of presentation to the developmental pattern of children's thinking. With this work in hand it may well be the case that non-specialist teachers may be educated in the phenomenological approach to R.E. just as they are currently being educated in modern mathematics.

In the meantime, however, it would be of particular benefit if teachers and students were to acquaint themselves with the thinking which underlies the phenomenological approach and become more familiar with the idea of seeing religion in terms of the six dimensions which Professor Smart has listed, i.e. ritual, mythological, doctrinal, ethical, social and experiential. Smart's book, *The Religious Experience of Mankind* (Collins Fontana Library, 1971), is invaluable in this respect although some will find its length somewhat daunting. Set out in the remainder of this chapter is a scheme for R.E. covering both primary and secondary schools which, without attempting to implement the phenomenological approach in its entirety, provides an opportunity for teachers and students to become accustomed to dealing with the six dimensions of religion in their work with children. As such it may be said to be a scheme which is within the scope of the non-specialist teacher of R.E. and which could prepare him for acceptance and use of the complete phenomenological approach when it is eventually made available in its fully developed form. As indicated earlier, this approach, the *Dimensional Approach,* is designed to complement the *Existential Approach* which was outlined in Chapter 5.

Level Two: The Dimensional Approach

We have already noted (p 28) that the six dimensions of religion are inter-related and inter-dependent. For example, a mystical or religious experience prompts the characteristic response of awe (experiential dimension) and this, in turn, prompts a feeling of need to adore, worship and pray and also to proclaim to others the experience which underlies and gives meaning to these acts. These needs are met by the creation of stories, hymns and poems and the incorporation of these into liturgies; sometimes these point to the special significance of an historical event or of a person (mythological and ritual dimensions). Those with similar types of experience (and those who seek such experiences) unite to form a community of believers—men and women holding common beliefs and advocating a particular life-style. They adopt a certain form of organisation and determine lines of conduct consonant with their beliefs (social and ethical dimensions). Their beliefs eventually come to be expressed in and through confessional statements, formularies and creeds, the truths of which are validated in terms of what has been "revealed" through an event, a person or a sacred scripture, or what continues to be revealed through the continuing existence of the community of believers and their common experience (doctrinal dimension). The aim of the *Dimensional Approach* to R.E. is to initiate children into religion as a unique mode of thought and awareness by helping them to become familiar with its six dimensions, especially with the way in which the experiential dimension provides the justification for the existence of the others. At the same time, through presenting selected religious concepts by way of these six dimensions and linking them with insights gained from work with the Existential Approach, it seeks to enable children to build conceptual bridges between their own experiences and what they recognise to be the central concepts of religion.

Educationally acceptable though these aims may be, at first sight they would appear to do little to resolve the central problem involved in teaching religion to children, namely, that of relating "religious material" to the developmental pattern of childrens thinking. In other words, although each of the six dimensions provides us with a different starting-point from which to examine religion, all, in their own way, are equally complex and involve material based on concepts and ways of thinking which, from an intellectual point of view, are largely outside the capacity of children who have not reached the stage of formal operational thought. The *Dimensional Approach,* however, attempts to meet this difficulty by emphasising that "understanding" religion is not only a matter of grappling with certain concepts at an intellectual level but also being aware of the sort of feelings or emotions which are involved in religious belief. Indeed, the approach begins with the premise that it is the "implicit" or feeling side of religion which provides the basis and the justification for the existence of "religious" as opposed to other types of concepts. How can this observation help us to relate "religious material" to the developmental pattern of children's thinking? In Chapter 4 we suggested that although intelligent, intellectual grasp of formal religious concepts is rarely possible before 13 or 14 years of age, even very young children can *feel* (a kind of knowing) things which they are capable neither of articulating nor fully understanding intellectually. Could it be, then, that our first priority when introducing children to religion should be to *sensitise them to the feelings* which underlie religious beliefs and practices rather than to give them an accurate *intellectual grasp* of its characteristic teaching? If this is so, our problem—at least with children in the primary school—is no longer one of trying to find material which is compatible with the stage of their intellectual development but one of selecting material which is best able to evoke in them a sense of religious experience and a perception of how adherents to a religious faith *feel* about life. Helping children towards an intellectual grasp of religious concepts is something with which we can become more concerned later—when we have already succeeded in giving them an appreciation of the "implicit" side of religion and when they have reached the stage of Formal Operations.

These observations provide us with guidelines for determining a framework for the *Dimensional Approach*. Faced with the six dimensions of religion, the ones which are *best* able to illustrate the "implicit" side of religion will need to be introduced to children before those in which it is less obvious. Thus, the experiential, mythological and ritual dimensions are logically prior, on this basis, to the social, ethical and doctrinal dimensions. Because the dimensions are inter-related and inter-dependent, however, provision needs to be made for work on them to overlap. This is facilitated if we link the experiential dimension with the mythological and ritual dimensions and the social dimensions with the ethical dimension. We are then left with three "areas" of subject-matter or material to be introduced into the framework: 1. experiential, mythological and ritual material; 2. social and ethical material; 3. doctrinal material. The diagram on p 50 shows how these three areas have been introduced into the framework in a manner which is similar to the accumulative process adopted for the three types of theme which comprise the Existential Approach, that is, introducing the different types of material in stages but ensuring that the scheme allows for work in each area to continue alongside that of the other areas. It is important to recognise that the scheme allows for work at Level 2 to be related to work at Level 1. Indeed, the *Dimensional Approach* may often provide illustration of how concepts arising from work, for example, on Depth Themes, are central to religion. Relating the two approaches in this way is crucial to the achievement of the common aim of the *Existential* and *Dimensional Approaches*—that of enabling children to build conceptual bridges between their own experiences and what they recognise to be the central concepts of religion. Further explanation

94

of the rationale underlying the *Dimensional Approach* and its relationship to the *Existential Approach* will be given in the following sections.

(a) *Experiential material*

Even in the over-simplified account of religion with which we began this consideration of the *Dimensional Approach* it is possible to see how the experiential dimension is central to religion and provides the justification for the existence of the other dimensions. It is this dimension which points us more precisely to the essence or nature of religion and religious belief. Indeed, it is the presence of an experiential dimension which distinguishes a "religion" from other types of belief-system. And yet, despite its crucial importance, it is this dimension which has been most neglected in traditional R.E. The *Dimensional Approach* attempts to compensate for this by making work on the experiential dimension the basis for work on the other dimensions throughout both primary and secondary schools. You will see from the diagram on p 50 that at Level 2, work on experiential material occupies a position analogous to that occupied at Level 1 by work on Depth Themes. But the relationship between the two is much closer than that they simply occupy analogous positions in their respective approaches; there is also a considerable overlap in their work both in matters of content and intention. Depth Themes, as we tried to show earlier, are designed to help children to practise the skill of looking into their own existential experiences at depth and expressing what they discern in contemporary, secular terms. Some of these experiences prompt feelings of awe and wonder and a sense of mystery—feelings which Depth Themes help them to explore and accept as essential constituents of man's experience. The teacher's task in using the Dimensional Approach is to try and bring work on material illustrating the experiential dimension of religion within the ambit of those insights which work on Depth Themes serves to promote. For example, he might choose to illustrate the traditional religious concepts of awe, wonder and mystery by referring to "religious" experiences in the lives of individuals (e.g. Jesus, Paul, Muhammad, the Buddha, saints and holy men and so on) or to the experiences which are felt to sustain the spiritual life of communities or faiths (e.g. the experience of the Presence of Christ in the Blessed Sacrament, of the Holy Spirit in the Church, and of the Buddha's response to the prayers of Mahayana Buddhists and so on). But having done this—or, more accurately, *while* doing this— he must seek to *link* these religious interpretations of awe, wonder and mystery with those insights into awe, wonder and mystery which the children have already developed as a result of reflecting

95

on their own "secular" experiences. In this way he can help them to become aware of the all-important "feeling" side of religion and, at the same time, gain more accurate and meaningful insights into traditional religious concepts. In subsequent work he will need to show how the religious interpretation given to these experiences results in a person committing himself to a particular perspective from which to view life, and how it accounts for his willingness to subscribe to religious doctrines and creeds and adopt characteristically religious practices such as taking the sacraments, praying, going on a pilgrimage and fulfilling other ritual and ethical obligations. With children aged 13 or 14 onwards a further aspect of the work will be that of examining the alternative interpretations which might be given to these experiences—aesthetic and psychological as well as religious.

Here we have an example, then, of how subject-matter dealing with the experiential dimension of religion may be linked with insights arising from work on Depth Themes. It is important to note, too, how the experiential dimension acts as a "baseline" for work on the other dimensions of religion—a point to which we will return in a moment. It would be wrong, though, to attempt to disguise the tremendous complexity of the accounts of "religious experience" which appear in religious writings—especially those which try to isolate the phenomenon itself. In actual fact there are very few examples of the latter because as soon as we venture into the realms of awe, wonder and mystery we find ourselves dealing with figurative accounts full of evocative, metaphorical and poetic language (e.g. Moses and the burning bush, Isaiah's vision in the Temple, Paul's experience of the Risen Christ on the Damascus road, Muhammad's revelationary experiences and so on). In view of the difficulties which these accounts present—especially to those who are unfamiliar with the special characteristics and pecularities of religious language—does it mean that we cannot use "religious material" to illustrate the experiential dimension of religion with children until they have acquired the necessary techniques to interpret it? (i.e. following work on Symbol and Language Themes and, therefore, not much before the age of 11 or 12). If our only concern when introducing such accounts was to foster understanding at an *intellectual* level, there would be little point in using them with children in the primary school. Indeed to use them with this purpose may well have the effect of reinforcing a literal interpretation of their symbolism. We have chosen, however, to give priority in our work with children of primary school age to the task of *sensitising them to the feelings which underlie religious beliefs and practices.* Let us look for a moment at the implications of this choice for a teacher of Infant and Lower Junior school children.

In Chapter 5 we spent some time considering how Depth Themes may serve to lay the foundations for an understanding of religious concepts even though this work is secular by nature. If this is to be achieved, however, it is necessary that the teacher selects themes which are not only relevant to the children's immediate experiences but which are also likely to involve them in exploration of concepts which have a place in religion. We spoke in this connection of the need for the teacher to determine in advance the "points of focus" of a theme. A particularly striking characteristic of young children is their capacity to find and enjoy a sense of awe, wonder and mystery in the world about them. We have already noted that awe, wonder and mystery are key-concepts in religion. Indeed these three concepts actually constitute the experiential dimension. Here, then, is a natural affinity between the children's experiences and thought-forms and certain crucial concepts in religion—an affinity which it is the teacher's responsibility to exploit and develop. Depth Themes provide the initial context for this to take place. The teacher will deliberately choose to involve children in work on themes which will lead them to an awareness of awe, wonder and mystery. Possible themes will include : Our Wonderful World, Sounds, Seeds, Animal Families, Colours, Our Favourite Things and so on. Work of this nature, however, will need to be augmented by opportunities for the children to actually experience these concepts within a *religious context* if conceptual bridges are to be made. This context may be supplied in three ways in particular : through acts of worship in school, through films and tapes, and through stories. In these three contexts the abstract nature of religious experience is given concrete or pictorial form, or, in other words, the *mythological and ritual dimensions* of religion are seen to fulfil their task as *expressions* of the experiential dimension. The teacher of young children, then, is likely to find that the task of sensitising children to the experiential side of religion will inevitably involve work on the mythological and ritual dimensions—despite their difficulties. It is for this reason that the diagram on p 50 shows mythological and ritual material being introduced to children as early as the Infant school. It is important to note, however, that when this type of material is introduced to young children the teacher's intention should be to allow the material to evoke a sense of the experience of which it is an expresion and not to foster *intellectual* understanding of the theological ideas that it contains. We will say more about this in the following section.

Further reading

J. G. Davies : *Every Day God. Encountering the Holy in World and Worship* (SCM Press, 1972).

W. James: *The Varieties of Religious Experience* (1902; Fontana, 1971).

H. D. Lewis: *Our Experience of God* (Allen & Unwin, 1959).

R. Otto: *The Idea of the Holy* (OUP, 1923).

N. Smart: *Philosophers and Religious Truth* (SCM, 1969).

N. Smart: *The Phenomenon of Religion* (Macmillan, 1973).

(b) *Mythological and Ritual material*

As a form of symbolic thought and expression, myth plays a central role in many, if not all religions. It is, however, very easy for 20th-century man to overlook the abiding value that myth has to religion, especially if his only idea of it is that of "a purely fictitious narrative usually involving supernatural persons, actions or events and embodying some popular idea concerning natural or historical phenomena" (Oxford English Dictionary). This sort of definition reflects the disrepute into which myth fell between the 18th and 20th centuries. Fortunately modern studies in depth psychology and the history of religions have brought about a rehabilitation of myth as a distinct mode of knowledge which can never be adequately reduced to rational discourse. Understandably myth occupies a more obvious position in early religions and in those which have a very limited historical basis (such as Hinduism) than it does in later religions and those which attribute special religious significance to certain historical events and persons (such as Christianity). In these latter religions the mythological elements have been subjected to a process of "de-mythologisation"—but not completely. In Christianity and Judaism, for example, history and myth are intertwined, myth being used to give expression to beliefs about the cosmic significance of the historical events. Thus we must learn to see myth as a construct of a believing community whereby its faith finds expression. As such it provides the matrix out of which the refinements of religious language, including theological or doctrinal language, have arisen. A study of myths, their nature and function is, therefore, a very useful starting-point for developing insight into religious language and into the nature of religion itself. This needs to be borne in mind when thinking about the education of R.E. teachers and, of course, when planning work for R.E. in schools. A number of books dealing with myth have been recommended at the end of this section.

Despite the criticism to which the "Myth and Ritual" thesis has been subjected in recent years, there is much to be said for seeing at least one aspect of myth's origin in the need to provide a kind of libretto to ritual action. Within the context of ritual the function of myth is both evocative and explanatory. It is evocative in that it points the worshipper to, what might be called, "cosmic truths" and projects him, symbolically at least, into "sacred" as opposed to "profane" time. It is explanatory in that it provides a commentary on ritual action which, in its turn, seeks to release the truths embodied in the myth into the here and now. Myth and ritual combine, therefore, to give both dramatic and concrete expression to those experiences which we have seen to be at the centre of religion. A particularly fine example of this, suitable for use with children from about nine years of age onwards, is the Babylonian "Enuma elish"—a ritual chant describing the victory of the god Marduk over the chaos-dragon, Tiamat, and the ensuing act of creation. This was used at the annual New Year Festival (Akitu) in Babylon when the king played the part of the god and the original act of creation was re-enacted. The purpose of this festival was to ensure the perpetuation of the created order but it also seems likely that it provided an opportunity for the people to re-affirm their allegiance to Marduk as their god (and to the king, his earthly representative) and to express their conviction that the world in which they lived had its origin in a divine purpose. The view that Israel celebrated a similar "New Year Festival of Yahweh" or a "Feast of Yahweh's enthronement" is not universally accepted by scholars but Psalms 47, 93, 96, 97, 98 and 99, dealing with the subject of Yahweh's Kingship over all the earth, possess a quality which makes them admirably suitable as the spoken part of a liturgy celebrating such an occasion. These psalms, like the "Enuma elish", not only illustrate man's response in worship to the feelings of awe and wonder which arise from his contemplation of the natural order of the universe, they evoke a sense of awe and wonder itself. The same is precisely true of the Hebrew Creation Myth in Genesis Chapter 1. Work with children on any of this material, therefore, needs to be undertaken with the intention of communicating to them something of its "feeling". How successfully this can be achieved will depend very considerably upon the methods chosen for its presentation. (See Chapter 8.)

So far we have been considering myth and ritual in a narrow and rather specialised sense. The *Dimensional Approach,* however, demands that we adopt much broader definitions of these words and so allow for the use of material other than that which illustrates the myth and ritual pattern. "Mythological material" may be taken to include, therefore, not only myths but all the many literary forms which a religion uses to express its beliefs *other than doctrinal formularies and creeds*. These include legends, epics, sagas, hymns, songs, poems, proverbs, discourses, biographies, autobiographies, oracles, letters, gospels and so on. Similarly, "Ritual material" may be taken to include any of the many acts or actions which a religion uses as expressions of belief. These include saying prayers, reciting creeds, making the sign of the cross, prostrating oneself on the ground in the direction of Mecca, taking the sacraments, fasting, going on a pilgrimage, pronouncing the sacred syllable "OM", making offerings to the gods, following a "rule" (such as the Ten Precepts of Buddhism), adopting a particular mode of dress (the Sikh turban or the Buddhist saffron robe) and carrying sacred objects and symbols (the Jewish tallith and phylacteries, the Sikh bangle and dagger). Useful though it is to extend the meaning of "myth" and "ritual" in this way, it does mean that we are faced with the problem of having to select material for use with our pupils from a wide range of possibilities. Let us look for a moment at some of the considerations that we might bear in mind when making our selection.

If we accept the view that a major aim of R.E. is to *sensitise children to the feeling side of religion,* we should recognise the extent to which feeling or emotion underlies many, if not all religious concepts and is present in religious literature and ritual. For example, the concepts of fatherhood, sonship, community, courage, sacrifice, trust, faith, loyalty, hope, reverence, joy, love and so on, gain their strength and meaning in Christianity from their emotional constituents rather than from the intellectual, doctrinal superstructure into which they are incorporated. Similarly, the function of religious literature—whether it is myth, legend, saga, oracle or gospel—and religious ritual is to express the *living* faith of a believing community—a faith which is sustained by experience of the divine. For example, the Gospel accounts of Jesus's birth, life, death and resurrection express the early Christian Church's experience of the Risen Christ and its accompanying conviction that Jesus is not only "Son of God" but "God made man". The same is true of the Old Testament, the Qur'an, the Vedas, the Granth, the Jataka Tales and so on—all are permeated with the experience and convictions of communities sharing a common religious faith. Thus, an essential skill which the teacher of religion must develop is that of seeing religious subject-matter in terms of the experiences and convictions of which it is an expression. Or, in other words, looking at religious literature and ritual "through the eyes of those who believe" whether they are Jews, Christians, Hindus, Muslims, Sikhs or Buddhists. Consequently, the subject-matter he chooses to use with children should be that which is best able to evoke in them a sense of the intensity of experience and conviction with which it is charged. R.E., at least with primary school children, thus becomes a matter of immersing pupils in the spirit of a religion by letting them participate in and enjoy the excitement and drama of its stories and ritual, not necessarily for the sake of understanding their subtle theological nuances or deep symbolic significances, but in order to give them a feeling of how man responds to his awareness of the divine.

Another consideration that we might bear in mind when selecting material to illustrate the mythological and ritual dimensions of religion is breadth or variety. If we are concerned to initiate children into *religion* as a unique mode of thought and awareness then the material which we use to illustrate religion should not be restricted to the Judaeo-Christian tradition but embrace all living faiths. While most teachers are prepared to admit to both the possibility and the desirability of this in the teaching of religion to secondary school children, many have reservations about including "World Religions" in primary school R.E. If our aim was to give children in the primary school an *intellectual* grasp of "Islam", "Hinduism", "Sikhism" and so on as distinct belief-systems, each with its own personal identity, characteristics and doctrinal structure, then reservations about such a suggestion would be justified (even though many teachers would be happy to accept this aim in relation to teaching Christianity in the primary school!). Our aim, however, is to help children to become aware of the phenomenon called "Religion" and to give them some appreciation of the sort of experiences and feelings which underlie religious belief. We have tried to show how Depth Themes contribute to the achievement of this aim and why, therefore, they should provide the basis for most of our work with children from the age of five to eight years. There is a need, though, for even very young children to be given an opportunity to come into contact with distinctively religious material, despite the problems presented by the pre-operational nature of their thinking. It has been customary for teachers to use Bible *stories* to meet this need and they have chosen stories which they have believed to be within their children's comprehension. These have usually been ones with an apparent historical basis. We have already seen in Chapter 4 something of the effect that this sort of teaching has had on children's religious thinking. An effect which we did not mention in our earlier discussion is the tendency for children to grow up with the idea that "truth" in religion needs to be *historical* truth—an idea which is more likely to retard their later theological understanding than assist it. This is a product of teachers satisfying children who ask, "Is it true?", with the answer, "Yes, it actually happened". We can, perhaps, avoid some of these problems if we introduce children of this age to stories, legends, myths, poems and hymns from *many* religious traditions without attempting to classify them within particular faiths or in terms of "historical" and "non-historical", and place our emphasis on the feelings which they express—especially on the feelings of any of the characters involved—rather than upon what the stories "mean". To adult minds this suggestion might appear to be most undesirable; children will be unable to distinguish between things that actually happened and between people who actually lived and

101

those that did not; they will confuse events in Jesus's life with those in the life of Muhammad—or worse still, in the life of Krishna!—they will be bewildered when they go to Church; they will lose their identity as "Christians" and so on, and so on. Certainly these are realistic objections to the *adult mind*, especially if it is the mind of a committed Christian who supports a confessional approach to R.E., but children's minds are different. Their "global" view of knowledge prohibits classification except in a very vague way; their identity as "Christians" can hardly be called conscious or voluntary at this age; their concept of history is undeveloped. They can, however, "feel" the spirit of stories even though they may not be able to communicate it in words. We should learn from their reactions to fairy stories; they *know* that a story about a knight and a dragon is about the conflict of good and evil because they *feel* it in the story. But if we were to ask them to tell us what the story is about they would answer, "About a knight and a dragon"! Is it not equally possible that they can *feel* what underlies a story such as Moses and the burning bush or even one of Jesus's miracles and still answer "About a burning bush" or "About a man who was blind"? It is, perhaps, a possibility which depends upon how we present the story to them.

In Chapter 5 we tried to show how religious language has a logical kinship with the language of poetry. This is not only to be seen in the use of language which is dramatic, evocative and symbolic, but also in the treatment that we must give the language if it is to "speak" to us. Poetry, as most of us are only too aware, can be dull, flat, monotonous, unchallenging when it is read aloud by a person who has no feeling for it. The same is true of religious literature, especially stories. This, like poetry, only begins to come alive and speak when we capture in our reading something of how the writer (and the religious community of which he is a member) *feels* about the thoughts, persons and events with which he is concerned. (See, for example, Isaiah Chapter 5.) Consideration about the presentation of subject-matter might very well begin, therefore, with some careful thinking about how effective we are as readers of stories. But a great deal of religious literature (especially in the Bible) has undergone a process of editing and compression and consequently the final literary form of a story—often designed to express a theological point—sometimes lacks the verve that the story may have had in its original oral form. While it may be possible to help children of about 13 or 14 years of age to understand not only the theological significance of the story but how theological considerations have contributed to its form, we can hardly have this intention in mind if we choose to use the same story with younger children. Instead we should be concerned to help them to *enjoy it* and sense something of the emotional or spiritual qualities it contains—qualities such as peace, courage, hope, joy, grandeur, fear, loneliness, love and so on. To do this we may have to *tell* it in our own words, with our own images, and even with our own interpolations, omissions and re-arrangements of its original outline. A good teacher knows which stories should be read and how to read them, and which stories should be told and how to tell them. For example, by any standards the Nativity of Jesus is a beautiful story. It has all the ingredients to capture a child's imagination and allow the eternal themes of love, peace and good-will to speak to him directly. With primary school children we should take care not to spoil the story's capacity to evoke a sense of wonder, beauty and mystery by too close an analysis of its different parts and features. In many ways we should approach it as we might approach a piece of music in a musical appreciation lesson; not breaking it down into pieces because, like a melody, it is the overall effect that is important, nor obstructing the child's own view of its beautiful message by raising our own objections and difficulties or by offering theological explanations. Here we are not teaching facts and knowledge; we are concerned with the communication of feeling. Thus, a sensitive *telling* of this story can teach a child more about the meaning of gifts and giving, the family, love, peace, humility and worship—not to mention an appreciation of awe, wonder and mystery—than any number of "explanatory" words. It can also, of course, disclose the meaning of the Incarnation to him *at his level*. Clearly, R.E. teachers cannot afford to neglect the need to be good story-tellers—especially if they are working with young children. Neither must they neglect to make use of other devices which can promote greater insight into the feeling side of religion—drama, dance, music, painting, films and radio broadcasts.

The considerations that we have noted in relation to our choice and presentation of mythological material—and the intention with which it should be used—are equally applicable to ritual material. Here, however, we are dealing with *actions* by and through which a man responds to his awareness of the divine—actions which reflect physically and externally his inner, spiritual experience and the beliefs to which he is committed. Ritual, the physical or overt side of worship, can never be fully understood, therefore, apart from the spiritual or covert side of worship, namely the believer's attitude of mind, or, more accurately, the disposition of his heart, for it is this which reveals both the significance and intention of the actions. And yet ritual *qua ritual* has a capacity to promote and heighten a sense of awe and wonder for those who engage in it; as well as being an expression of their faith it can also be a means by which their faith is sustained and deepened. Even those who are not committed to religious belief may gain a greater insight into the nature of religion and religious belief through involvement in ritual or an act of worship (e.g. the Mass, a pilgrimage, a Bar Mitzvah and so on) than through an academic examination of beliefs and a technical knowledge of what ritual symbolises. Through involvement they place themselves in a position where the feeling side of religion is able to be disclosed to them through the splendour, colour, solemnity and mystery of a liturgy, or, more importantly, through the sincere devotion of those who participate in it.

It is the visual appeal of ritual and its close association with the feeling side of religion which makes it a valuable source of religious material for use with children. It contributes most effectively to their development of religious understanding, however, when opportunities are arranged for them to *participate* in ritual and acts of worship—preferably those of a variety of faiths. The school's "Morning Assembly" should provide such an opportunity. In an article entitled "World Religions in the Infant School" ("Child Education", Autumn 1970), Elizabeth Wilson describes how Diwali, the Hindu festival of lights, provided an opportunity for children in an Infant school to share the songs, music, dances, stories and rhymes of their Asian class-mates. It also enabled them to participate in an act of worship which involved ritual. She writes :

Last year, at Diwali, we put a number of small lamps—some were night lights which we stood in jam jars surrounded by coloured tissue paper—on the tables in the school hall. The children came quietly and wide-eyed into the hall for assembly while Indian classical music was being played. We sang one of our well known hymns, "Teach me to love, teach me to pray", which ends with the words, "Guard me when Mother turns out the light", and then we talked about fear of the dark, how glad we are to have lights, and how we burn candles at Christmas and at birthday parties when we are happy. In India, in October the summer rains are over, and people are happy because the skies are clear and they can see the stars at night. The festival of lights, called Diwali, is held then, and the story of Prince Rama is remembered. I told the story at assembly. . . . At the end of the story I said the following prayer: "Dear God, thank you for the joy of light and candles and twinkling stars. Help us not to be afraid when it is dark, but to be brave and helpful to all your creatures as Prince Rama was." We then sang the hymn, "All things bright and beautiful", and afterwards the Asian children, each holding a candle, stood in the middle of the hall while we wished them "A happy Diwali". In this assembly, which lasted about a quarter of an hour, we recognised that joy, light and homecomings are experiences enjoyed by children of all faiths.

Experiences of this nature may be extended and enriched by visits to places of worship (churches, cathedrals, mosques, temples, gurdwaras, synagogues, meeting houses) organised with the intention of helping children to find out more about faiths and become more familiar with their worship at first hand. Their attention should also be drawn to objects used in worship and the way in which buildings are designed to facilitate participation in the liturgies. If opportunities for such visits are limited, films and tapes which capture the "atmosphere" of the different faiths (especially as it is expressed in worship) can provide substitute experiences. Visits from priests, monks, imams and so on, willing to talk about their faith to the children may also be useful, provided that they are able to avoid involving children, especially in the primary school, in the complex dimension of doctrine. A rabbi might be invited to talk about some of the ceremonies of the Jewish faith and illustrate these by bringing with him some of the ritual objects and dress they include.

In conclusion, we should note that work on material illustrating the experiential, mythological and ritual dimensions of religion begins *prior* to the introduction of Symbol and Language Themes. (See the diagram on p 50). This means that children should already have a *feel* for stories and ritual—especially for the drama and mystery which lies behind them—and a *sense* of their importance to religion *before* we begin to concentrate our efforts upon helping them towards an understanding of the special characteristics of religious language and symbolism at an *intellectual* level. They should also have an acquaintance (not an over-familiarity) with some of the central stories of religion which can then be used as illustrations of some of the features which Symbol and Language Themes try to identify. Indeed, mythological and ritual material, allied to the experiential side of religion, is likely to provide most of the illustrations for work on Symbol and Language Themes at both Junior and Secondary levels.

Further reading

R. Bultmann : *Jesus Christ and Mythology* (SCM Press, 1960).

E. Cassirer : *Language and Myth* (Harper & Row, New York, 1946).

G. Cope : *Symbolism in the Bible and in the Church* (SCM Press, 1959).

J. G. Davies (Ed.) : *A Dictionary of Liturgy and Worship* (SCM Press, 1972).

F. W. Dillistone (Ed.) : *Myth and Symbol* (SPCK Theological Collections, No. 7, 1966).

M. Eliade : *Patterns in Comparative Religion* (Sheed & Ward, 1958).

M. Eliade : *The Sacred and the Profane* (Harcourt, Brace & World, 1959).

M. Eliade : *Myth and Reality* (Harper & Row, New York, 1963).

T. Fawcett : *The Symbolic Language of Religion* (SCM Press, 1970).

T. Fawcett : *Hebrew Myth and Christian Gospel* (SCM Press, 1973).

G. Ferguson : *Signs and Symbols in Christian Art* (OUP, 1961).

F. H. Hilliard : *How Men Worship* (RKP, 1965).

J. A. Hutchinson : *Language and Faith; Studies in Sign, Symbol and Meaning* (Westminster Press, 1963).

J. M. Kitagawa and C. H. Lang (Eds.) : *Myth and Symbol* (Univ. of Chicago Press, 1969).

C. E. Padwick : *Muslim Devotions* (SPCK, 1961).

E. G. Parrinder : *Worship in the World's Religions* (Faber, 1961).

N. Smart : *The Concept of Worship* (Macmillan, 1972).

(c) *Social and Ethical material*

The task of distinguishing between social and ethical dimensions of religion is an exceedingly difficult one and cannot be undertaken within the limited confines of this book. Professor Smart defines the social dimension as "the mode in which the religion in question is institutionalised, whereby, through its institutions and teachings, it affects the community in which it finds itself". He goes on to observe that the ethical dimension, together with the mythological and doctrinal dimensions, expresses "a religion's claims about the nature of the invisible world and its aim about how men's lives ought to be shaped : the social dimension indicates the way in which men's lives are in fact shaped by these claims and the way in which religious institutions operate." (*The Religious Experience of Mankind*, p 21.) In terms of our work in schools, there would appear to be fairly strong grounds for emphasising the inter-relatedness of these two dimensions at the expense of blurring some of their individual features. Thus, within the *Dimensional Approach,* we have taken the "social" side of religion to mean the organisational and institutional structure of a religion, the corporate life of the faithful and the sort of relationships they have with each other, and the way in which a religious community bears witness to its faith in the wider context of society and the world; and the "ethical" side to mean a religion's teaching about the conduct of the faithful, both in their individual lives and as members of a community and of society.

It is crucially important that provision is made for work on

106

either of these dimensions to be linked with a religion's experiential dimension and, later, with its doctrinal dimension. For example, it is all too common for children to be given the impression that religions *enforce* a number of rules upon people. This impression is often the result of teachers failing to help their pupils to transfer their understanding of the nature of religious belief to the sphere of ethical teaching. Commitment to a religious belief, arising as it may from the experience of a "disclosure situation", brings about a changed perspective on life—a perspective which issues in the adoption of certain attitudes and ways of behaving. It is this perspective of faith and belief, then, which provides the underlying rationale for a person's actions and leads him to accept whatever ethical code his religion teaches. The observance of ethical teaching thus becomes yet another mode in and through which a person may express his religious commitment. We do religion and the children whom we teach a great disservice if we imply that the notion of "duty" has no life of its own apart from enforcement, compulsion, punishment and fear. Similarly, when considering the social side of religion, we should take care to show how the particular form of organisation that is adopted by a religion reflects the beliefs which it upholds—beliefs which in some cases are directly attributable to a founder, and in others, are the outcome of the corporate experience of its faithful. In other words, in our work with children we are as much concerned with the examination of man's *religious experience* within a social and organisational context as with the organisational structure itself.

As indicated in the diagram on p 50, it is suggested that work on material illustrating the social and ethical dimensions of religion should be deferred until the beginning of the secondary school. There are various reasons for this. Firstly, most of the material illustrating these dimensions lacks the visual and dramatic quality characteristic of mythological and ritual material and its connection with the "implicit" or feeling side of religion is more subtle and, consequently, less obvious. This means that it is unlikely to be particularly effective as a means of sensitising children to the feelings which underlie religious beliefs and practices—something which we have seen to be of special importance in our work in the primary school. Secondly, although work on material illustrating these dimensions involves discerning how religious beliefs are translated into social and ethical consequences, these consequences are usually of a very practical nature (e.g. the institution of an ordained ministry, religious orders, ministries of preaching, healing and teaching and so on; keeping the Torah, loving one's neighbour, refraining from the taking of life and so on). The work thus forms a useful transition from the predominantly concrete material of myth and ritual to the abstract material of doctrine at a time when

107

children's thinking is moving out of Concrete Operations into Formal Operations. Thirdly, research into children's moral thinking (especially Piaget's work on moral judgment) has shown that insight into the nature of rules is determined by the growth of social awareness, the achievement of "reversibility" in their cognitive development and the replacement of adult restraint by opportunities for personal and group decision-making. For most children the transition from "heteronomous" morality (i.e. blind rule-following and equating culpability with the size of the consequence) to "autonomous" morality (i.e. accepting that rules may be modified according to the circumstances and that culpability is determined by intention) occurs towards the end of the primary school and at the beginning of the secondary school. It is appropriate, therefore, that subject-matter dealing with the ethical and social dimensions of religion should be introduced at a time which is consonant with this development. Fourthly, it is also appropriate that this subject-matter should be introduced alongside Situation Themes which, as we have seen, are introduced at the beginning of the secondary school with the intention of helping children to perceive the connection between beliefs, values and attitudes and behaviour. The ethical and social dimensions of religion can provide not only examples of situations in which religious belief is seen to issue in particular attitudes, values and actions (both on the part of individuals and communities), they can also offer principles which may be applied to situations which require a moral choice or judgment to be made. Thus, once again we see the importance of relating work within the *Dimensional Approach* to the insights gained through work within the *Existential Approach*.

As children move towards the stage of Formal Operations, therefore, we can begin to place greater emphasis on helping them towards an *intellectual* grasp of religious beliefs and teaching. This is not meant to infer that once children have reached Formal Operations we should no longer seek to sensitise them to the feeling or experiential side of religion, but rather that at this stage we should begin to help them to become more aware of the way in which religions translate religious experience into beliefs and beliefs into practice. The use of social and ethical material (i.e. how beliefs and teaching are put into practice) would appear to be more appropriate as a means of introducing this emphasis than the use of doctrinal material. For example, work on the social and ethical dimensions of religion will inevitably involve giving close attention to the idea of "community". We have already seen how this is an appropriate topic for exploration by way of both Depth Themes and Symbol and Language Themes. The task of the *Dimensional Approach* is to help children to build conceptual bridges between whatever insights they have developed into "community" (through work on these types of theme) and the way in which the concept is understood within a religious context. But despite the centrality of the concept to most religions, the communal life of *each* religion reflects its own distinctive interpretation of its significance—especially of its significance for the individual who is a member of the community. This "distinctive interpretation" is, in fact, a *theological* interpretation—it relates to the *particular* beliefs of a *particular* religion. Thus, work on the special characteristics of a religion's communal life (e.g. the role of communal worship; the role of the bishop, priest, monk, nun, rabbi, imam, guru, minister, elder, granthi and so on; the importance given to the celebration of feasts in the home and in a place of communal worship; the ethical and social demands that are made on the individual as a member of the community; the community's participation or non-participation in the life of the society in which it exists and so on, and so on) may be found to be an effective way of introducing children to the special characteristics of its theology (i.e. to its doctrine). Indeed, doctrinal material is only likely to be seen as important if children have an opportunity to perceive the necessity for it within the life of a religious *community* (e.g. the need for a statement of communal belief). It is important to remember, however, that work on the experiential, mythological and ritual dimensions of religion should continue throughout the secondary school parallel to work on the social and ethical dimensions. Here too there should be an increasing emphasis on the "truths" which lie behind the material and which the material seeks to "release" or express. In this way it is likely to be less difficult for pupils to appreciate how myth merges with doctrine and how doctrine attempts to give "system, clarity and intellectual power to what is revealed through the mythological and symbolic language of religious faith and ritual" (N. Smart, *op cit,* p 19).

Further reading

W. Barclay: *Ethics in a Permissive Society* (Collins, 1971).
P. L. Berger: *The Social Reality of Religion* (Faber, 1969).
D. Bonhoeffer: *The Cost of Discipleship* (SCM Press, 1948).
H. F. A. Catherwood: *The Christian Citizen* (Hodder & Stoughton, 1969).
R. N. Flew: *Jesus and his Way* (Epworth, 1963).
R. H. Fuller and B. K. Rice: *Christianity and the Affluent Society* (Hodder & Stoughton, 1966).
W. H. Hudson: *Ethical Institutionism* (Macmillan, 1967).
J. Knox: *The Ethic of Jesus in the Teaching of the Church* (Epworth, 1962).
P. L. Lehmann: *Ethics in a Christian Context* (SCM Press, 1963).

E. L. Long : *A Survey of Christian Ethics* (OUP, 1967).

D. M. Mackinnon *et al* : *God, Sex and War* (Collins Fontana, 1963).

I. T. Ramsey (Ed.) : *Christian Ethics and Contemporary Philosophy* (SCM Press, 1966).

P. Ramsey (Ed.) : *Faith and Ethics* (Harper Torchbook, 1965).

P. Roubiczek : *Ethical Values in an Age of Science* (CUP, 1969).

Sociological Yearbook of Religion in Britain 1, 2, 3, 4 and 5 (SCM).

G. Winter : *Social Ethics* (SCM Press, 1968).

(d) *Doctrinal material*

Although many references to beliefs will occur in R.E. at all levels, it is logical that the examination of *doctrine*—the systematic and intellectual account of a religion's beliefs—should be deferred until children are well into the stage of Formal Operations and have had some experience of thinking in abstract terms and of formulating, applying and testing hypotheses. Most of this experience one hopes, will be gained in subject areas other than religion—in mathematics, science, history, geography and the literary arts. An important task in R.E., therefore, is to help children of 14 or 15 years of age to extend these skills into the sphere of religion and develop some insight into the sort of thinking and verification procedures which are appropriate to it, contrasting these, perhaps, with mathematical, scientific, historical and aesthetic forms of thought. Doctrinal material, especially credal confessions, provide a useful basis for this work. Our earlier comments on the nature of religious language are particularly pertinent to this task. I. T. Ramsey, in *Religious Language* (SCM Press Ltd, 1957—especially Chapter 4), and Paul van Buren, in *The Secular Meaning of the Gospel* (SCM Press Ltd, 1963—especially Chapters 6, 7 and 8), both provide refreshingly new insights into the language of Christian Doctrine which may be helpful to teachers in their own thinking and in suggesting lines of approach for dealing with doctrine with their pupils, especially in the sixth form. J. L. Goodall's book, *An Introduction to the Philosophy of Religion* (Longmans, 1966) is also likely to be of value.

But work on doctrinal material should not only be undertaken as a means of cultivating techniques of thinking—important though this is to the achievement of Religious Understanding. "Doctrine" means "that which is taught" and so a major concern in R.E. with older secondary school pupils should be that of acquainting them with the distinctive teaching or doctrines of the world's living faiths. For children who have followed a scheme of R.E. such as the one outlined in this book, much of this later work will consist of *linking* their earlier insights into religion (gained through work within the *Existential* and *Dimensional Approaches*) into a coherent whole. In actual fact, this is precisely what doctrine attempts to do—organise those religious "truths" expressed in and through experiential, mythological, ritual, social and ethical categories into a coherent whole called "a faith" or "a religion". It is appropriate, then, that our scheme for R.E. should culminate in work on doctrine. This material may be organised and presented in a variety of ways, depending upon the abilities and background knowledge of the pupils. For example, an over-view of the principal doctrines of the major faiths can be given during a unit of work devoted to "Sacred Scriptures". This is likely to involve children in reading, discussing and presenting (through drama, wall charts, tapes and so on) *selected* passages from the Qur'an, the Bhagavad Gita, the Dhammapada, the Milindha panha, the Granth, and, of course, the Bible. Alternatively, a thematic approach may be used : "How men think of God", "Salvation in World Faiths", "Religion and Suffering", "Incarnation and Re-incarnation", all provide an opportunity for children to become aware of both the diversity and the unity of religious thinking to be found in world faiths.

Giving children an over-view of the beliefs of world faiths in this way is frequently contested on the grounds that it leads to a superficial estimate of each religion. Certainly we must avoid "caricaturing" faiths in our treatment of them at this level, and yet we should remember that for the vast majority of our pupils who leave school at 16 this is the only opportunity that they have (apart from personal interest) for examining different belief systems and that a detailed examination of one religion—even if it is the religion which is dominant in their own culture—is unlikely to provide them with the perspective or the inclination to approach religion and the question of religious belief with sensitivity and understanding. One further point. Although one should not underestimate the value of devoting a great deal of time in the final years of secondary education to give pupils "opportunities for coming to terms with situations which make Christian teaching relevant to life as the pupils know it" (*Religion and Life,* Agreed Syllabus, Lancashire Education Committee, 1968, p 153), it is, perhaps, unfortunate that many teachers fail to introduce distinctive religious teaching at the very time when their pupils are most capable of comprehending it. It is only when we balance "discussion" with purposeful and systematic teaching about religion that we prevent R.E. in the fourth and fifth forms from degenerating into repetitive "conversations about life" and contribute effectively to our aim of "creating in pupils certain capacities to understand and think about religion as a unique mode of thought and awareness". There are grounds for believing, then, that even giving children an over-view of world faiths is less likely to encourage superficial learning than much of what currently passes for R.E. in these last years of school. For those pupils who stay at school after 16, R.E. in the sixth form (called, perhaps, "Religion, Ethics and Philosophy" or "R.E.P.") should be concerned with deepening these initial insights and with adding to them new insights into non-theistic or atheistic belief-systems such as Marxism, Atheistic Existentialism and Scientific Humanism.

Set out below are some of the major doctrines of seven living faiths which could feature in a teacher's *selection* of doctrinal material for use with older secondary school pupils.

Judaism : the unity and oneness of God; the doctrine of man and his relationship to God the Creator; the Messianic expectation.

Christianity : the Fatherhood of God and the Sonship of Christ; the Incarnation; teaching on salvation and eternal life; the Church as the Body of Christ; the Holy Spirit; the Trinity; the Sacraments.

Islam : the unity and oneness of Allah, the Compassionate, the Merciful; the six basic doctrines of the Qur'an (belief in God, angels, the Holy Books, the Prophets, predestination, the Day of Judgment/Resurrection); the five Pillars of Faith.

Hinduism : the Universe having neither beginning nor end; Brahman, the impersonal essence and synthesis of good and evil, pain and joy, life and death and so on; Atman (the Soul); Samsara and Karma (the round of births); Mukti (salvation) and Nirvana; karma-yoga (works), jnana-yoga (knowledge) and bhakti-yoga (devotion); the trimurti (Brahma, Vishnu and Siva); doctrine of avatars (Krishna and Rama).

Jainism : its atheistic outlook; karma; ahimsa (non-violence).

Sikhism : its ties with Islam and Hinduism; the uniqueness and personality of God, distinct from the human soul but loving all his children; rebirth; the need for Guru Granth Sahib.

Buddhism : its atheistic outlook, especially Hinayana; the differences between Hinayana and Mahayana; the four Noble Truths; the Eightfold Path; rebirth; Nibbana.

Further reading

S. G. F. Brandon (Ed.): *A Dictionary of Comparative Religion* Weidenfeld & Nicolson, 1970).

112

J. Bowker : *Problems of Suffering in Religions of the World* (CUP, 1970).

T. O. Ling : *A History of Religion East and West* (Macmillan, 1968).

W. Macquitty : *Buddha* (Nelson, 1969).

J. B. Noss : *Man's Religions* (Collier-Macmillan, 1963).

E. G. Parrinder : *The World's Living Religions* (Pan, 1964).

E. G. Parrinder : *A Book of World Religions* (Hulton Educational, 1965).

E. G. Parrinder : *What World Religions Teach* (Harrap, 1968 edition).

E. G. Parrinder : *A Dictionary of Non-Christian Religions* (Hulton Educational, 1971).

H. Ringgren and A. V. Strom : *Religions of Mankind* (Oliver & Boyd, 1967).

N. Smart : *The Religious Experience of Mankind* (Collins Fontana, 1971).

N. Smart : *World Religions: A Dialogue* (Penguin, 1966).

R. C. Zaehner (Ed.) : *A Concise Encylopaedia of Living Faiths* (Hutchinson, 1964).

Chapter 7

Planning Schemes of Work and Lessons in Religious Education

Now that we have considered at some length the theoretical bases for the *Existential* and *Dimensional Approaches* to R.E. and the sort of content appropriate to each one, we are in a position to look more closely at some of the ways in which they may be implemented in the classroom. In Chapter 2 of this book, we noted that Curriculum Development demands that prior to teaching anything, we decide (on the basis of our knowledge of the subject and of the children in our class) on a number of educational objectives which we wish to achieve through our teaching, and that we state these in precise terms before going on to select content and method which is best suited to their achievement. These objectives—often classified under Knowledge, Skills and Attitudes—should be determined by at least three factors :

1 The overall or general aim of R.E. (i.e. to create in pupils certain capacities to understand and think about religion as a unique mode of thought and awareness).
2 The structure of religion (i.e. the key-concepts of religion and the way in which these are expressed through six inter-related and inter-dependent dimensions—experiential, mythological, ritual and so on).
3 Pupil characteristics (i.e. the developmental age, interests, needs, knowledge and experience of the children in the class).

In other words, the objectives that we choose should contribute to the achievement of (1), highlight an aspect of (2), and relate to one or more features of (3). Let us see how this works out, first in relation to the *Existential Approach*.

   In presenting the three types of theme which constitute the *Existential Approach*, we have been careful to list aims appropriate to each one. (The aims of Depth Themes are given on p 57, the aims of Symbol and Language Themes on p 75, and the aims of Situation Themes on p 84.) All these aims may be said to contribute to the achievement of the overall aim of R.E. The Conceptual Framework which we have adopted for R.E. indicates where special emphasis may be placed on a particular type of theme and, therefore, on particular types of aim. For example, work on Depth Themes has special importance with children between the ages of five and nine; the aims of this type of theme are, consequently, also especially appropriate to this age-range (e.g. to provide the child with an opportunity to practise the skill of reflecting on his own experiences at depth, of developing insight into himself and his feelings, and so on). Similarly, work on Situation Themes has special importance with children from the age of 11, and so too have their aims (e.g. to provide the child with an opportunity to learn how to assess situations in terms of the consequences of attitudes and actions, to perceive the connection between beliefs, values, attitudes and actions and so on). The task of choosing objectives within the *Existential Approach* is, therefore, fairly straightforward. We simply adopt one of the aims appropriate to whatever type of theme we happen to be using and then decide on subject-matter most likely to lead to its achievement. This subject-matter will be purely "secular" in the case of Depth Themes and partly secular in the case of Symbol and Language Themes and Situation Themes. It should, however, involve concepts relevant to an understanding of religion or religious belief and be related to "pupil characteristics" (i.e. their developmental age, interests, needs, knowledge and experience). Let us look at some examples of this.

1 Depth Themes

As the four aims given for Depth Themes are very closely interrelated there is no need to choose one aim in particular; all Depth Themes will inevitably contribute to the achievement of all four aims at the same time.

An example of a Depth Theme for use with children aged seven.

Aim: To provide the child with an opportunity to :

1 practise the skill of reflecting on his own experiences at depth;
2 develop insight into himself and his feelings;
3 develop insight into other people and their feelings;
4 develop insight into what constitutes a distinctly human relationship between self and others.

What subject involving concepts relevant to religion and able to be related to pupil characteristics might be used to achieve these aims? Of the many possibilities we will choose the subject of "Caring". Our *Objectives* for this theme thus become :

To provide the child with an opportunity to :

1 develop insight into the concepts of kindness, helpfulness, friendliness and compassion as means of understanding the concept of caring;

2 practise the skill of looking at depth into personal experiences of kindness, helpfulness, friendliness, compassion, and caring;

3 acquire a sensitivity to the value of being kind, helpful, showing friendliness and compassion, and caring.

We should note that (1) constitutes Knowledge, (2) is a Skill, and (3) is concerned with the development of Attitudes. Having identified our Objectives (i.e. the points of focus for the theme) we are now in a position to choose subject-matter or content likely to lead to their achievement. This could include :

Everyday examples of kindness and friendliness at home, in the street, at school.

How animals care for their young. Why do they care?

How people care for animals (e.g. bird protection, bird sanctuaries, treatment of injured or oil-covered birds, the work of the R.S.P.C.A. and the P.D.S.A., nature reserves, rescue of big-game in danger of extermination). Why do they care?

How people care for each other (e.g. parents and children, caring for members of the family, relatives, neighbours, people in need, the work of hospitals, homes, organisations committed to caring Dr Barnado's homes, Save the Children Fund, Oxfam, the work of religious organisations at home and abroad, V.S.O. and so on). Why do they care?

How we can care (e.g. feeding birds in bad weather, a class bird table, not being cruel to birds or animals, sheltering injured or stray birds and animals, not neglecting pets, being helpful and considerate at home, being kind to children at school, helping neighbours, the elderly, foreigners and so on). Why should we care?

Stories involving acts of kindness, helpfulness, friendliness, compassion and caring. Why do they care?

Some of these examples of caring are taken from *Suggestions for R.E.*, West Riding Agreed Syllabus, p 18—an indication of how Agreed Syllabuses may be used in relation to the *Existential Approach*.

116

An example of a Symbol and Language Theme for use with children aged ten.

Aim: To provide children with an opportunity to recognise the special characteristics of religious language and symbolism by acquainting them with language which is evocative, poetic, metaphorical and dramatic and educating them in its use.

Theme: Rocks, Fortresses and Refuges.

Objectives: To provide children with an opportunity to:

1 acquire sensitivity to the *feelings* of strength, security, reliability, dignity, awe and wonder which are evoked by the images of rocks, fortresses and refuges;

2 discern how these images may be used as a way of talking about God (e.g. Psalm 18 : 2, "The Lord is my rock, and my fortress . . . my God, my rock, in whom I take refuge").

Content and Learning Experiences:

Examination of different types of rock on field trips or in the classroom (e.g. specimens and slides).

Finding words for talking about the quality and character of rocks (e.g. smooth, rough, sharp, hard, durable, strong, long-lasting, heavy and so on).

Some famous rocks and rock formations (e.g. The Cow and Calf on Ilkley Moor, The Devil's Arrowheads at Boroughbridge, The Norber Boulders in the Pennines, Ailsa Craig in the Firth of Clyde, The Bass Rock in the Firth of Forth, Haytor on Dartmoor, The Giant's Causeway in N. Ireland, Penmaen Mawr in N. Wales and so on).

Pictures and slides of these and similar rocks. Finding words to describe the impression that these rocks make on us (e.g. they tower above us and make us feel small; they look as if they will last forever; their hugeness takes your breath away!)

Listening to poems and stories about rocks and to legends associated with famous rocks. Writing poems and stories about rocks. Making rock models and pictures; painted rocks, collages, rock and stone jewellery, rock mosaics and so on.

Examples of common expressions using the word "rock"—"as firm as a rock" may be said of both objects and people. Why? But why did Jesus call Peter "Cephas" (Rock) in Mt 16 : 18?

Uses of rock (e.g. foundations, churches, castles, houses, roads). Many Fortresses and Castles are built on rock (e.g. Edinburgh Castle (the rock comes through the floor of the Scottish National

War Memorial Chapel in this castle), Stirling Castle, Conway Castle, Rhuddlan Castle, Clifford's Tower in York, Tintagel Castle, Richmond Castle and so on). Pictures and slides of these and similar castles. Drackenfels Castle on the Rhine is particularly impressive. Finding words to describe the impression that these castles make on us.

Why were they built? To whom did they give protection and safety? Stories of people taking refuge in fortresses and castles. Project on Masada—Herod's rock fortress. The story of the Alcazar de Toledo during the Spanish Civil War.

Why other buildings give refuge? Churches and monasteries. Is this only because they are strong buildings? Why do people go there for refuge? It is God rather than the building which is the refuge.

Looking at ways in which people have expressed this belief, e.g. Psalms 9 : 9; 18 : 2; 31 : 3; 46 : 1f; 62 : 2; 71 : 3; 73 : 26; 89 : 26; 91 : 2; The Song of David, 2 Sam. 22 : 2f.

Is this a useful way of talking about God? Is it sufficient to say that he is a Rock, a Fortress and a Refuge?

Making up psalms and songs using these images and any others which are felt to be appropriate.

3   Situation Themes

An example of a Situation Theme for use with children aged thirteen.

Aim: To provide children with an opportunity to explore, examine and discuss situations which call for a moral choice or judgment to be made about the situation and/or about the attitudes and actions of persons involved in it.

Theme: Family Relationships.

Objectives: To provide children with an opportunity to :

1   examine areas in family relationships which are subject to stress, strain and conflict;
2   identify with characters involved in family situations and gain insight into the attitudes they adopt;
3   assess the attitudes displayed by characters in terms of their consequences for family life;
4   formulate possible solutions to these conflicts.

Content and Learning Experiences:

The Thompson family consists of Margery and Harold (15 and 13 respectively), Mr and Mrs Thompson, and Granny, who is 70. The children are normal for their age—rather noisy, and

118

full of life. They like playing their discs at full volume, and they run downstairs two at a time. On one occasion, Granny is particularly annoyed because she can't settle down for her afternoon nap. She gives the two children a thorough telling-off. As she is finishing, Mrs Thompson enters the room and wonders what she should do—agree with Granny, or side with the children. She feels her children ought to be free to live normal lives, but then she knows Granny is getting on in years. What should she do? (A. Durband: *New English,* Hutchinson, 1967, Book Three, p 61).

This situation could be approached through role-play and followed by discussion. Similar situations would be used to develop the theme, some of which should be written and presented by the pupils themselves.

These three examples should serve to illustrate the sort of thinking and planning which needs to precede the work we do with children in the classroom. If we first select "worthwhile" aims and objectives and then choose subject-matter which we think is most likely to lead to their achievement, we are far more likely to be teaching children something which is "worthwhile" (i.e. educational) than if we merely begin with subject-matter. It is important to note, however, that Schemes of Work such as we have been looking at, are sufficiently flexible to allow for spontaneous, individual interest on the part of pupils to be accommodated within their structure. In most circumstances, however, this leads to an extension of the scheme in time rather than a substantial alteration in its direction. This is especially so when a scheme is developed entirely through group and individual work.

It is inevitable, however, that occasions will arise, especially when using the *Dimensional Approach,* when a teacher will wish to impart a particular body of "religious knowledge" to his pupils because he feels that it makes an essential contribution to understanding religion. (This will occur when a teacher is following an Agreed Syllabus.) How will this affect his choice and statement of aims and objectives? Does it mean that in such circumstances they can be dispensed with? First of all, when deciding upon a body of knowledge the teacher needs to be clear in his own mind as to *why* and *how* it makes an essential contribution to understanding religion. Is it, for example, material which embodies certain key-concepts in a particular religion? Does it illustrate an important aspect of a religion's teaching? Does it illustrate one of the six dimensions of religion in an especially apposite way? Does it provide insight into the historical or social context out of which certain religious ideas have grown? In short, the teacher needs to be aware of the *theological significance* of the material because it is this which he ultimately wishes to convey to his pupils. For example, a teacher in the secondary school may feel that he should spend some time looking at Jesus's parables with a class of 13 year old pupils. But faced with such a wealth of parabolic material as there is in the Synoptic Gospels, where is he to start? How is he to make his selection? A decision to "do the parables" is clearly inadequate on its own; if his teaching is to be purposeful it must be planned—and planned in the light of what he hopes to achieve. In this case his intention will be to help children to become aware of the theological insights afforded by the parables—an intention which is closely related to the overall aim of R.E., that of creating in pupils "certain capacities to understand and think about religion". Accordingly, he should start by choosing and stating aims which reflect, and even identify, the theological insights which he hopes will result from work on parabolic material. Possible aims include providing children with an opportunity to:

1 understand that parables were a common teaching method used by Jewish rabbis in the first century;

2 appreciate that the images employed in the parables were taken from the daily life of Palestine and that they would have immediate appeal to first century Jews;

3 appreciate how Jesus used parables to illustrate aspects of his teaching about God's relationship with man;

4 appreciate that in their original form each parable was designed to teach a single theological point;

5 appreciate how the Early Christian Church, in its preaching of the Gospel, collected and arranged Jesus's parables according to their subject-matter, often created a new setting for them, sometimes modified their original form (e.g. allegorised them), and always sought to relate them to the Church's own situation.

All these aims, taken together or individually, provide guidelines for the selection of subject-matter. These guidelines become even clearer if we translate them into objectives. For example, objectives appropriate to the first aim might be to provide children with an opportunity to:

(a) become familiar with some of the parables to be found in the Old Testament and in the rabbinic writings;

(b) discern how Jesus modified existing rabbinic parables to express new religious perspectives (e.g. the different treatment given to parables about "The Kingdom of Heaven"; how Jesus modified "The parable of the Good Israelite" so that it became "The parable of the Good Samaritan" and why).

Similarly, objectives appropriate to the third aim might be to provide children with an opportunity to :

(a)   examine parables illustrating God's willingness to forgive man's wrongdoings;

(b)   relate the insights gained to the attitudes which Jesus showed towards the outcastes of society;

(c)   relate the insights gained to Jesus's ethical teaching in the Sermon on the Mount.

Mapping out aims and objectives in this way causes us to think very carefully not only about the way in which we can structure subject-matter but also about how one set of subject-matter may be related to another set. For example, in choosing the fourth aim for our work on parables (i.e. encouraging children to look for the theological point in each parable) we are equipping pupils with a technique which they can apply beyond the field of parables— to miracles for instance. By structuring our Scheme of Work so that work on parables is followed first by work on acted parables and then on miracles, we are providing opportunities for children to *transfer* their learning and apply it in a new setting. This is an important educational principle. But we would need to state this intention in our aims and objectives and then select content which is most appropriate for assisting transfer.

So far we have said little about "method"—i.e. the various ways in which subject-matter may be presented to children. There is a growing consensus of opinion among educationists that it is unwise to make too rigid a distinction between "subject-matter" and "method" largely because "child-centred" education places its emphasis on involving children in "experiences"—a concept which transcends the notion of communicating "subject-matter". Accordingly, it is becoming increasingly common for books on Curriculum Development to speak of aims and objectives being achieved through the creation of "Learning Experiences". Let us look at a Scheme of Work, dealing with material illustrating the mythological and ritual dimensions of religion, in which the term "learning experience" might be said to be appropriate.

121

An example of a Scheme of Work involving mythological and ritual material for use with children aged ten.

Aim: To provide children with an opportunity to appreciate the importance of Holy Books (or Sacred Scriptures) in the life of religious communities living in Britain.

Objectives: To provide children with an opportunity to:
1 learn the names of the Holy Books of the Jews, Christians, Sikhs, Muslims and Hindus;
2 gain insight into their origin and age;
3 read and discuss selected passages from them;
4 become sensitive to the awe in which they are held and the reverence shown to them;
5 recognise the part that they play in public and private worship.
6 recognise the part that they play in teaching men about God.

Learning Experiences:
Films, pictures, slides and tapes showing:

1 *The procession and reading of the Torah in a synagogue.* Pictures to include the ark, the ark doors or curtain, the decorated velvet mantle covering the scrolls, the religious symbols on the ark, mantle and scrolls—i.e. the two tablets of the Law, the crown, bells and breastplate—the carrying of the covered scroll, the uncovering of the scroll, the spreading of the scroll, the reading of the Torah to the congregation (with heads covered, wearing tallith and tefillin), the use of a silver pointer, the Hebrew script, the tying of the scroll with a sash, the replacing of the embroidered mantle, the breastplate, crown and pointer, and the returning of the scroll to the ark.
Tapes to include the chanting of The Shema (Deut. 6 : 4-9) in Hebrew and English, the chanting of Numbers 10 : 36, Psalm 132 : 8-10; Proverbs 4 : 2; 3 : 17 and 18 by the congregation as the Torah is returned to the ark.
Follow up by looking at the account of how Moses received the Torah from God on Mount Sinai (Exodus 19 and 20—preferably told in the teacher's own words) and also The Shema.

2 *The procession and reading of The Gospel in a church or cathedral.*
Pictures to include the preparation of the procession, the

122

thurifer, the processional cross, the acolytes, the Subdeacon, the Deacon carrying the Gospel, the censing of the Gospel, the reading, the carrying of the Gospel to the Celebrant, the return of the procession (pictures too of the congregation standing and making the sign of the cross).

Tapes to include the singing of The Gospel—preferably one of the parables or something descriptive—and the responses made by the congregation.

Pictures showing the altar of a Lutheran Church (with its open Bible), the lectern with an open Bible, individuals (priests, monks, nuns, laymen) reading their Bibles and so on may be included. Follow up by looking at selected passages, showing Greek script and talking about the number of languages into which the Bible has been translated.

3 *The procession of Sikhs to the throne of the Guru Granth Sahib in a Sikh temple.*
Pictures to include the Golden Temple at Amritsar where the original Guru Granth is kept, a Sikh temple in Britain, the "takht"—the Granth's throne, a garlanded Granth, an open Granth showing the 16th century Punjabi script, the Granthi (the Granth's custodian), his "chauri" which he waves over the Granth, the worshippers walking towards the Granth, kneeling before it and then sitting cross-legged on the floor before it, the chanting of hymns taken from the Granth.

Tapes to include the chanting of hymns in Punjabi.

Follow up by showing pictures of Guru Nanak (b. 1469 A.D.) the founder of the Sikh religion; telling the story of his vision of God holding out to him a cup of nectar and inviting him to "Go and repeat my name, and make others do so. This cup is a pledge of my regard"; explaining how the Granth ("book") became the "guru" ("teacher") of the Sikhs ("disciples") after the death of Guru Gobind Singh.

4 *Muslims attending the Friday "Salat" at a mosque.*
Pictures to include mosques (e.g. The Dome of The Rock in Jerusalem, The Sultan Hamed mosque in Istanbul, the mosque in Preston, Lancashire), an interior showing the pulpit, the "mihrab", the lectern supporting the Holy Qur'an, a page from the Qur'an showing its Arabic script, Muslims performing the "Wudhu" (ablution), entering the mosque, facing the mihrab, performing the "rak'as" (prayer movements and prostrations), reciting the prayers from the Qur'an. (The midday prayer on a Friday is replaced by a congregational service when the Imam delivers a sermon (usually based on the Qur'an) followed by two rak'as.

123

Tapes to include the call of the muezzin standing in the minaret, the first Sura from the Qur'an and the recitation of the "Tashahud" and "Du'ah".

Follow up by telling the story of how the angel Gabriel appeared to Muhammad in The Cave of Hira'a on Mount Light (Jabal-al-Noor) and told him to "Recite" (Sura 96); how he had other revelations during his life; how the first caliph, Abu Bakr, ordered all the memorised verses to be compiled into a standard copy of The Holy Qur'an after Muhammad's death in 632 A.D.

5   *A Hindu engaging in his devotions at home.*

Pictures to include the worship room or the home shrine, ritual bathing, the recitation of "The Mother of the Vedas" (i.e. "Let us meditate upon the most excellent light of the radiant sun; May he guide our minds"), the sacred thread over the left shoulder and across the body to the waist, water-sprinkling, repetition of "OM" or a sacred verse from the Vedas or the Vedanta, the use of prayer beads, offerings of flowers, scent, incense, lights and food to the god of the image—perhaps Vishnu or Shiva, or the popular Rama or Lord Krishna, the Sanskrit text of the Vedas, an illustrated page from the Upanishads or Bhagavad Gita—"The Song of the Lord", men and women reading and meditating on passages from the Scriptures by river banks, in parks, on buses and so on.

Tapes to include readings in Sanskrit and English from the Vedas, the repetition of the sacred syllable "OM" and so on. Follow up by telling the story of Lord Rama and explaining the importance and popularity of the Bhagavad Gita (i.e. its teaching on love and devotion—"bhakti").

It is important to note that this Scheme of Work, unlike the previous one, is primarily concerned with giving children a sense of the *feelings* that the adherents to various faiths have about their Holy Books (i.e. Objective 4: "to become sensitive to the awe in which they are held and the reverence shown to them"). Because of this intention, the success of the Scheme, especially with children in the Late Junior school, will depend almost entirely upon the *visual impact* of the material. The visual materials—the films and the tapes—are not, therefore, merely optional extras, visual *aids,* they are the learning medium itself. *They* make it possible to deal with so complicated a subject with such young children. "Subject-matter" and "method" are thus combined to create a "learning experience"; indeed, in this case, matter and method are closely interwoven, they are inseparable. What this Scheme is trying to do is to provide an "emotional backcloth" against which pupils may *eventually* view the religious ideas that arise in later lessons. Accordingly, lessons devoted to it should be more attuned to fostering sensitivities (as in a music or poetry appreciation lesson) than to imparting knowledge. Their whole emphasis should be on allowing the child to experience for himself the significance of Holy Books from what is *done* by the worshippers rather than from what is *said* by the teacher. In other words, great care needs to be taken to avoid debasing the experience by seeking to use the Scheme merely as an introduction to more detailed work on Holy Books —the experience itself constitutes the learning. Naturally a teacher should seek to answer those questions which may arise from the experience, but the temptation to develop explanations into detailed accounts of distinctive beliefs should be resisted at this stage. With this Scheme every opportunity should be given for the material to "speak for itself".

As a final example of Schemes of Work let us look at some material where the relationship between content and method is less obvious. In the Lancashire Agreed Syllabus, *Religion and Life,* p 66, under the heading "Obedience and Forgiveness", it is suggested that teachers might like to use the story of Esau and Jacob to illustrate how quarrels begin and how they can eventually be overcome through forgiveness. This work is suggested for children aged nine years. Various points may be made about this suggestion. By restricting the choice of subject-matter to Gen. 25 : 27-34; 27 : 1-41; and 33 : 1-16, the syllabus implies that we should ignore the *theological significance* of the material and simply use it as a good example of how quarrels may be resolved between brothers. But this story is *not* a good example of the latter, mainly because it was never intended to be ! Besides, the story is full of details (e.g. birthrights and blessings) which makes it incongruous to a child living in the 20th century. It would appear, then, that this is a classic example of "using the Bible for the Bible's sake" rather than using it is an aid to developing the child's theological understanding. Certainly one can think of any number of secular stories dealing with quarrels and forgiveness which are far better suited to children of nine than this one. But having mentioned this story let us consider if there is a place for it in R.E. and if so where and how.

Earlier in this chapter we stressed the importance of the teacher being aware of the *theological significance* of the material he uses because it is this which he ultimately wishes to convey to his pupils. What is the theological significance of the story of Esau and Jacob? Crucial to the Jacob Saga, of which this story is a part, are three incidents dealing with the experiential side of religion— Gen. 28 : 10-22 (Jacob's dream at Bethel), Gen. 32 : 24-32 (Jacob wrestles with God at Penuel) and Gen. 35 : 1-3 and 9-13 (God appears to Jacob on his return from Paddan-aram). These experiences, expressed in symbolic terms, serve to give some theological and moral justification for placing the unattractive Jacob (crafty, scheming, coolly ambitious and suspicious compared with the generous, impulsive, adventure loving, forgiving Esau) in the line of grace and giving him the name of "Israel". Thus the theological significance of the Jacob saga lies outside his quarrel with Esau and is to be seen in Jacob's eventual acknowledgement of the fact that all through his wanderings and trials God's hand has been over him, shaping him for a part in the salvation drama. At one level, therefore, it is a story about a man who eventually "finds" God through his own experiences. But there are other levels—theological levels—to the story. Whereas Abraham represented the ideal Israel, faithful and unquestioning, Jacob represents the Israel of history, continually sinning and suffering yet ever seeking the birthright and blessing. Like the story of Israel herself, the story of Jacob points us to the Hebrew doctrine of Election and Grace and to the inevitability of the divine will prevailing over the natural will. To see this story only in human terms is to miss an essential dimension; irrespective of outward appearances Jacob the salvation agent must prevail over Esau the "natural man". At yet another level we see how the Yahwist has skillfully combined ancient historical traditions about the relations between the Hebrews and neighbouring peoples (Esau would appear to be Edom) into a continuous narrative of God's dealings with the "patriarchs" of the Hebrews prior to their emergence in history as "Yahweh's People" at the Siniatic Covenant. One cannot help but be amazed at the way in which such unpromising material can fulfil these theological functions and still express a wide range of human emotions which are recognisable as those of 20th century man.

In the Scheme of Work that follows we have attempted to do justice to some of the story's theological points while disregarding others. For example, all three incidents dealing with the experiential side of religion have been introduced. This not only allows children to examine the part played by symbolism in the communication of religious ideas and experiences but also provides them with an opportunity to discern the significance of religious experience as an influence on man's attitude and behaviour. It also enables them to compare the attitudes of a man before he becomes aware of God with the attitudes he displays afterwards. The main intention for using the Jacob Saga, however, is *to provide children with an opportunity to examine and discuss material illustrating the mythological dimension of religion.* It should, therefore, be used with children who already have some sensitivity to the function of myth and legend within religion. For this reason we would

126

suggest that the Scheme is most appropriate to children aged between eleven and thirteen, if not older.

An example of a Scheme of Work involving mythological material for use with children aged eleven onwards.

Aim: To provide children with an opportunity to examine material illustrating the mythological dimension of religion and to discern some of the theological insights that it contains.

Material: The Jacob Saga (Gen. 25-36).

Objectives: To provide children with an opportunity to :

1 explore the concepts of ambition, honesty and integrity (and their opposites, deceit and cowardice), jealousy, duty, responsibility, happiness, adventure, danger, fear, awe, generosity, tolerance, love, wealth, forgiveness, reconciliation, thankfulness and commitment;

2 recognise the part played by symbolism in the communication of religious ideas and experiences;

3 discern the significance of religious experience as an influence upon a man's attitude and behaviour;

4 practise the skill of assessing both character and situation and making moral judgments on the basis of information given;

5 examine the place of custom, rights and status within the family situation.

Content:

Stage 1 The twins when they were young boys (Gen. 25 : 19-34). Esau sells his birthright to Jacob.

Stage 2 The twins when they were young men (Gen. 27 : 1-45). Jacob tricks Esau out of his father's blessing and has to leave home because of Esau's anger.

Stage 3 Jacob's adventures among the people of the East.
Part 1 Jacob's first experience of God in a dream at Bethel (Gen. 23 : 10-22).
Part 2 Jacob goes to work for his uncle Laban; his love for Rachel; his uncle's trickery; his marriages. (Select material carefully from Gen. 29 : 1-28.)
Part 3 Jacob's family and wealth increase; his decision to leave Laban and begin life on his own; he arrives at Esau's territory and because of the deceit he had practised on Esau is afraid. (Select material carefully from Gen. 32 : 1-21.)

127

Part 4 Jacob's second experience of God; he decides to go and meet Esau.

Stage 4 The twins when they were fathers (Gen. 33).
Jacob is forgiven by Esau and the quarrel ends.

Stage 5 Jacob's third experience of God; he accepts him as his God; his name is changed to "Israel" and God promises that from his family a nation will grow. (Select material from Gen. 35 : 1-4, 9-16, 22b-29; 37 : 1-2.)

Stage 6 What does this ancient saga tell us about the Hebrew ideas of God and man? Which of these ideas do you find difficult to accept? There are several parallels between the story of Esau and Jacob and the parable of the Prodigal Son in Luke 15 : 11-32 (a better title is The Parable of the Two Sons). Look at some of these parallels and see how the view of God differs in Jesus's parable. Are ideas of God still changing? How? Why?

How can a dry skeletal framework such as this be transformed into a series of imaginative, child-centred "experiences" capable of promoting those insights which we have stated to be our objectives? Certainly *not* by reading the Bible passages to the class or by getting them to read them! Fortunately, there are more "methods" at our disposal than these, some of which may help us to bring our skeleton to life. For example, there are several points in the Scheme where we can find parallels with the children's own experiences and interests. Most useful will be the children's experiences of quarrels, of the nagging anxiety experienced when they have treated someone badly, of the fear that accompanies deceit and of the relief and happiness which follow from a reconciliation. On a different level, there are parallels in the story with children's interest in dreams, their curiosity about love (the romantic variety!) and their enjoyment of a story involving danger, trickery and mystery. These parallels will need to be exploited in our presentation of the material. The presentation itself will undoubtedly involve us in story-telling with a liberal and imaginative approach to the story's original outline. There will also be a place for questions and discussion—both perhaps leading to a number of activities. Let us look at a few which are appropriate to Stages 2 and 3 of the Scheme.

Stage 2 How do you think Isaac felt when he discovered that Jacob had tricked him? How do you think Esau felt? Imagine a conversation between Isaac and one of his old friends on the day that it had happened. Would he want to talk about it? Act out the situation. Imagine a conversation between Esau and one of his friends on the day of the incident. Act it out or write about it. Do you think that Isaac and Esau would still feel the same about Jacob a year later?

Stage 3 Imagine the sort of thoughts that Jacob had when he was running away from Esau? Do you think he was glad to leave home? What do you think he was thinking about when he went to sleep in the sanctuary at Bethel? Do you think he went to sleep there on purpose? Why?

Part 1 When you have dreams, what sort of things do you dream about? Are you sometimes surprised by the strangeness of dreams? Do they always make sense? Can you remember them when you wake up? Do you think about them later? Are your dreams in colour or in black and white? What is the difference between a "dream" and a "nightmare"? What do you feel like when you wake up after you have had a dream or a nightmare? Write an account or draw a picture of a dream that you have had which you can still remember. Why do you think you still remember it? After his dream Jacob was afraid. Why? What did he do which shows that he took his dream very seriously? Find out more about the importance that people of the past used to give to their dreams. Look up passages in the Bible which tell about dreams. Are they as strange as this one? Do they have things in them which are the same as in this one? Create a dance drama based on the incidents in the story of Jacob up to and including his dream at Bethel.

It is important to remember, that whatever methods we select for use with a Scheme of this kind—story-telling, questioning, discussing, acting, writing, drawing and so on—they must not simply be selected on the basis of their appropriateness to the subject-matter and their appeal to pupil characteristics (or their convenience to the teacher!) but on their value *as a means of facilitating the achievement of our stated aims and objectives.*

Now that we have looked at some of the ways in which Schemes of Work may be devised we must turn our attention to the task of planning lessons for classroom use. Many of the observations that we have made about planning Schemes are also applicable to planning lessons, especially the importance of beginning, wherever possible, with the selection of aims and objectives and then choosing content and methods most likely to result in their achievement. There are, however, several additional requirements which we must bear in mind when selecting and stating lesson objectives. Two are particularly important:

1 Whereas Scheme objectives define what the *teacher* intends to do, lesson objectives should define what the *pupils* should be able to do at the end of the learning experience.

129

2   Whereas Scheme objectives should be as precise as possible, lesson objectives should be *specific* and expressed, wherever possible, in *behavioural* terms.

Let us look at these two requirements a little more closely. In our examples of Schemes we have begun with a fairly general aim and then translated this aim into a number of objectives. We have preceded the aim and the objectives with the phrase, "To provide the children with an opportunity to . . .". This may be seen to be a statement of the teacher's intention, or, in educational jargon, "teacher behaviour". When we come to planning lessons, however, we must orientate our statement of objectives away from "teacher behaviour" towards "pupil behaviour"—what behaviour we expect the pupils to exhibit at the end of the learning experience. In this case the phrase preceding our objectives will simply become, "The children will . . .". Why is it necessary to do this? The answer is quite simple; it enables us to evaluate the success or failure of our teaching. By knowing in advance what sort of outcome we require on the part of the child, we are in a much better position to see if this has occurred as a result of the lesson. This leads us to the second requirement—that we should be specific in our statement of lesson objectives. Unless we are specific the task of evalution is not only difficult it is virtually impossible. This is why it is recommended by those working in the field of Curriculum Development that lesson objectives should be stated in "behavioural", "functional' or "observable" terms and should contain at least one *strong* verb. For example, although it is reasonable to state the objective (i.e. teacher objective) of a Scheme as, "To provide children with an opportunity to *learn* the names of the Holy Books of the Jews, Christians, Sikhs, Muslims and Hindus", when we translate this objective into a Specific Objective for a lesson (i.e. pupil objective) it is advisable to rephrase it as, "The children will state (orally or in writing) the names of the Holy Books of the Jews, Christians, Sikhs, Muslims and Hindus". The verb "learn" in the former objective (like the verbs "understand", "appreciate" and "know") is less than completely satisfactory as a lesson objective because it does not make clear what "learning" implies in terms of the pupil's behaviour. (The same is true of "understanding", "appreciating" and "knowing".) By using the verb "state" (orally or in writing), the teacher is in a good position to actually see whether or not learning has taken place. He can then either proceed with the next stage of the scheme or, if learning has not taken place, try to identify the cause of the failure : e.g. Was the material too difficult? Were the methods of presentation inappropriate? Was too much material introduced too quickly? Were the learning difficulties of some of the pupils underestimated? Should the work have been graduated in difficulty and easier work given to slower children? Were there distractions in the classroom? Did the lesson fail to arouse interest? Why? and so on. Selecting and stating lesson objectives in specific, behavioural terms is, then, a useful way of ensuring that learning is purposeful, systematic and, therefore, more successful. It is necessary, however, that in order to allow for evaluation a lesson or a number of lessons should provide an opportunity for pupils to engage in an activity which permits the teacher to observe if the intended objective has been achieved. The choice of specific objective, therefore, will inevitably affect not only the way in which the lesson is planned but, more particularly, the way in which it is concluded.

In making these observations we must recognise that there are likely to be special difficulties encountered when we try and apply this technique to the field of R.E. By far the easiest objectives to select and state are those concerned with Knowledge—facts and concepts. Although the learning of facts and the development of concepts are integral to much of R.E., by far the most important area in R.E. is that concerned with promoting attitudes and values. Not only are these exceedingly difficult to state in specific terms, but they often defy all attempts to be recognised in pupil behaviour within a classroom. Besides, attitudes and values may take a considerable time to form and develop so that the actual outcome of R.E. may only be evident many years after children have left the school! In this book we have emphasised the importance of providing children with an opportunity to gain insight into the "implicit" or feeling side of religion—of experiences such as awe, wonder and mystery. These by their very nature defy definition in behavioural terms or at least it is unlikely that any form of objective test is able to reflect the true range or depth of feeling which constitutes a person's experience of awe, wonder and mystery. Despite these difficulties and limitations, however, the technique has much to offer to the R.E. teacher and in the following examples of lesson plans we have attempted to implement the two requirements given earlier. (For further reading on curriculum development see the books listed at the end of Chapter 3.)

Set out on pp 133-137 are two lesson plan formats. There can be no "universal" format for a lesson plan as much will depend upon a school's form of organisation (e.g. grouping according to age, ability; vertical grouping; integrated day; team-teaching and so on) and, of course, upon individual teacher's preferences. The formats have been designed to help the teacher to keep his Specific Objectives in mind while teaching. The first one may be used when teaching the whole class as a single unit and the second when a theme or topic is to be approached through group work. It is important to note, however, that both group and individual work is possible and desirable within the context of the first format. Behind a lesson plan, whether it is a Class Unit or Group Unit plan, lies the Scheme of Work. The Scheme, therefore, especially its aim(s) and objectives, should be a constant reference point during both the planning and teaching of individual lessons. You will notice that the aim and objectives (i.e. teacher objectives) given in the Scheme do not need to be re-stated in the lesson plan. Instead, each plan contains Specific Objectives (i.e. pupil objectives) and provides for the evaluation of these at the end of each lesson and at the end of a sequence of lessons. Good teaching, however, is characterised by continuous evaluation, a corollary of which is willingness to alter direction when it is apparent that things are going badly or in order to capitalise on spontaneous interests and questions. Lesson plans should be sufficiently flexible to accommodate this. It is important to note, however, that where lessons depart radically from their plans some modification of Specific Objectives of the lessons which follow will be required. One further point. It is not a good idea to choose too many Specific Objectives for a single lesson because this makes evaluation difficult. Neither is it a good idea to include all three types of Specific Objectives in a single lesson—Knowledge, Skill and Attitude. Even where a lesson provides Knowledge it is perfectly legitimate to choose a Skill Objective if it is this which is seen to be important, i.e. analysis and application of facts and concepts to a particular task or problem.

To conclude this chapter we have set out in lesson plan form the first lessons of two of the Schemes of Work given earlier—a Situation Theme based on the Jacob Saga and a Depth Theme on "Caring".

132

CLASS .... AGE RANGE ....

DEVELOPMENTAL STAGES ....

TIME AVAILABLE .... NUMBER OF

CHILDREN .... THEME TITLE OR

SUBJECT ....

NO. OF LESSON IN THE SCHEME ....
(e.g. Introduction; No. Six)

PART 1   *Specific Objectives:* (Indicate whether Knowledge, Skill
or Attitude)

The children will :

1 .... (Knowledge)

2 .... (Skill)

3 .... (Attitude)
and so on.

Preparation.   List the pictures, slides, models, charts
and so on, to be used. Indicate the read-
ing done in preparation. Say how the
blackboard and other aids are to be
organised.

Organisation.   Describe how the materials and aids are
to be obtained and distributed and how
the children are to be organised.

133

PART 2 *Learning Experience to achieve Specific objectives*

SUBJECT MATTER	METHOD
Introduction What information is to be given or what questions are to be asked to link e x i s t i n g, appropriate, common interests with the new material.	How the information is to be given and how the questions are to be phrased.
Development The core of the lesson. Set down in note form the content of the information and the stages by which it is to be passed on.	The technique to be used. Describe the proposed form of activity—oral, written, dramatic, discovery, enquiry from books, work cards and so on.
Conclusion Summary, recapitulation, revision, reconstruction, application, r e v i e w, evaluation, initiation or preparation of further work and so on. Clearing up.	How this is to be done, i.e. blackboard summary, notes, illustration, exercises, model-making, questions, dramatisation, test, discussion.

PART 3 *Evaluation:* Were the Specific Objectives achieved?

Specific Objective No.	*Comments*
1...............	....
2...............	....
3	....
4...............	....
and so on	

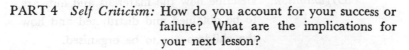

PART 4 *Self Criticism:* How do you account for your success or failure? What are the implications for your next lesson?

CLASS .... AGE RANGE ....
DEVELOPMENTAL STAGES ....
TIME AVAILABLE .... NUMBER OF
CHILDREN .... NUMBER OF
GROUPS .... THEME TITLE
OR TOPIC SUBJECT ....

Preparation	List the aids, pictures, films, tapes, books required. Indicate preparatory reading.
Materials	List all materials and equipment needed by each group.
Organisation	Describe how the materials and aids are to be obtained and distributed. Give the criteria for division into groups (e.g. friendship, ability, free-choice and so on). Describe the allocation of accommodation for each group and how the furniture is to be re-arranged.
Introduction	How the theme or topic will be introduced to the class to give an overall concept of the work to be done. How individual children will be informed of their part in the work of the group, and that of each group in the overall work of the class.
Development	Make a forecast of work to be done by each group together with a specific objective(s) for each group. This may be done in tabular form, the column for results being completed at the end of the first lesson.

Aim of the Theme or Topic (i.e. Teacher aim and objectives) *Aim:* *Objectives:*		
Forecast of work to be done	*Specific Objectives*	*Results obtained*
Group 1	....	....
Group 2	....	....
Group 3 .... and so on	....	....

Conclusion	How the work will be co-ordinated and displayed.	
Clearing up	How the clearing up is to be carried out after the lesson and after the final display.	
Evaluation	Did each group achieve their Specific Objective?	

Group No.	Specific Objective	Evaluation
Group 1	....	....
Group 2	....	....
Group 4	....	....
and so on		

Self Criticism	How do you account for your success or failure? Were your aims and objectives realistic? Were your Specific Objectives realistic? What are the implications for the next lesson involving group work?

The format of this lesson plan assumes that the theme or topic will be completed in a single lesson (a realistic assumption for some themes, especially when a whole morning or afternoon is devoted to the work). If the theme is to continue over a number of lessons the following table may be used.

Week 1

Forecast of work to be done	Specific Objectives	Results obtained
Group 1...............	....	....
Group 2...............	....	....
Group 3...............	....	....
and so on		

Week 2   *Materials*   List all the materials and equipment needed by each group.

Group activity and guidance to be given	Specific Objectives	Results obtained
Group 1...............	....	....
Group 2...............	....	....
Group 3...............	....	....
and so on		

Week 3 *Materials* List all the materials and equipment needed
by each group.

Group activity and guidance to be given	Specific Objectives	Results obtained
Group 1...............	....	....
Group 2...............	....	....
Group 3...............	....	....
and so on		

Continue as above until the theme or topic is completed.
Then use the following for evaluation :

Work completed	Specific Objectives	Evaluation
Group 1...............	....	....
Group 2...............	....	....
Group 3...............	....	....
and so on		

Self Criticism As given earlier.

CLASS : 1X. AGE RANGE : Eleven-plus. DEVELOP-
MENTAL STAGES : Concrete—Formal. TIME
AVAILABLE : 45 mins. NUMBER OF CHILDREN :
35. THEME TITLE OR SUBJECT : The Jacob Saga.
NUMBER OF LESSON IN THE SCHEME : Introduction. The twins when they were young boys (Gen.
25 : 19-34). Used as a Situation Theme.

PART 1 *Specific Objective*

The children will :

1 distinguish in writing between aspects of Esau's
character and aspects of Jacob's character. (Skill.)
(See Teacher objective no. 4);

2 state orally or in writing their preference for Esau or
Jacob and justify their choice by referring to the
story. (Attitude.)

137

Large pictures of identical twins and fraternal twins (taken from magazines, newspapers, advertisements and so on) to be used as teaching aids.

Reference made to Peake's *Commentary on the Bible* pp 194-200; *A Source Book of the Bible for Teachers* (edited by R. C. Walton) pp 102-106; also Gen. 25 prior to devising the lesson.

Preparation of the story in own words to be told to the class.

Blackboard to be used for title, spellings and for stating the pupil task.

Organisation No special organisation required. Pupils will work individually in their usual seats.

PART 2 *Learning Experience to achieve Specific Objectives*

<table>
<tr><td align="center">SUBJECT MATTER</td><td align="center">METHOD</td></tr>
<tr><td>

Introduction
Presenting an opportunity for the children to recognise that identical physical appearances need not necessarily indicate identical character, interests and ambitions, through :
(a) Reference to identical twins.

</td><td>

Questioning after displaying visual aids of identical twins. What do you notice about these two people? What is so special about being an *identical* twin? (Have the same appearance as well as having the same birthday; are close to each other in a special kind of way.) Expand by referring to examples of one twin feeling the other twin's pain, incidents of telepathic communication between twins and so on. If you can't distinguish between identical twins because of their identical appearance, imagine the tricks they can play on people! Example of changing places in class. Do you think they could

</td></tr>
</table>

138

(b) Reference to fraternal twins.

Biological explanation of the reason for identical and fraternal twins. Identical: one egg is fertilised and then it divides. Fraternal: two eggs are fertilised simultaneously.

Development

The story of Esau and Jacob.

Directing attention towards aspects appropriate to the Specific Objectives of the lesson.

play tricks on their mother and father as easily as they could on people who don't know them? Why not? Mothers and fathers don't just go on appearances; they *know* them by the *sort of persons* they are.

Give examples; one prefers to read, the other to play football and so on. One is more affectionate than the other?

Some twins don't look alike, they are not identical. Show pictures of fraternal twins.

Explain the difference between identical and fraternal twins if children ask or if they show special interest.

Just as we find differences in character among identical twins, so too do we find differences among fraternal twins. But they are still twins; they are still close to each other in a special kind of way.

Listen to another story made up by the ancient Israelites to account for their origin as a nation with a special relationship with God. This is a story about Esau and Jacob. They were fraternal twins but they were not at all alike. See how many differences you can notice between them while I tell the story.

The following points to be brought out in the story:

Esau, firstborn, red hair : Jacob, dark and smooth-skinned.
They developed different interests :
Esau: skilful hunter; brave and adventurous; loved to be away from home on hunting expeditions; could think of little else; was he irresponsible? His father, Isaac, did not think so but Rebekah, his mother, did.
Jacob: quiet and serious-minded; loved to be at home helping his mother; keen on growing plants and looking after the house; preferred to have possessions rather than Esau's adventurous life; was he a cissy? His mother, Rebekah, did not think so but Isaac, his father, did.
Introduction of background custom—the eldest son inherits his father's possessions when he dies. He has the "birthright".
Although Esau had this right, he lived for the moment and never gave the future a thought. Jacob, on the other hand, could not get the unfairness of this custom out of his mind. He, Jacob, spent all of his time at home looking after the place so why should Esau get it? If Esau did not value the birthright, why should he have it? He looked for an opportunity to trick Esau out of it.
How Esau sells his birthright to Jacob for a bowl of soup.
If Esau could give up his birthright for such a small price and with hardly any thought, perhaps he did not deserve to have it. But did Jacob deserve to have it after he had used a trick to get it? Try and make up your own mind about this. What do you think of Esau and Jacob? Which one do you like more, Esau or Jacob? You will have to think about this carefully in order to do the piece of work I'm now going to set.

Conclusion

Children are set to use what they have perceived in the story as a basis for a character assessment. The lesson will be evaluated in terms of the number of distinctions noted between the characters and the sort of reasons given for their preference for one of the characters.

"Imagine that you have gone to spend your summer holiday with this family. Write a letter to a friend at home telling him about Esau and Jacob, about what they are like and which of the two you prefer as a person."

Clearing up Not applicable. Written accounts to be collected at the end of the lesson if they are complete. If they are incomplete time for their completion to be allowed at the beginning of the next lesson.

PART 3 *Evaluation* Were the Specific Objectives achieved?

Specific Objective No.	Comments
1....................	....
2....................	....
....	....
....	....
....	....
....	....

PART 4 *Self Criticism* How do you account for your success or failure. What are the implications for your next lesson?

CLASS: 3. AGE RANGE: six-seven. READING AGES: six-twelve. TIME AVAILABLE: 1½ hours. NUMBER OF CHILD-REN: 35. NUMBER OF GROUPS: seven. THEME TITLE OR TOPIC SUBJECT: "Caring". Stage One. People who help us.

Preparation Newspaper and magazine cuttings and pictures of policemen, nurses, firemen, postmen, life-boat men, fishermen, farmers.

Materials Copies of number one, two, three, four, five, seven and sixteen of the *Ladybird* Easy Reading Series 606B—"People at Work".
Sheets of writing paper.
Seven large sheets of sugarpaper.
Sheets of drawing paper.
Scissors for each group.
Crayons, pencils, felt-tipped pens.
Paste.
Workcards for each group.

Organisation Materials to be placed on the children's tables before the lesson.
Grouping by reading age.
Furniture to allow for seven groups.

Introduction When children come into the class they will sit on the floor around the teacher's chair. Short discussion about ways in which we help each other. Focus of discussion moved to people who help us. Explanation of the work to be done. The work to be displayed on the wall at the end of the afternoon. Allocation of children to groups.

141

Development

Objectives: To provide children with an opportunity to :
1 develop insight into the concept of helpfulness as a means of understanding the concept of caring;
2 gain knowledge of the work of policemen, nurses, firemen, postmen, life-boat men, fishermen and farmers;
3 gain practical experience of sharing and co-operating in group work;
4 practise reading, writing, drawing, cutting and study skills.

Forecast of work to be done and Specific Objectives

Group 1 The children will describe through writing, pictures and drawings the ways in which policemen help us.
Result obtained

Group 2 The children will describe through writing, pictures and drawings the ways in which nurses (doctors and dentists) help us.
Result obtained

(Group 3, firemen; Group 4, postmen; Group 5, life-boat men; Group 6, fishermen; Group 7, farmers. The same Specific Objective is applicable to each group.)

Examples of Workcards

1 *The policeman*
Write about these four things on a piece of paper.
Begin with the words I have given you.
Look at the book on "The Policeman" to help you.
(a) The policeman wears a uniform because ....
(b) The policeman helps children to ....
(c) The policeman looks after our houses by ....
(d) The roads are safe for us because the policeman ....
Each member of the group chooses one of the ways in which the policeman helps us and draws a picture of him doing it.
Write under the picture what he is doing.
Paste your picture on the sugarpaper.
Find a picture of a policeman in the newspapers and magazines. Cut it out and paste it on the sugarpaper.
At the top of the sugarpaper write in large letters : "How the policeman helps us."
(The instructions may be given by the teacher orally instead of writing them on the workcard. Individual help will need to be given to non-readers, e.g. "Tell me what a policeman does to help us. Draw a picture of him doing one of these things. Tell me what

142

to write under your picture. Now you can copy the sentence underneath.")

2 *The nurse*
Write about these four things on a piece of paper.
Begin with the words I have given you.
Look at the book "The Nurse" to help you.
(a) The nurse wears a uniform because ....
(b) The nurse helps people in hospital by ....
(c) The nurse helps the doctor and the dentist by ....
(d) Inside the nurse's bag there are ....
and so on.

3 *The fireman*
Write about these four things on a piece of paper.
Begin with the words I have given you.
Look at the book "The Fireman" to help you.
(a) The fireman wears a uniform because ....
(b) On his fire engine the fireman carries ....
(c) When a house is on fire the fireman ....
(d) To call the fireman we have to ....
and so on.

Conclusion   All the children's work will be displayed on the classroom wall under the heading, "People who help us".

Clearing up   Members of each group will be made responsible for clearing away different items. Some children will be asked to help with putting up the display.

Evaluation   Did each group achieve their Specific Objective?

Group No.	Specific Objective	Evaluation
1	The children will describe through writing, pictures and drawings the ways in which policemen help us.	
and so on.		

Self Criticism   How do you account for your success or failure?
Were your aims and objectives realistic?
Were your Specific Objectives realistic?
Did the children experience difficulty with the workcards? How? Why?
What are the implications for the next lesson involving group work?

143

Chapter 8

Teaching Methods in Religious Education

There are no distinctive teaching methods uniquely applicable to
R.E. Like his colleagues dealing with other subjects, the R.E. teacher
makes use of the common "pool" of methods—discovery and activity methods, project work, story and essay writing, workcards,
stimulus material, painting, dramatisation, questioning, discussion
and so on—by adapting them to his subject-matter, to his own style
of teaching and to the needs, interests and abilities of his pupils. A
detailed examination of such a wide variety of methods and how
they may be applied to the teaching of religion in schools is inappropriate within the plan of this book, and so in this chapter
we will concentrate only on those methods whose potentialities
would appear to have been least explored by many teachers within
the context of R.E. These are :
A Educational drama
    (a) Scripted and extempore drama.
    (b) Sociodrama or role-play.
    (c) Dance drama.
    (d) Stylised drama.
B Music and Art
C Films, tapes and communication media

A Educational drama

The term "educational drama" is a very broad one; it includes
mime, movement, improvisation, play-acting, role-play, sociodrama,
dance drama, stylised drama and even story-telling. It is important
to make a distinction between this term and "theatre". Educational
drama is interested in the *process* of dramatisation (i.e. its value to
the person engaging in it) while "theatre" is interested in the *outcome* or *performance* (i.e. its value to those watching it). "Theatre"
has only a very limited place in schools whereas "educational

drama" has an important contribution to make in schools at all levels.

Most teachers are aware that drama's capacity to capture and stimulate interest makes it a good motivator. But drama should not be seen merely as an educational aid or a teaching method. On the contrary, drama is an "imaginative, living experience", it is a "learning experience" or "learning situation" in its own right. Through drama we seek to provide the child with an opportunity not only to expand his personal experiences but also to *examine them at depth* from a number of different viewpoints. As we saw in Chapter 5 of this book, this is precisely what we are seeking to do when we use Depth Themes in R.E. Indeed, there is a very close link between the aims of the three types of theme which comprise the *Existential Approach* to R.E. and those of educational drama. This should be apparent from the following statement of the aims of educational drama :

1 To develop the personality.
2 To develop the powers of imagination, self-expression and communication.
3 To develop an awareness of the other's position and the ability to empathise.
4 To foster group identification.

These aims serve to indicate how drama is a *process* (rather than a subject) which seeks to contribute to *personal awareness* (i.e. awareness of self) and to *social awareness* (i.e. awareness of others). For example :

Personal awareness

Drama is useful in assisting the growth of physical, emotional and intellectual confidence and independence. At the same time, like play, it affords an acceptable means by which a child may satisfy basic needs—the release of physical and mental energies, aggression, hate, fear, violence, wish-fulfilment and so on. Through drama children can project themselves into their future adult roles or safely regress and give expression to unfulfilled infantile needs. Through drama they can be themselves as they feel they are, rather than as others expect them to be. Thus, on an imaginative level they can overcome difficulties and problems that in real life would be insoluble or insupportable.

Social awareness

Drama is useful as a means of promoting feeling for, and awareness

145

of, other people and their attitudes and needs. It teaches a child to adopt attitudes towards problems and situations faced by other people. It is a way of exploring other people, their needs, fears and joys, so making possible close, empathetic identification. Just as drama has a therapeutic value for the socially maladjusted, so too does it help to give children and young people confidence to face the ever-growing demands of the 20th century.

Drama, then, has an educational value in its own right and there should be occasions when children are encouraged to engage in it for its own sake. There should, however, be other occasions when drama is used as an additional tool in the teaching of other subjects. With reference to R.E., we may identify three broad types of purpose for which it may be used.

1 Using drama as:
   (a) a means of *introducing* and *exploring* themes, stories, characters and situations;
   (b) a means of pulling together the threads of experience at the end of a topic;
   (c) a means of promoting discussion, research and writing.
2 Using drama as:
   an aid to *understanding* religious concepts and ideas both on an intellectual and an emotional level (e.g. religious symbolism, myth and ritual).
3 Using drama as:
   a means of *evaluating* the success or failure of lessons with Attitude Objectives (i.e. the quality and level of feelings and sensitivities).

Other purposes for using drama in R.E. might include:
(a) providing light relief after a formal lesson;
(b) stimulating interest in a story or topic and so motivating reading;
(c) fostering group identification in a class lacking social cohesion;
(d) promoting confidence and developing communication skills;
(e) helping children to memorise an incident or story.

Educational drama and R.E. Some general principles

1 A teacher may be defined as a person who "creates learning experiences and learning situations for others". Thus, in relation to drama and R.E., a teacher is a "stimulator and structurer of learning experiences and situations for children". At

146

primary school level he may be a "designer of incidents and situations" for dramatisation; and at secondary school level he may be a "designer of problem situations" which young people can then attempt to understand and solve largely through role-play.

2 Using drama in R.E. does not simply mean requesting children to "act out" certain well-known Bible stories as an alternative to writing about them—although this may legitimately happen occasionally. As we have seen, R.E. should be very broad in outlook; its content should reflect the principle that the essence of religion is to be found in life itself, in all experiences and in all "subjects". Thus, encouraging a group of Infants to play out mother, father and children roles in the Wendy House is more likely to foster insight into the significance of "Homes and Families" than telling them the story of Jesus's boyhood in his Nazareth home with Mary and Joseph without such parallel experiences. There may, then, appear to be very little difference to an observer between a "drama" lesson and an R.E. lesson using drama. The difference if any may be in *intent or aim,* although in view of the closeness of R.E. and drama aims this does not necessarily follow. The Specific Objective chosen for such an R.E. lesson, however, may be related far more closely to involving children in experiences which provide a basis for developing insight into distinctively religious concepts (such as awe, wonder, mystery and worship) although, once again, this need not necessarily follow for are not "religious" concepts really "secular" concepts viewed from a different angle?

3 An over-riding concern, especially when encouraging children to dramatise Biblical material, should be to help them towards an appreciation of the significance of the incident rather than merely providing them with a knowledge of the details of the story. Thus, although it is inevitable that the concrete features of the story will predominate in dramatisations in the Infant and Lower Junior school, in the Late Junior school dramatisations should be moving away from these to a greater preoccupation with what the children think and feel the incident really points to or reflects in terms of meaning and significance. For example, Late Infant and Junior school children delight in presenting, either through mime or improvised drama, the parable of the Good Samaritan. Their dramatisation is usually very "factual", following the parable's original literary structure closely. Few would realise the strength of the parable's point even if they were told that Jews were not on speaking terms with Samaritans at that time! But Late Junior school children *can* be helped

147

towards an appreciation of this point, especially if they are encouraged to give the parable a new setting, a very different "cast" (who knows about Levites today, anyway?) and a much developed dialogue. With children in the Late Secondary school dramatisation may only involve dialogue exploring the *motives* lying behind the actions of the persons involved in the incident. Indeed, by this time the original story may have disappeared altogether. Thus, a general principle which might be observed in this work is to *decrease* the extent of the narrative and "plot" as children become older. Whereas Early Junior school children would dramatise the whole of an incident (e.g. the parable of the Prodigal Son), Middle Secondary school children may wish to concentrate on a single aspect of the incident or even on a single moment (e.g. the moment of reunion between the prodigal son and his father).

(a) *Scripted and extempore drama*

There is little doubt that extempore or improvised drama has a much greater educational value to children than scripted or written drama. Indeed, the aims given at the beginning of this chapter are only really applicable to extempore drama. There may, however, be occasions when a teacher may wish to offer his pupils an opportunity to *write* their own plays, playlets or incidents for dramatisation rather than rely entirely on extempore work. If this is the case, he should be very clear in his own mind as to *why* a scripted or written play is preferable to an extempore one. Is it because it provides them with an opportunity to improve their writing ability? Is it because he wishes them to give much closer attention to a text than they would normally give if they were only asked to read it? Is it because he wants them to produce material suitable for use in Assembly? Whatever his reason he should recognise that it is the process of creating and writing the play wherein the value of the activity is to be found and not in its eventual "performance". Few children are likely to be able to "explore" the character they are playing if they are preoccupied with the technical difficulties of reading a script, coming in at the right moment and making sure that they are standing in the right place! "Exploration of character" in this instance will only occur when they are discussing the incident *after* the performance.

Assuming that a teacher wishes to involve a class of Late Junior school children in writing their own play, how might he go about it? Unless he has considerable expertise in this area he would be well advised to abandon all thought of a *class* play and concentrate instead on a number of *group* plays. If he so wished he could suggest that the class might take a common theme (e.g. "Groups we belong to", "People in need" or a Biblical theme such as "People whom Jesus helped" and so on) and each group contribute a different situation or incident. Considerable discussion with the class on possible subjects should obviously precede this work, the teacher guiding choices rather than dictating them. Friendship grouping is advisable for work of this kind with special care being taken over the placing of isolates and rejectees. The classroom furniture will need to be re-arranged so that groups may sit and work together, and a "Producer" (i.e. a co-ordinator of the work) should be selected from each group. As this situation usually leads to a rise in the level of classroom noise, some signal (such as a handclap) should be adopted by the teacher so that the class may be called to order should the necessity arise. Groups should begin by reading the incident carefully if it is taken from the Bible and then producing a written outline of the incident. For example :

The Stilling of the Storm (Mark 4)

1 Jesus preaching and talking to the people.
2 The crowd presses forward to hear.
3 Jesus and his disciples get into a boat.
4 They row away from the shore and put up the sail.
5 Idle conversation while Jesus sleeps.
6 The storm breaks.
7 The disciples are terror-stricken.
8 The disciples wake Jesus.
9 Jesus speaks to them and to the sea.
10 The reaction of the disciples.

Once the outline is complete the groups may begin to fill it out with spoken dialogue. The number of "characters" in the incident will have to be determined by the number of children in the group although it is sometimes possible for one or two children to take more than one part each. Depending on the incident, "stage" directions may be included. All members of each group will need to write out the final version of the group's play—another disadvantage of scripted drama. The initial play-reading may be done within the group. For the actual "performance" a central area of the room will need to be cleared or the front of the classroom may be used. With the above example chairs might be used to represent the boat. Each group would then perform their play with the rest of the class acting as the audience. It is very important that if the significance and meaning of the play is to be brought out, each performance is followed by a discussion involving the whole class. With the incident of the stilling of the storm the teacher should emphasise

149

Jesus's capacity to calm the disciples through his own lack of fear —something that they found as strange as the calming of the sea. Questions such as, "Why wasn't Jesus afraid?" or "Was Jesus afraid but didn't show it?" might be asked, and the children's attention could be directed to Psalm 107 : 23-32—a passage which, perhaps, this incident was originally intended to remind people of; a passage which shows the stilling of the storm to be the prerogative of God. What conclusions should we draw from this about Jesus? What did Mark think about this? It may well be that after such a discussion, groups could go on to suggest less literal approaches to their incidents. Certainly, children of this age (9-11 +) are more likely to begin to appreciate the *nature* of the miracle stories in the Gospels through drama followed by discussion than if discussion is introduced after only a cursory reading of the Biblical account.

Extempore or improvised drama provides a much greater opportunity for children to "play out" their own feelings (and so come to grips with them) and to look more deeply into character and situation than is provided by scripted drama. Consequently, with extempore drama accuracy should be sacrificed to imagination for the child and his feelings are more important than any text or script. This does not mean, however, that when using a Biblical incident or symbol as the basis for improvisation a careful reading of the text is unnecessary. On the contrary, a careful reading of the text (especially if the teacher is able to read it sensitively to the children) often provides a "springboard" for a great deal of imaginative, creative and original thinking. As we noted earlier, young children, at least initially, require a far more structured situation than older ones. This is true even when they are engaging in mime and movement—both of which are useful as an introduction to extempore drama involving speech. Both the Old and New Testaments contain a wealth of material involving action which are appropriate as a stimulus for mime and extempore drama. There are many different ways of approach but two which are particularly successful with Late Junior and Early Secondary school children are :

1   Presenting the situation to the children in a brief outline or asking them to read about it, and then encouraging them to act it out in their own words.

2   Asking the group to imagine that they have witnessed the incident (or heard about it) and that they are now discussing it (especially its significance) among themselves. Some characterisation is often helpful, e.g. a mother and her daughter, a couple of workmen, a businessman and an elderly lady and so on.

150

This second approach may be used in relation to Biblical incidents and to contemporary events. In the former case it might involve a Temple Official talking with a Pharisee; Mary Magdalene talking to Simon the Leper (Matthew 26) or to Judas; the disciple talking to a sceptical neighbour about Jesus's identity; groups of people (disciples, soldiers, merchants, Pharisees and so on) talking about the verdict at Jesus's trial. In the latter case, children might be given situations such as taking a tramp home to dinner, an argument among a group of people about the arrival of a family of immigrants in their street, a disagreement among a group of friends about how they should spend Saturday afternoon, a bullying incident in the playground, a stolen purse and so on. This sort of work is closely connected with "role-play" or "socio-drama".

(b) *Role-play and Socio-drama*

Everyone plays a number of different "roles" in life according to the demands of their "role-set". (A teacher's professional role-set comprises his headmaster, his deputy headmaster, his head of department, other members of staff, H.M.I.'s, examiners, College tutors, parents and pupils. If the teacher is married and a parent his role-set will also include his wife, his sons and daughters, his relatives, his neighbours, friends which he has in common with his wife, his children's friends and so on. He may also be a member of the local Rugby team and this too will add to his role-set by incorporating into it his team-mates, his drinking companions, his fans and so on.) Emotional stability or good mental health depends largely upon how successfully we play our different roles in accordance with the different demands of our role-set. How successful we are at this will depend upon two main factors:

1 Our knowledge of the expectations of our role-set and why they have such expectations.
2 Our ability to fulfil these expectations in our behaviour without undue stress and strain.

"Role-play" has to be learned in life often through bitter experience. Fortunately children and young people can be helped to gain knowledge of the feelings and attitudes of their role-sets and practise the skill of adapting their responses in accordance with these by being involved in "situational" or "socio" drama. Within the same situation a person can "rotate" through the members of his role-set by playing each role in turn (e.g. in a family argument about "being in at night on time", a pupil can play himself, then his father and finally his mother). In rotating through the roles he is able to objectify and analyse the distinctive characteristics of each position and so evaluate their viewpoints in relation to his own. Work of this nature may eventually lead to the pupil acquiring a much greater flexibility in his adaptation to other people as well as to a greater sensitivity to their feelings and values. Thus, the approach is invaluable in helping children to deal with the conflicts and division of loyalties which occur in adolescence. Furthermore, role-play may provide the means by which anti-authority feelings and attitudes may be channelled into constructive rather than destructive behaviour. The approach is particularly applicable to work on Situation Themes within the *Existential Approach.*

(c) *Dance drama*

In playing out their feelings through *physical movement* children objectify them and so are able to examine and evaluate them. This form of self-expression is particularly desirable in R.E. where the "subject-matter" is so very difficult to translate into words, largely because "understanding" also depends on "feeling". Furthermore, the physical symbolism of dance or movement assists the development of the child's awareness of the nature of symbolism —both physical and linguistic. This can greatly facilitate the child's development of religious concepts and his appreciation of the nature of religious language.

Dance may be either with or without music and with or without a story, plot or incident. The older the children the greater the freedom they should be given to interpret symbols, images and situations for themselves. Younger children may require the security of a story whereas older children may find that this is a hindrance rather than a help. It is important to note that almost every symbol, image and situation can be interpreted at different levels according to the maturity of the pupils. For example, even very young children are able to explore through dance such concepts as awe, wonder, mystery and worship—concepts which we have seen to be central to religion. Dance, however, may also provide children with new insights into well-known stories. Late Juniors, for instance, might find more significance in the parable of the lost sheep through dance than through merely hearing it read. In this case they could identify first with the sheep and then with the shepherd. For example:

1 *Identification with the sheep*
   The dance might follow a sequence of: the security of the flock; innocent or deliberate straying; the excitement of being alone; the fear of being alone; a frantic search for the way back; despair; nightfall; the approach of the shepherd; fear turning to joy; feelings of security, peace and belonging.

2   *Identification with the shepherd*
The dance might follow a sequence of : vigilance; dangers;
distractions; nightfall; counting the flock; concern for the
missing sheep; resolution to leave the flock and search; the
search; finding the sheep; relief; joy; the return; celebration.

Although both Old and New Testaments contain abundant
material which can act as a stimulus for dance, particular attention
should be given to the vividness of symbolism and imagery in this
material. The task of dance drama is to heighten the effect of these
symbols and images by placing them within a context of movement
which helps to bring them to life. The following abstract contains
an account of the work of a class of ten year old children and their
teacher in which this is done.

When this same class and teacher became absorbed in the theme
of "Light and darkness" during the next term, the significance
of dance drama and movement and music in R.E. became more
apparent. The class had not previously explored the use of movement or music in relation to their themes but when they heard
some of the primitive creation myths of North American Indians
and some from Babylonian sources, they found movement a way
of exploring and entering into these searchings of primitive man
for an explanation of the beginnings of the elements around him.
These myths and the use of the music of Holst's *The Planets* and
The New Music—with its electronics effects—acted as inspira-
tion for both moving and writing. These myths set the Genesis
creation story into a context for them and enabled these children to see it as truth expressed in story and poetry rather than
as a scientific account.

Out of this work on creation the children devised a kind of
mime of the canticle the *Benedicite Omnia opera* for one of their
class assemblies. . . . The children adapted the canticle using
mainly the first part, and they made exciting masks for the sun,
moon, fire, snow, winter and summer lightning—each line was
mimed with vivid movement by those wearing the masks, while
others sang the chant, or clashed the cymbals, or drums or played
the recorder during the refrain "Praise ye the Lord". This assembly deeply impressed the rest of the school, but for this particular class it was the experience of working on it together, the cooperation and the sharing and the creative involvement which
were for them true religious education. . . ."

(Joan Clark, an article entitled "The Junior School" in *Learning
for Living*, The Journal of the Christian Education Movement,
SCM Press Ltd, January 1971.)

Here then is an example of how dance drama can involve children not only in the exploration of religious symbolism but also give them first-hand experience of myth and ritual. It also provides a context in which most of the basic human emotions may be explored—love, hate, fear, courage, anger, cruelty, sorrow, joy, excitement, horror, compassion, sympathy, humour and so on.

(d) *Stylised drama*

In Chapter 5, pp 59-75, we noted that the task of educating children towards an appreciation of the nature of religious language, especially its logical kinship with poetry, requires us to acquaint them with evocative and dramatic language being used within the context of religion as an expression of faith and commitment. Provided the approach is not over used, "stylised drama" or "choral verse speaking" has value in this respect. For example, the theme of "Creation" might be presented through verse-speaking being interwoven with music and drama. In this case a careful selection of appropriate verses from Psalms 8, 29, 33, 47, 93 and 148 could be made and these combined into the framework provided by Gen. Chapter 1. Groups of voices might be employed in contrast to solo voices and a narrator. A modern translation of the Bible could be used. Similarly, the story of the Exodus might be presented in this way using Psalms 78 and 105. This approach has the advantage of providing a link between the classroom and Assembly as much of the work is suitable for use in school worship.

B Music and Art

Many modern "pop" and "folk" songs deal with topics or ideas which, in essence, are "religious". Indeed these songs are remarkably successful in communicating *in the language of today* some of those "truths" which traditional religious language fails to communicate. Clearly, then, such music has an important contribution to make to our task of educating children towards religious understanding. Various approaches are possible. For example, listening to songs and exploring their lyrics; incorporating songs within lessons to illustrate and develop points; involving the class in writing their own songs and then, perhaps, introducing them into Assembly. At a different level, the R.E. lesson should provide children with an opportunity to examine "Pop Culture" in terms of the values and attitudes which underlie it—values which are often in conflict with those which most teachers regard as normative.

With Middle and Late Secondary school children some attention may be given to the great classical masterpieces in music which have been inspired by religious ideas or a religious faith. Here again one should be trying to help children to appreciate that religious truth cannot be confined within purely "rational" categories but belongs more to the realm of aesthetics—especially in the part played by emotional or personal response to its "impact". Works which are likely to be particularly appropriate are : Handel's *Messiah* (especially "For unto us a child is born", "Glory to God in the Highest", "I know that my Redeemer liveth" and "Hallelujah"); Bach's *Christmas Oratorio* and *Saint Matthew's Passion;* Haydn's *Creation;* Verdi's *Requiem;* Elgar's *Dream of Gerontius;* Stravinsky's *Symphony of Psalms;* Walton's *Balshazzar's Feast;* Britten's *Noye's Fludde* and *Saint Nicholas's Cantata.*

Similarly, a series of lessons on how different artists have depicted Christ and the Christian faith would not only help older children to appreciate the nature of symbolism but also how symbols change to meet man's changing circumstances and demands. A consideration of trends within contemporary cinema and theatre might also help them to understand how man's beliefs and values and how they may be expressed "evolve" in accordance with his present existential situation. An examination of literature affords a similar opportunity. In this way we can provide a context in which to place current trends in theology.

C Films, tapes and communication media

With the development of a "phenomenological" approach to the teaching of religion, films and tapes have assumed a much greater significance to R.E. than ever before. A good film is one which is able to project into the classroom something of the "feel" or atmosphere of a religion as well as portraying its distinctive external features. This is unlikely to be achieved by film strips unless they are accompanied by a sound recording giving an authentic audio account of the situation or events that the film covers. A mere commentary on what is seen on the film is no substitute for this; indeed one of the failings of a commentary is that it often becomes obtrusive and destroys the film's impact. This is rarely so of the actual sounds which accompany the events. For example, a film dealing with pilgrimage in Islam should communicate something of the atmosphere of pilgrimage, the feelings of those participating, the brotherhood existing between pilgrims, the holy actions and prayers, the sacrifice and the ensuing celebration. The "noise" of pilgrimage is distinctive; it has a character of its own; it is part of the experience of pilgrimage. To replace this with a monotonous description is to reduce the effectiveness of even the very best photography. Fortunately much greater care is now being given by commercial companies to these requirements, although there is still a deficiency in the number of films dealing sympathetically with worship. Many potentially valuable films, however, are ruined by their "confessional" approach. This is particularly true of films dealing with the Christian faith.

The tape-recorder, especially the portable cassette recorder, is now a well established teaching tool in the classroom. We may distinguish between its use as a means of presenting material to the children and its use by the children to present their work. Teacher-made tapes often take a long time and much patience to produce but they are very useful in presenting a "stimulus" for development in the lesson. For example, a Depth Theme on "Sounds" for a class of Infant children may be introduced by a tape of home, school and street sounds for the children to identify and discuss. Pupil-made tapes are not easily produced but the time and effort expended on overcoming the technical difficulties is easily compensated for by the enthusiasm and enjoyment which work of this nature arouses in the children—enthusiasm and enjoyment which is transferred to the topic or subject-matter. From simply recording their own poems and songs, descriptions of their homes and families and accounts of their experiences, young children contribute to their own linguistic development as well as practise the skill of looking more deeply into the things around them.

With children in the Late Junior school the tape-recorder may be used for interviews, a news programme and a "radio play". Unlike interviews, programmes need to be scripted and timed, each section being the responsibility of a group of children. A really "professional" programme requires introductory theme music, "on the spot" reporting and realistic background noises (traffic, crowds, storm, sea and so on). The tape may have to be built up in sections with judicious use of the pause button. Crowd scenes are difficult to record because of the variability of sound level. Music can be used to good effect but copyright laws should not be infringed. Depending on the choice of topic, pupil-made tapes may be used in Assembly but if this is to be the case they should be recorded at a fairly high sound level so that they are audible in a large hall. For those who would wish to use this approach in relation to Biblical material suitable topics might be : events in David's reign, incidents from the lives of the Prophets, the Exodus, the trial of Jesus, interviews with New Testament characters, Saint Paul reporting on events in his missionary journeys and so on.

With the exception of radio and television, newspapers are still the most important medium of communication in society. Producing a class newspaper with Late Junior or Early Secondary school children is another way in which they can be involved in a "learning experience" which has ramifications beyond their immediate situation. For example, work on a class newspaper, especially with secondary school children, should begin with a careful consideration of the reasons for newspapers, what a newspaper tries to do (e.g. influence public opinion), what a newspaper should contain and what goes to make a *good* newspaper (e.g. reporting style, format, illustrations and so on). The job of a reporter, a columnist, a political commentator, a cartoonist and so on, needs to be examined, and also the functions of the different editors. Some consideration should also be given to newspaper owners and advertisers, especially how they are able to influence a newspaper's policy. Here we are attempting to lay a foundation of knowledge upon which the slow growth of discrimination can rest.

If a class newspaper is decided upon it is essential that care is taken over the allocation of different tasks to pupils. Initially it is a good idea for the paper to reflect the class's or school's news. This will involve work being produced in class, interviews with teachers, caretaking and kitchen staff, school sports results, articles by pupils on their hobbies, reports of visits, cartoons, a correspondence page, photographs, crosswords, advertisements, information about forthcoming events at the school and so on. It may be seen that such a "topic" as a newspaper is likely to become an "integrated curriculum" in its own right. The more ambitious schemes may result in the publication of a newspaper by means of spirit-duplicating, while others may be content to produce a single copy for display on the classroom wall. In the latter case each group of six pupils could be made responsible for producing one page (i.e. a large sheet of sugarpaper) covering certain specified topics.

Where the newspaper is to relate specifically to work in R.E. both the Old and New Testaments as well as Church History and World Religions provide a wealth of material for incorporation. For example, something as dull as 1 Kings Chap. 12, the division of the monarchy after Solomon, can be transformed into an exciting and informative account of Civil War. Three group newspapers might be produced by Early Secondary school children to deal with this topic, each with a headline showing the course of events:

Nisan 9, 922.   NORTH GIVES KING REHOBOAM AN ULTIMATUM.
Nisan 12, 922. REHOBOAM STILL AT TALKS WITH ADVISERS.
Nisan 13, 922. CIVIL WAR! NORTH REJECTS REHOBOAM AND MAKES JEROBOAM KING.

The papers would need to reflect the conditions of the time, the attitudes of people from the North and the South, the difference of opinion between the young men of the nation and the old men, the ambitions of the two kings and so on, and this would involve preliminary research into the Old Testament and Jewish history. The whole scheme would inevitably raise questions about Civil Wars in more recent history, including today.

The crisis events in Jesus's life provide ideal subject-matter for a newspaper. So too do the events of Passion Week. For the latter each group could undertake to report the happenings of one day of the week so producing a series of "dailies" concluding with a Sunday newspaper dealing with the Christian claim that Jesus had risen from the dead. Older children are capable of producing papers with a political slant (e.g. a pro-Roman, pro-Pharisee or a pro-Christian paper) and also of attempting political cartoons. Once again the newspapers should reflect the conditions and opinions of the time. Other subjects for coverage might include a report on Pentecost, an exclusive interview with Peter following his sermon on Jesus's resurrection, the death of Stephen (which might include a statement from an eye-witness called Saul) and an interview with Paul after his conversion.

Where a teacher is concerned with introducing children to World Religions, a newspaper might be produced which gives information about the beliefs and practices of different faiths, especially if they are represented in the local community, and also about the customs and life-styles of their adherents. Provided the accounts were accurate a great deal of good might be done if such newspapers were distributed by the children to people living in the area who knew only about Christianity.

Further reading

V. Bruce: *Dance and Dance Drama in Education* (Pergamon, 1965).
V. Bruce: *Movement in Silence and Sound* (G. Bell and Sons, 1970).
C. Herbert: *The New Creation* (Dance Drama; REP, 1972).
C. J. Kitchell: *Radio Jerusalem* (Ginn and Co. Ltd, 1972).
J. Russell: *Creative Dance in the Primary School* (Macdonald & Evans, 1965).
J. Took and V. Bruce: *Lord of the Dance—an approach to R.E.* (Pergamon, 1966).
B. Way: *Development through Drama* (Longmans, 1967).

158

Appendix One

Practical Examples of the Existential Approach

1   DEPTH THEMES

Aim: To provide the child with an opportunity to :
1   practise the skill of reflecting on his own experiences at depth;
2   develop insight into himself and his feelings;
3   develop insight into other people and their feelings;
4   develop insight into what constitutes a distinctly human relationship between self and others.

(a)   Some Depth Themes may be developed like a Topic and take several lessons to complete. In this case they will normally have a title and the work will be done in individual or group topic books. For example :

Infants
(5-7 years)
Homes and Families, Our Pets, Things we share, People who help us, Our Happiness Book, Seeds, The food we eat, The clothes we wear, Our Book of People, Our Book about Mothers and Fathers, Our Holiday Book, Our Book of Plants and Flowers, Our Book of Games, Things we like to touch, Things we like to see, Things we like to smell, Colours, Shapes, The games we like to play, The songs we like to sing, Spring, Summer, Autumn, Winter, Our Wonderful World, Myself, and so on.

159

| *Early Juniors* (7-9 years) | Families and Relatives, Friends and Neighbours, Highways and Journeys, Travel and Travellers, Gifts and Giving, Holidays, Our Weekend Book, Lending a hand, Our Book of Dreams, Things we like to make, Caring, Books we like to read, Visits and Visitors, My Favourite Things, and so on. |

(b) Some Depth Themes will simply be "experiences"—often only of a moment's duration. These may be created within the context of topics and other subject areas or through stories and activities. For example: experiences of awe, wonder, mystery, peace, stillness, listening, touching, feeling, smelling, moving, leaping, dancing and so on.

(c) Some Depth Themes will involve the exploration of previously selected concepts. For example: courage, sacrifice, forgiveness, adventure, danger, fear, tolerance, loneliness, honesty, truthfulness, worry, temptation, quarrelling, fighting, disappointment, jealousy, hatred, aggression, ambition, confidence, responsibility, loyalty, pride, prejudice, rejection, isolation, greed, fairness, kindness, love and so on.

(d) All Depth Themes will begin with, or relate to, the child's immediate situation, experiences and interests.

An example of how a Depth Theme may be explored at different depths according to the ages, interests and developmental levels of the pupils.

Theme: Homes and Families.

Aim: To provide the child with an opportunity to :
1 practise the skill of reflecting on his own experiences at depth;
2 develop insight into himself and his feelings;
3 develop insight into other people and their feelings;
4 develop insight into what constitutes a distinctly human relationship between self and others.

Objectives: To provide the child with an opportunity to :
1 examine the nature of human relationships, especially those within a family situation;
2 examine the nature of family life in his own and other cultures;

3 gain insight into the concepts of love, consideration, obedience, duty, responsibility, punishment, forgiveness, suffering, need, security, tolerance, loneliness, sharing, unity, community and "relationship";

4 examine his own position in, and responsibility towards, his own family and towards the wider "Family of Man".

Summary of the theme's structure:

Infants (5-7 years)	Our Homes and Our Families.
Early Juniors (7-9 years)	"Adventures with the Family"; "The Family at Work"; "The Family at Play"; "The Family at Home"; "Homes in other lands".
Late Juniors (9-11 years)	Stories about families with children aged 9-11. "Families without homes"; Families on the move".
Early Secondary (11-13 years)	"Families of the World"; "People without Families".
Middle Secondary (13+)	"Family Conflicts".
Late Secondary (14-16 years)	"New Families".

Content and Learning Experiences

Infants
Stage One

Talking about our houses and our families. A house needs a family in order to make it into a "home". Paintings of our houses and families.

Stage Two

A class family, e.g. Mr and Mrs Jones and Sarah and Jim; their grandma and their pets. Stories about the family.

Stage Three

"The Move"; What happened on the day that the Jones family moved into their new home? What did father do? What did mother

161

do? What did the children do? What happened to the pets? Did anyone help the family to move? This work could be presented through pictures, short descriptions with pictures and so on. The children could draw pictures of the new house, of the removal van, of Mr and Mrs Jones carrying belongings, of the children helping; a simple "map" of the street (to help the removal men find the house) could also be drawn.

Stage Four

"Exploring the new house"; comparisons with the old house; a plan of the house; pictorial and verbal descriptions of the children's rooms. "How the family worked together to make the new house into a home." What did father do? (decorating). What did mother do? (cleaning and putting up the curtains). What did the children do? (helped, looked after the pets and so on). What did the pets think of the new home? Emphasis on excitement.

Stage Five

"Meeting the neighbours"; "Finding the shops"; "Finding the way back to the new home".

Stage Six

"Starting at a new school"; the new teacher; the new class; making new friends. (This aspect would be particularly useful if there are new pupils in the class; it is a way of reminding the others of how they feel and how they might help them.)

Stage Seven

"Helping at home". (The theme could be linked with reading, e.g. the Ladybird "Learning to Read" series 563 contains a book of this title. Sentences include: "We are helping to lay the table. We are helping to wash up. I am helping Mummy to make the bed. We are helping Mummy to feed the animals" and so on.)

Stage Eight

"How do we know that the members of the family love each other?" Making up sentences:

Father He goes out to work. He gives Mum a kiss. He pays the bills. He buys presents for the family at Christmas. He looks after the others. He plays with the children.

Mother She buys and cooks the food. She makes the house comfortable. She cleans the house and makes it nice. She looks after the others when they are ill. She smiles when she says "Goodnight!". She gives the children a hug.

Children They do as they are asked. They do jobs and run errands. They don't shout when Mum has a headache. They keep quiet when the baby is asleep. They give their parents a hug and a kiss.

Pets The dog wags his tail when he finds you. The cat purrs when she is stroked. They do not go far from home. They like to sit in front of the fire with the family. The budgie sings for us. The rabbit comes to the front of his hutch to say "Hello!".

Stage Nine

"The family enjoy doing things together", e.g. going on holiday, visiting auntie, watching T.V., having a meal together. Discussion, pictures, poems, mime, a class frieze.

(This scheme would be particularly appropriate for use with a class of children who had just moved to a new housing estate as part of an urban reconstruction or slum clearance programme. The material could also be adapted for use with children aged seven to nine years.)

Early Juniors
Stage One
Some animal families and their homes

Possibilities include: birds (especially chaffinches, goldfinches, warblers, flamingos, swallows, kingfishers, storks, eagles, green woodpeckers, penguins); insects (especially ants, wasps, bees, spiders); fish (sticklebacks); mammals (especially otters, beavers, badgers, doormice and harvestmice, rabbits, foxes, squirrels, lions, elephants and so on).

Group work using work cards (if Reading Age permits). Each group undertakes to find out about the family life of one of the animals, e.g. What does the home look like? What is it called? How is it built? How do the parents look after the young when they are born? How do they feed them, keep them warm, protect them? What do the parents teach their young? and so on. Work assembled into a display, e.g. a classroom frieze depicting animal families and their homes. The topic may also be explored through mime, dance, creative writing, modelling and painting.

Stage Two
Human families and their homes

The topic should be presented in such a way as to allow for comparisons to be made between animal family life and human family life, e.g. How do human parents look after their children? How do they feed them, keep them warm, protect them? What sort of things do human parents protect their children from? What do human parents teach their children? Further comparisons might be made between animal homes and human homes, e.g. Do human families live close to each other or far apart? Why do they live in roads, streets, towns? This could lead into a subsidiary theme on "Help", "Lending a hand" or "Neighbours".

Stage Three
Pets in the family

Oral, written and pictorial descriptions of pets and how the family looks after them. Instruction on how to care for pets.

Stage Four
Adventures with the family

A further development of Stage Nine in the Infant scheme. Would you enjoy doing these things as much if you did them on your own?

Stage Five
When things go wrong in the family

It is important that children are helped to appreciate human failing and fallibility as an inevitable and painful part of human

164

life. So too should they grow up recognising that life has its own difficulties, disappointments and sorrows and that few are spared this experience. Topics to be considered might include illness, pain, worry, anger, quarrels, punishment and, if circumstances demand, death. These topics, especially death, must be approached with great skill, tact and understanding on the part of the teacher. In most cases discussion with individual children is preferable (especially about death) and at all times great care must be taken to avoid reference to a specific family. The safest approach is by way of a story—perhaps one that does not have the traditional "happy ending".

Stage Six
Family occasions

Emphasis here should be on the unity of the family as illustrated by a family wedding, the arrival of a baby, a christening, a birthday party, an anniversary, Christmas celebrations. Each of these occasions provide departure-points for other Depth Themes.

Stage Seven
Homes in other lands

Group work on "Homes like ours" (in Western societies of an advanced technological nature) and "Homes very different from ours" (in Eastern societies and in underdeveloped countries). Homes considered might include igloos, tents and tepees, tree-houses, long-houses, stilt-houses, underground houses and so on. This is a useful way of promoting interest in the people, their beliefs and customs and so extending the theme to "Families in other lands" (see later).

Late Juniors
Stage One
Stories about families with children aged nine-eleven

There are many possibilities here, e.g. stories from the "Classics" or from modern fiction, true-life stories, newspaper stories, the teacher's own stories and so on. The class might like to decide on a fictitious family, discuss the members of the family and then, in groups, write a series of playlets dealing with events in the life of the family. These could be acted out or taped and some might be used in Assembly. Other stories could include the Von Trapp Family

165

(i.e. "The Sound of Music"), the Swiss Family Robinson, the Bach family, the Kennedy family, the Royal family and so on.

Stage Two
Families on the move

(a) Nomads. This might include a consideration of nomads and settlers, their different ways of life, the conflict between the two. Why? The Bedouin Arabs, their life and customs, little changed for 3,000 or 4,000 years. This could lead into work on Abraham, his nomadic life and the problems he encountered. (This could be developed into a theme on "Pioneers" which would include figures such as Jesus, Saint Paul and Gautama Buddha, all of whom lived nomadic lives during their teaching periods. The theme could be extended to include modern pioneers, e.g. Thor Heyerdahl, Captain Scott, Gladys Aylward and so on).

(b) Gypsies. This might include stories about gypsies and their families, their Romany origins, their preference for an outdoor life, their work, caravans, animals, campfires, campfire songs, their difficulties and hardships. Why do some people dislike gypsies? A comparison of the reasons for conflict between nomads and settlers. Gypsies are "modern nomads". Gypsy children; how they amuse themselves, their knowledge of nature, what they do to help their parents, their problem of always having to change their school and their friends. The reluctance shown by gypsies to change their way of life; their happiness together; their unhappiness when people are unkind to them; their close family ties and their strong community spirit. Activities might include models and pictures of old and new gypsy caravans, poems about gypsies, writing gypsy campfire songs, creative writing on topics such as "A day in the life of a gypsy boy", "The day the gypsies camped at the bottom of our garden", "The gypsy they wanted to live in a house" and so on.

(c) Fairground and Circus families. There are many stories available about circus families. The emphasis should be on the continuity of the family (e.g. the family tradition of being an acrobat, juggler, clown, lion-tamer and so on), how the children learn the skills from an early age, how circus folk are devoted to their work and to each other. What would happen if they did not care about each other? (e.g. a family of acrobats). Their insistence that whatever the difficulties, "The Show Must Go On". The responsibilities which are given to circus children. Is their life all fun and excitement? There are times of difficulty and sorrow (e.g. when someone becomes ill, has an accident, is too old to continue or when their act is no longer popular). The comfort given to individuals by the family and the circus community.

166

Activities might include murals, friezes, models, posters, poems, songs, mime, dance and stories written about "The acrobat who was afraid", "John's first act", "The clown who could not laugh" and so on.

Stage Three
Families without homes

The aim here is to provide children with an opportunity to understand that family life has an inner strength in the love that each member feels for the others and that it is not dependent upon material objects and material comfort for its continuance. Provided that circumstances are not too adverse, difficulties often have the effect of drawing the family closer together. The children should be helped to see the responsibility of others to help those in need not only by contributing to their material comfort but by extending friendship and understanding to them.

Refugees. There are three broad types: refugees from war, from natural disaster such as earthquake or plague, and from oppressive governments. In addition to using stories, plays and poems about refugees, current national and international events receiving news coverage might provide a starting-point for the development of this topic. A balance should be maintained between the difficulties experienced by families in such circumstances and providing insight into the work of relief organisations such as Save the Children Fund, Oxfam, Christian Aid.

Activities. The work might lead to a desire on the part of the children to make some practical offer of help to refugees, e.g. a school collection in aid of one of the organisations, a jumble sale, a sale of handmade cards, models, ornaments and so on. It may also stimulate sufficient interest in the country concerned to justify setting a whole day aside for learning more about its people, their way of life, customs and beliefs. This topic is a way of sowing the seeds from which the concept of the "Family of Man" can develop —a concept which the next stage of the theme is designed to promote.

Early Secondary
Stage One
Families of the World

The topic might be approached either by way of nationalities or by way of beliefs and customs. Either: a Jamaican family, a Chinese family, a Pakistani family, an Indian family, a Japanese

167

family, a Thai family, an Israeli family and so on. Or : a Christian family, a Tao family, a Muslim family, a Shinto family, a Buddhist family, a Jewish family, a Sikh family, a Hindu family and so on. The families might be explored either in the context of their own country or as immigrant families in Britain.

Individual or Group projects might be undertaken on "Family Festivals". The festivals might be selected from the following :

Christian: Christmas, Epiphany, Easter, Whitsun, Ascension.

Tao/Shinto: Moon Festival, New Year Festival, Lantern Festival; Japanese festivals of Shichi-Go-Sen and Hina Matsuri (doll festival); Hill Climbing Festival.

Muslim: Id-ul-Fitr (end of Ramadhan), Id-ul-Adha, Islamic New Year (Hijra), the Birthday of Muhammad.

Buddhists: Enlightenment Day (Mahayana Buddhists), Magna Puja (Full Moon Festival for Theravada Buddhists), Full Moon Festival (Vesakha-Puja).

Jewish: Rosh Hashanah (Jewish New Year), Feast of Tabernacles (especially Simchath Torah), Passover, Feast of Weeks, Hannukah (Festival of Dedication and Light).

Hindu: Durga Puja (Kali Festival), Diwali (New Year Festival of Lights), Lohri (children's fire festival), Birthday of Lord Rama, Holi (colour-sprinkling festival), Rath Yatra, Janam Ashtami (birthday of Lord Krishna, the Hindu nativity festival).

Sikh: Guru Nanak's birthday, Lohri, Baisakhi, Raksha Bandham.

Choice of festivals will be determined by information available. At this stage concern should be with "explicit" religion, i.e. the outward forms of worship, ritual and ceremony, and these seen as expressions of belief and commitment.

Stage Two
People without families

(a) Tramps. This might include a consideration of the reasons why people become tramps—force of circumstance as well as choice. What advantages does a tramp enjoy? What disadvantages? What do you think about the attitude of the tramp who says, "I keep myself to myself; I mind my own business; all I want is to be left alone."? Is this selfish? Is it as selfish as the person who, when it comes to money and possessions, always wants more than anyone else? Is it a waste of life to be a tramp? Is he missing out on life by not having a job and a family? Children should be encouraged to answer questions like these for themselves and be helped towards tolerance and understanding of those who do not appear to fit in with society. They should learn to be willing to see the other's point of view rather than dismiss people by using

168

labels. "Oh! he's only a tramp" is close to the statement, "Oh! he's only a negro/dustman/roadman and so on". At the same time they should be made aware of the dependence of such people on the goodwill of others; they belong to the "Family of Man".

Activities might include creative writing ("A tramp's view of us"), poems, mime and drama.

(b) Monks and Nuns. This might include information about religious orders—male and female, Christian and non-Christian—life in a monastery, its daily routine and so on. What prompts a man or woman to give up his family for this? Does he really give up family life? Could we call this escapism? What about enclosed orders?

Activities might include research into different orders, stories of monks, Saint Francis of Assisi, Buddhist monks in Tibet, a visit to a monastery or convent or a visit from a monk or nun to describe their work, attitudes and beliefs.

(c) Old people. This might include a consideration of the problems of old age—loneliness, illness, fear, difficulties experienced doing the necessary things in life, e.g. shopping, taking a bus, completing forms, keeping the home clean, looking after the garden and so on. Also the independent and proud attitudes of old people. Emphasis on tolerance and understanding but also on the need for practical help.

Activities might include a census of old people in the immediate neighbourhood, research into their difficulties, the encouragement of children to volunteer to visit old people (with parental permission), send them cards on their birthday, go and sing carols to them at Christmas (especially if there is an Old People's Home nearby), run errands, spend time on odd jobs around their homes.

Stage Three
Families in need

Similar to earlier work on "Refugees" but with the emphasis on the needs of people in this country, e.g. problems of housing, play areas for children, problems of unemployment, motherless or fatherless families and so on.

Practical activities might include collecting newspapers and selling them (in bulk) to a local paper merchant, holding fairs and concerts all in aid of charitable organisations (e.g. "Shelter").

169

Middle Secondary
Family Conflicts

The theme, at this point, merges with Situation Themes based on adolescent conflict at home. This may be seen as problem-centred discussion with use being made of sociodrama or role-play. Discussion may be "impersonalised" by introducing a fictitious family. (It is inadvisable to prompt a child to talk directly about himself and his family, although this may occasionally happen. Topics should be determined by the pupils' problems although the following are general to this age group : lack of communication between parents and children (e.g. questions of freedom, authority, attitudes), antagonism between older and younger children, parental expectations (e.g. job, marriage) conflicting with adolescent ambitions, the presence of relatives in the home (e.g. grandparents) and so on.)

Late Secondary
New Families

The aim here is to give young people insight into the complexities of adult life and adult responsibilities especially in relation to marriage. The topic is best developed as an integrated curriculum dealing with the financial, economic, legal, emotional and physical aspects of married life. Sex Education and education in responsible parenthood should be included. Lessons on mothercraft and fatherhood with something on child-development would be appropriate in this context.

It is important to note that each *stage* in this scheme should be preceded by the selection of Specific Objectives and the determination of ways in which individual lessons might be evaluated.

An example of a Depth Theme for use with children aged five-seven.

Aim: To provide children with an opportunity to practise the skill of reflecting on their own experiences at depth.

Theme: Sounds.

Objectives: To provide children with an opportunity to :
1 become more aware of the sounds in their lives;

170

2 become more sensitive to the wonder and beauty of sounds;
3 become more appreciative of the wonder of hearing;
4 extend their experience of sounds;
5 extend their vocabularies;
6 improve sound discrimination as a pre-requisite to accurate reading.

Learning experiences:

"Sounds of the morning"—a tape-recording made by the teacher. This might include : the dawn chorus, the milkman, the postman, an alarm clock, footsteps going downstairs, running water in the bathroom, cleaning teeth, the radio announcing the 8 o'clock news, a kettle beginning to boil, a kettle whistling, boiling water being poured into a teapot, the breakfast table being laid, the "snap, crackle and pop" of cereal as the milk is poured over it, cups clinking against saucers, knives and spoons being scraped against plates and so on.

The tape could be played through without comment and then played again with pauses to allow for identification and discussion. What sounds were missing? Conversation. The conversation can make these sounds "happy" or "sad". What sort of things do you say in the morning? What sort of things do your parents and brothers and sisters say? Do you like the mornings? Pictures could be drawn and sentences written about "The beginning of the day in my house" or "My family at breakfast". Children could be encouraged to listen more carefully to the "sounds of the morning" and tell the class about them next day. Alternatively, they could be asked to listen to the "Sounds of the street" as they go home and tell about them in the next lesson. The children might make their own tape-recording of "Sounds of the classroom" or "Sounds of the school", especially the happy "Sounds of the playground".

Possible development of this theme includes : "Sounds of nature" (the whistling of the wind, the tapping of rain against the window, the rumblings of thunder, the gurgling of a brook, the roar of a waterfall, the sounds of the sea and seashore, bird sounds and animal sounds), "Warning sounds" (shouts, cries, whistles, police sirens, fire engine sirens, fire and burglar alarms, motor car horns), "Happy sounds" (a birthday party, children's games, clapping, laughing, giggling, cheering, singing, dancing, whistling), "Musical sounds" (the sounds made by different musical instruments, simple pieces of music which tell a story), "Mechanical sounds" (pieces of machinery, clocks, tractors, harvesters, pneumatic drills, railway engines). Children should be encouraged to make their own sounds, find words to describe sounds, distinguish between "high" sounds, "low" sounds, "harsh" sounds, "dull" sounds and so on, beat out simple rhythms, compose their own tunes, sing songs, make and play

171

simple musical instruments. The theme also lends itself to development through dance (e.g. a dance based on mechanical sounds—"The dance of the machines").

(*"Sounds"* by Peggy Blakeley, published by Adam and Charles Black Ltd, provides further ideas and an excellent poem to use with children of this age.)

Here is an example of a poem on "Sounds" written by a first year College of Education student for use with children aged five to seven years :

Sounds

What are the sounds we hear every day?
Alarm clocks ringing, mother singing,
Water splashing, dustbin lids crashing,
Children chattering, saucepans clattering,
Gates that squeak, gates that creak,
Factory sirens wailing and moaning,
Firebells clanging, engines groaning,
Traffic booming, aeroplanes zooming,
Workmen hammering, bumping, banging,
Drummers drumming, guitars twanging.
These are the sounds we hear every day.

What are the quiet sounds of the night?
Rain on the windows, pattering, stuttering,
Leaves on the trees are rustling, muttering,
Parents whispering, night birds fluttering,
Satellites bleeping, we are sleeping,
Gentle breathing, gentle sighing,
We don't hear the quiet sounds of the night.

Brenda Howarth

Depth Themes on "Sights", "Smells" and "Things we like to touch" would follow naturally from this work. They might be combined under the title "Our Senses" or "Our Wonderful World". All of these themes provide an opportunity to involve children in experiences which prompt feelings of awe, wonder and a sense of mystery.

172

An example of a Depth Theme for use with children aged five-seven.

Aim: To provide children with an opportunity to practise the skill of reflecting on their own experiences at depth.

Theme: Things we like to touch.

Objectives: To provide children with an opportunity to :
1 experience pleasure in touching and handling objects;
2 experience a sense of mystery, wonder and awe through handling objects;
3 extend their vocabularies.

Learning Experiences:
The theme might begin with children being asked to bring small objects to school which they like to touch. Alternatively, children might be taken on a nature walk and encouraged to find objects which they like to touch. Individual objects could then be examined and talked about and then placed on a "Touch Table". The following objects might be provided by the teacher for the table : sandpaper, dough, holly, thorns, twigs, dry sand, dimpled paper, tissue paper, a piece of very smooth driftwood, clay, fur, rope, polystyrene, velvet, sheepskin, a piece of lambswool, sponge, shells, cork, seaweeds, dead leaves, foam rubber, smooth and rough pebbles and rocks, a page of braille and so on.

Some of the objects lend themselves to discussion. Where did they come from? How did they get like this? (e.g. a smooth piece of driftwood, a highly polished stone, a piece of coral). What sort of words could we use to describe this object? (e.g. a piece of sponge, velvet and so on).

Handling and looking at rocks and minerals through a magnifying glass can evoke a sense of awe and wonder in children. The following might be placed on a "Touch Table" :

Quartz : (smooth, round pebbles, egg-shaped or spherical, and with crystals.)

Calcite : (crystals which break into rhomboids : pure calcite is as clear as glass and has the property of "double-refraction"; stalactites and stalagmites are made of millions of tiny, radiating calcite crystals formed from the lime in the water which trickles through the rocks—illustrate with good quality colour photographs.)

Fluorite : ("fluorspar", "Blue John", cuboids which can be yellow, brown, green and pink as well as blue.)

173

Galena :	(lead ore, has a metallic lustre, cuboids; this should be shown to children but they should not be allowed to handle it.)
Barite :	(flat, heavy crystals.)
Graphite :	(soft, soils the fingers, marks paper.)
Mica :	(comes in sheets which can be split.)
Schist :	(splits into irregular shapes, very shiny and crinkled.)
Granite :	(has shiny surfaces.)
Sandstone :	(breaks down into sand; interesting textures.)
Shale :	(breaks easily; often contains plant fossils.)
Limestone :	(often contains shells and other animal fossils.)
Coal :	(also can contain plant fossils.)
Pumice :	(floats.)

(Very realistic casts of all types of fossils can be supplied by Ammonite Ltd, Cowbridge, Glamorgan at prices ranging from 30-60p.)

The age of the rocks and the uses to which man has put them are two possible developments. Fossils are especially interesting to young children. Children can be introduced to "evolution" through the story of how fossils came to be formed. A sensitive telling of this story is capable of arousing even more of a sense of awe than the telling of the Genesis Creation story. Activities might include dance ("Under the Sea", "Primeval Forests"), making fossils by pressing objects against plasticine, fossil-rubbings, paintings of mountains and trees under the sea, a visit to the local museum to see the fossils and so on.

An example of a Depth Theme for use with children aged nine-eleven or with less able early secondary school children.

Aim: To provide the child with an opportunity to :
1 practise the skill of reflecting on his own experiences at depth;
2 develop insight into himself and his feelings;
3 develop insight into other people and their feelings;
4 develop insight into what constitutes a distinctly human relationship between self and others.

Theme: Adventure or Proving a theory.

Objectives: To provide children with an opportunity to :
1 gain insight into the concepts of adventure, courage, danger, fear, ambition, loyalty, friendship, trust, faith, belief and commitment;

174

2 recognise the relationship between belief(s) and actions;
3 become involved, at an imaginative level, in the spirit of adventure;
4 gain insight into what motivates men and women to embark on dangerous adventures;
5 gain insight into the demands made by friendship, especially that of self-sacrifice.

Content and Learning Experiences:

Stage One

What sort of things do you think about when you hear the word "adventure"? ("The Famous Five", "The Secret Seven", films about Cowboys and Indians, "cops and robbers", spy stories, war stories, stories about the conquest of mountains, space and deserts and so on.) We talk about *"exciting* adventures", *"daring* adventures", *"thrilling* adventures", *"dangerous* adventures", *"spine-chilling* adventures", *"breath-taking* adventures" and even about *"horrifying* adventures". What does an adventure have to have in order to make it an "adventure"? (risk, hazard, danger, excitement). All adventures start without us knowing how they will end—it is this "uncertainty" which makes them exciting. If someone tells us the ending of the story we are reading or the film that we are watching, it spoils it for us. It takes away the excitement because it removes the uncertainty. We usually are rather annoyed when this happens. Why do we like adventure and excitement? Do we need it? Why? (discussion). Are fictitious adventures more exciting than real-life adventures? (Compare one of Enid Blyton's adventure stories with an Apollo Moon Mission.) Have you ever had an adventure? What was it? Did it involve risk, hazard, danger, excitement and uncertainty? Did you have it when you were alone or did others share it with you? Do you think adventures are likely to be more exciting if you have them on your own or if you have them with other people? (discussion). Write an account of an adventure using the first person singular. Don't say whether it is "real" or "imagined"; you can then read it out to the rest of the class and they can then try and say if it actually happened or if you have made it up.

Stage Two

Some people set out to have adventures deliberately while others suddenly find themselves in the middle of adventures they don't

175

want. Make up a list of people who deliberately look for adventures. (The list can be either one of historical personalities (e.g. Thor Heyerdahl, Captain Scott, Christopher Columbus, Marco Polo and so on) or one of occupations (discoverers, ꜱlorers, mercenaries, test-pilots, detectives and so on.)) Why do people choose to get involved in adventures? For money? For fame? For the love of excitement? To prove their own courage? More often than not they do it "to prove a theory".

Stage Three

The theme could be developed by way of an examination of real-life adventure such as Heyerdahl's anthropological explorations, Scott's expedition to the South Pole, the Ascent of Everest and the American Moon Landings. Heyerdahl's "Kon-Tiki" expedition in 1947 and his "Ra" expeditions (1969) are especially appropriate. Although Heyerdahl's own accounts are too difficult for Junior school children to appreciate, the teacher can easily adapt them, introducing quotations from the book into his own account. The following framework may be used for both adventures, and even for *most* adventures involving groups of people (except Scott's) :

Introduction : The man and his theory.
1   Getting the team together;
2   Finding out about the job;
3   Setting out on the adventure;
4   The adventure runs into difficulties;
5   Everything goes very well;
6   The adventure suddenly becomes very dangerous;
7   The adventure begins to be a disaster;
8   The adventure begins to end in tragedy;
9   All's well that ends well. The adventure wins through;
10 What have people said about the adventure?

In introducing Heyerdahl as a "man with a theory" (i.e. Kon-Tiki : that prehistoric people of South America might have crossed the 4,300 miles from Peru to Polynesia on a balsa raft; Ra : that the ancient Egyptians crossed the Atlantic in papyrus boats long before Columbus), it is important to emphasise that both expeditions were also concerned with demonstrating how men depend on each other and can work together to achieve a common goal. This was especially true of the Ra expeditions. For the ill-fated "Ra I", Heyerdahl had a crew of seven. He writes :

In gathering a crew I had decided to assemble as many nationalities as space would allow : seven. The voyage itself was intended as an experiment, a study trip into the dawn of civilisation. But there was room for an experiment within an experiment : our boat would be a micro-world, an attempt to prove that men can work together in peace, regardless of politics, religion or colour. (Thor Heyerdahl, *The Ra Expeditions,* 1971, George Allen and Unwin, Ltd.)

These men were :

Norman Baker : American; a civil engineer and a commander in the U.S. Naval Reserve.

Yuri Alexandrovich Senkevich : Russian; a doctor who specialised in the problems of astronauts under acceleration and weightlessness.

Carlo Mauri : Italian; a professional mountain guide with no sailing experience.

Santiago Genovés : Mexican; a professor of anthropology who was the ship's quartermaster.

Abdullah Djibrine : African; a carpenter and papyrus expert who knew nothing about the sea.

Georges Sourial : Egyptian; a chemical engineer, professional frog-man, judo champion.

Thor Heyerdahl : Norwegian; anthropologist and experienced sailor.

For the "Ra II" expedition, Abdullah was replaced by Kei Ohara from Japan and an eighth member, a Berber named Madani Ait Ouhanni, was added. Heyerdahl comments :

To my own mind our main problem was not so much the papyrus as how we seven passengers would survive our inter-action with each other. The most insidious danger on any expedition where men have to rub shoulders for weeks on end is a psychological condition which makes even the most peaceful person irritable or even furious, because his perceptive capacity shrinks until he sees only his companions' faults. (*op.cit.*)

Details of this kind can provide the basis for class discussion, e.g. How do you think these men felt when they first met? What was common to all of them? (They believed in the theory and were prepared to risk their lives proving it.) What would be the effect of living together on a small boat for 57 days (Ra II)? What if one of them had become afraid and wanted to return? What would the captain have done? What happened during a storm when someone was washed overboard? The men learned to work as a team; they had trust in their captain and in each other. Even when things went

177

wrong they learned to "stick together". What did they have in common when the expedition was over? (Their friendship.)

Activities might include : making models and paintings of Kon-Tiki and Ra I and Ra II; plotting the courses taken on the expeditions, marking the dangers and difficulties that occurred; writing personal accounts in a ship's "log"; acting out situations, especially arguments, that threatened the success of the voyages; devising similar expeditions and considering how one would find a crew— what sort of qualities would you look for? Can you ever be sure of a person? Can you be more sure of him if he is your friend? Why?

Stage Four

The theme could be developed into a simple "Life of Jesus". Jesus was a man with a theory—that religion is about loving each other, including social outcasts and enemies, and not merely a matter of keeping laws and engaging in ritual and ceremony. Religion is *inward* and concerned with attitudes to people rather than *outward,* concerned with things. God is loving, like a father, and he wants men to be loving too. Man learns to love God by first learning to love his fellow human beings. How did Jesus set out to prove his theory? By showing men how to love; by living a life of love for others even to the point of dying for them. He was a man who was prepared to die for his beliefs and he actually did so. In its own way, Jesus's "adventure" was as difficult and dangerous as the adventures of Thor Heyerdahl. It involved getting men to change their ideas about God, about themselves and about how they should behave towards others. And people living in Palestine at the time of Jesus were so convinced that their ideas about God were right that they were prepared to kill a man who disagreed. To help him to prove his theory Jesus needed a "crew"—men who trusted him and believed in his theory; men who were also prepared to show others how to love.

The story of Jesus can be presented within the framework given earlier for other adventures :

1 *Getting the team together.* Mark 1 : 16-20; 2 : 14; John 1 : 43f. Research into the disciples.
2 *Finding out about the job.* Matthew 5-7; 10.
3 *Setting out on the adventure.*
   (a) Watching Jesus at work. Some healing miracles; Matthew 9 : 35-38.
   (b) Trying to do the same. Mark 9 : 14-29.

178

(c) Finding out the secret of Jesus's power. Mark 4 : 35; Mark 1 : 35-39; Luke 3 : 21-22; 5 : 16; 6 : 12-13; 9 : 18, 28-29. Jesus teaches the disciples to pray. Luke 11 : 1-4. Peter and John heal a lame man. Acts 3 : 1-10.

(d) Finding out about the work. Luke 15.

4 *The adventure runs into difficulties.*
Opposition from the Scribes, Pharisees and Sadducees. Mark 2 : 1-10; 2 : 15-28; 3 : 1-6. Jesus overcomes the difficulties. Matthew 2 : 15-28, 29-33; Mark 11 : 27-33.

5 *Everything goes very well.* Mark 11 : 1-11.

6 *The adventure suddenly becomes very dangerous.*
(a) A friend becomes a traitor. Matthew 26 : 14.
(b) A final meal together. Matthew 26 : 17-35.

7 *The adventure begins to be a disaster.*
The team breaks up. Matthew 26 : 36-56.

8 *The adventure begins to end in tragedy.*
Selected passages from Jesus's trial and crucifixion.

9 *All's well that ends well. The adventure wins through.*
The disciples meet Jesus again. Luke 24 : 1-53.

10 *What have people said about the adventure?* Acts 2.

It is important to note that this stage of the scheme should be related to the Objectives given earlier. For this reason it is advisable to restrict content to those New Testament passages given above.

Stage Five

Possible development of the theme might include : an examination of the beliefs and work of people in the 20th century who have tried to put Jesus's theory into practice (e.g. Gladys Aylward, Father Borelli, Trevor Huddleston, Martin Luther King and so on. A series of study books for the ten-thirteen year old age group on 20th century personalities is available under the title *People with a Purpose,* edited by Ian H. Birnie and published by SCM Press).

Alternatively, the theme could focus upon people who have suddenly found themselves involved in an "adventure" which has had the effect of changing their view of life. Classic examples are provided by Saint Paul and Muhammad, both of whom spent their lives teaching others about their discovery about God.

With older children it might be useful to explore the "adventures" of poets, dramatists, musicians and painters—their search for new ideas and ways of presenting them, the difficulties they have in persuading people to take these new ideas seriously and think about them carefully. This could develop into a theme on "New Ideas of God"—a simple introduction to some of the ideas being put forward by 20th century theologians.

179

An example of a Depth Theme for use with children aged thirteen.

Aim: To provide the child with an opportunity to :
1 practise the skill of reflecting on his own experiences at depth;
2 develop insight into himself and his feelings;
3 develop insight into other people and their feelings;
4 develop insight into what constitutes a distinctly human relationship between self and others.

Theme: Barriers.

Objectives: To provide children with an opportunity to :
1 gain insight into the concepts of suspicion, mistrust, enmity, intolerance, prejudice, fear, envy, hatred, greed, selfishness and their opposites;
2 recognise that these concepts divide men and cause both physical and mental suffering;
3 distinguish between "useful" and "harmful" barriers;
4 become sensitive to the need to work for the removal of barriers which hinder unity and understanding between men.

Content and Learning Experiences:

Stage One
Necessary barriers

Physical barriers, road barriers, crash barriers on motorways, barriers in football stadiums, fairground and circus barriers, barriers at the zoo, sea walls, harbour walls, railings at the top of cliffs, at the top of stairs and next to water, barriers around electricity stations and pylons and so on. These barriers "bar the way" to danger.

What about other man-made, physical barriers such as prison walls and prison bars?

Are these "necessary" and are they "good"? These are barriers which, for some men and women, "bar the way" to freedom, to work and to their families. (Discussion on prisons, their function and place in society. What are the alternatives to having prisons? Reference to "open prisons". How do you think prisoners feel when they are in prison? How can being in prison change a person, for good or for ill? Prisoners still find prisons a "barrier" when they have served their sentences. Why? (attitudes of people, especially employers, to ex-convicts). What is done to rehabilitate prisoners to life in society? and so on).

Reference might be made to the "Berlin Wall"—a physical

180

barrier which causes a mental barrier between East and West Germany? How?

Activities might include writing a letter, as a West Berliner, to a member of his family living in East Berlin. What sort of details would the person in East Berlin like to read about? Alternatively children might be asked to write their impression of a day in the life of a "lifer"—a person serving a life-sentence in prison. The account should concentrate on his thoughts rather than his actions.

Stage Two
Natural barriers

Mountains, deserts, seas, blizzards, heavy snowfalls, storms and so on. The challenge that these have presented to man and how he has overcome them. Stories of men and women who have conquered these barriers. Note that in so doing they had to overcome another type of barrier—the barrier of fear (another natural barrier). Reference might be made to the motives of lone, round-the-world yachtsmen, mountaineers, astronauts—the importance of personal challenge and "proving oneself to oneself" and so on. What sort of personal qualities would you expect these people to have?

Language is also a "natural barrier" between men. Why, do you think, has "Esperanto"—the international language—failed to "catch on"? People are proud of their own language, it is a symbol of their special identity. It is the medium through which their "culture" is expressed—another thing of which they are proud. Is "nationality" and "nationalism" a good thing or is it a harmful barrier? What other things are symbols of national pride? What difference would it make to us if we went to live in another country? How would we behave? Would we eventually lose our national identity if we were there a long time? Do you think this would be a good or bad thing? We tend to associate certain characteristics with particular nationalities. Make a list of the characteristics of the following: a Scotsman, an Irishman, a Frenchman, a Spaniard, a German, a Russian, an American and an Englishman. How have we come to have these ideas? Do you think they are true? (For further ideas see *Connexions*, "Foreign places, foreign faces". Penguin Education.)

Stage Three
Barriers against disease

This provides an opportunity for a lesson on Health Education. Inoculation, vaccination, drugs and medicines but also personal hygiene. One of the worst barriers to health is ignorance—ignorance about our bodies and how to keep them healthy. This work could lead on to "Barriers to normal life"—physical and mental handicaps, deafness, blindness and dumbness. The aim here is to remove the element of fear and insensitivity which pupils often display towards handicaps, especially mental handicap.

Stage Four
Barriers to unity, harmony and understanding

This part of the scheme should concentrate on the different ways in which "colour, creed and nationality" are used as an excuse for hatred and intolerance. What do we mean by "xenophobia"? Consideration of this in animals and humans. Why are people afraid of others who appear to be different? What do they represent? A threat to their well-being and security. How often is this actually true? How often is it based on ignorance? A consideration of the meaning of "prejudice"—"pre-judging".

A special consideration of the way in which religion can act as a barrier between people—also politics. How can people learn to disagree with each others' ideas without having to hate each other and wish harm to each other? Relate this to the ethical teaching of a number of faiths.

Stage Five
Barriers to happiness

This might include a consideration of illness, physical and mental suffering, anxiety, poverty, the love of money and possessions, dissatisfaction, greed and selfishness. What is your idea of perfect happiness? Can a man be happy in a world in which there is still such misery? What are the responsibilities of man to each other?—to the "Third World"?

Going against one's conscience is a barrier to happiness. Is conscience a useful or harmful barrier? How is your conscience formed? How does it function? and so on.

As much of this scheme has involved symbols the children might be asked to create their own summary of "Barriers" in symbolic form. A large wall chart could be made depicting the different types of barrier, how they are formed, how they function and the effects that they have on man.

182

Examples of Depth Themes for use with children aged fourteen-sixteen.

As we have seen, Depth Themes should begin with, or relate to, the child's immediate situation, experiences and interests. The following topics are likely to be relevant to pupils in the fourth and fifth forms :

Ambition, education, school, work, relationships (including sex, marriage and family planning), authority, rules, law and order, freedom, responsibility, conflict, demonstration, violence, war, pop culture, drugs, sport, the mass media (national, local and commercial radio and television, newspapers, magazines, posters, advertisements, records and so on), prejudice, minority groups, money and possessions, politics, pollution, space, technology, science, community and so on.

A large number of publications designed for use with this age-range are now available on most of these subjects. For example :
Connexions (Penguin Education)
  All in the game (sport)
  Break for commercials (advertising)
  Disaster
  Fit to live in? (conservation)
  For better, for worse (marriage and the family)
  Foreign places, foreign faces (relations with foreigners)
  The language of prejudice
  The lawbreakers
  Living tomorrow (the impact of science and technology on life)
  Out of your mind? (drugs)
  Standards of living
  Violence
  His and hers (masculinity and femininity)
  Food
  Shelter and housing
  Work

Probe (SCM Press Ltd)

1	*Population and Family Planning*	9	*Conservation*
2	*Drugs*	10	*The Future*
3	*Racial Discrimination*	11	*Violence*
4	*Human Rights*	12	*Technology*
5	*Protest*	13	*Folksong*
6	*Pop*	14	*Community Relations*
7	*Housing*	15	*Education*
	Revolution (Probe Special)	16	*Christmas*
8	*Industry*	17	*Women and Men*

("PROBE is a series of short booklets which have been designed to provide school groups and teachers with information about important topics, as a basis for discussion. . . . Their aim is merely to open up particular subjects and raise a few relevant questions. The title PROBE is meant to convey, not what the booklets do, but what we hope its readers will want to do when they have read them.")

Living Issues (SCM Press Ltd)

1 *Conflict*
2 *Communication*
3 *Behaviour*
4 *Power*
5 *Freedom*
6 *Hope*

("In this series of lesson books contemporary issues which have also been a feature of other periods of history are discussed in an open-ended way. The underlying hope is that through the study of contemporary life in the context of history the relevance of past struggles for contemporary man can be understood, leading to a growth in understanding of certain aspects of the Christian faith.")

The following publications are also useful as "discussion-starters" with older secondary school pupils :

A. Adams : *Life in the Family* ("Explorations" series, Pergamon, 1968).

A. Adams : *Loneliness and Parting* ("Explorations" series, Pergamon, 1968).

R. G. Cave and D. A. F. Conochie : *Living with Other People* (Ward Lock, 1965).

A. Crang : *Growing Up* ("Explorations" series, Pergamon, 1969).

H. Cunningham : *Challenge and Response*. Vol. 1 *The Work we Live by;* Vol. 2 *Governing Ourselves* (Pergamon, 1968).

P. Grosset : *What's your opinion?* (Evans, 1964).

P. Grosset : *Things that matter* (Evans, 1966).

P. Grosset : *Link Up* (Evans, 1971).

G. Hacker *et al* : *Conflict 1;* conflict in home and school (Nelson, 1969).

G. Hacker *et al* : *Conflict 2;* conflict in adult life (Nelson, 1969).

E. Jones : *Making Contact* ("Explorations" series, Pergamon, 1968).

E. Jones : *Work and Leisure* ("Explorations" series, Pergamon, 1968).

D. C. Prowles: *Standpoint* ("Javelin" series, Collins, 1967).

J. Skull (Ed.): *Conflict and Compassion* (Hutchinson Educational, 1969).

S. Southworth: *Prospects* ("Javelin" series, Collins, 1967).

J. Watts: *Encounters* Stage 1, 2, 3, 4 and 5 (Longmans, 1970).

V. Whitcombe: *Love and Marriage* ("Explorations" series, Pergamon, 1970).

2 SYMBOL AND LANGUAGE THEMES

Aim: To initiate children into Religion as a unique mode of thought and awareness by providing them with an opportunity to :

1 express their own ideas, thoughts and feelings in appropriate symbols and language;
2 recognise the special characteristics of religious language and symbolism by :
   (a) acquainting them with language which is evocative, poetic, metaphorical and dramatic (firstly within a secular context and then within a religious context) and educating them in its use;
   (b) acquainting them with the context (country, life and customs) out of which the traditional language and symbols of religion have grown;
   (c) acquainting them with the feasts, festivals, ceremonies, ritual and myths of religion as symbolic expressions of the faith of adherents.

It is suggested that children are introduced to Symbol and Language Themes at the age of nine or ten and that this type of theme is continued throughout both junior and secondary schools.

The following words may be said to have a theological cash value as symbols or images which reflect important religious concepts :

Water, power, spirit, fire, heat, light, darkness, blood, wine, bread, body, cup, door, life, sheep, lamb, cross, wheel, sun, birth, end, death, king, master, servant, lord, hands, feet, head, heart, self, soul, creature, creator, guide, lamp, evil, goodness, friend, saviour, sower, suffer, father, son, bride, mother, prince, covenant, sacrifice, redeem, anoint, bless, elect, flesh, judge, miracle, ransom, word, glory, height, depth, far, near, in, out, with, without.

Some of these words may form themes in their own right, e.g. Light, Water, Hands and so on, while others will need to be incorporated within other themes. Initially, however, children will need to be introduced to the concept of symbolism itself. The theme of "Gifts and Giving" is especially appropriate to children of nine or ten years of age. It forms a useful transition from Depth Themes to Symbol and Language Themes. In the following example, the aims are those of a Depth Theme with one additional aim.

An example of a Symbol and Language Theme for use with children aged nine.

Aim: To provide the child with an opportunity to :
1   practise the skill of reflecting on his own experiences at depth;
2   develop insight into himself and his feelings;
3   develop insight into other people and their feelings;
4   develop insight into what constitutes a distinctly human relationship between self and others;
5   *recognise the part played by symbolism in communicating ideas and feelings.*

Theme: Gifts and Giving.

Objectives: To provide children with an opportunity to :
1   recognise that the relationship between giver and receiver is symbolised by the gift;
2   consider why the intention of the giver is more important than the gift itself;
3   recognise that giving involves self-sacrifice;
4   recognise that the most valuable gifts are not necessarily material gifts;
5   gain insight into the Christian doctrine of the Incarnation.

Content and Learning Experiences:

Stage One
Material gifts

What sort of gifts do you like to receive? (Discussion.) Would you mind who gave you the gift?
Use of "open-ended" situations, modern parables and so on, e.g. Stories about Peter and his uncles.

1   Peter always enjoyed being with Uncle Bob; he always knew what sort of games Peter liked to play and he always took an interest in everything he did. Uncle Jim, on the other hand, never seemed to realise that Peter was there; he rarely talked to Peter and he never played with him. By chance both uncles gave Peter the same birthday present one year—the same book. Do you think Peter should keep both presents? Do you think he should give one away? If so, whose present do you think he should keep? Uncle Bob's or Uncle Jim's? Why?
2   Uncle Bob has a large family and that means that he does not have much money left to spend on birthday presents for his

nephews. Uncle Jim, on the other hand, doesn't have any children of his own. One year both uncles heard that Peter wanted a bicycle for his birthday. Uncle Jim bought him one but Uncle Bob, who couldn't afford it, bought him a record instead. Do you think that Peter would now like Uncle Jim more and Uncle Bob less? If Peter did not like the record do you think he should keep it?

3 Uncle Bob once gave Peter his old stamp album that he had had when he was a boy. Peter was very keen on stamp-collecting to begin with but he lost interest and began to be very interested in model aeroplanes. A boy at school offered to swap a model Tigermoth plane for Peter's stamp album (the one that Uncle Bob gave him). Do you think Peter should swap? If Uncle Bob found out about the swap, what would he think and feel? Do you think he would say anything to Peter?

Stage Two
Transition from material to abstract gifts

A brief recapitulation of points raised in relation to these three stories, e.g. we enjoy receiving gifts most from the people we like and admire; we also enjoy giving gifts to people whom we like; gifts are closely connected with happiness—they are "symbols" that we like the other person and are happy to be with them. Gifts show that someone cares for us and, when we give them, that we care for them.

Stories about the twins, John and Timothy.

1 The twins, John and Timothy, have been invited to William's birthday party. John makes an effort to find out what present William would like and for four weeks before the party he saves something from his pocket-money to spend on the present. Eventually he goes to the shops and buys the present, wraps it carefully and puts it in a safe place. Timothy, however, doesn't bother about William's present; he spends all his pocket-money on things for himself hoping that his mother will give him something for William's present. On the day of the party Timothy persuades his mother to buy something for him to give William; he doesn't go to the shops himself as he wants to play football with some boys from school. The twins go to the party and William is pleased with their presents, but especially with John's as it is just what he wanted—an electric torch. Which of the twins do you think enjoyed giving the present more? Do you think both twins enjoyed the party as much? What did John

give William that was more than Timothy gave William? (He gave him his friendship.)

Development of the following points through discussion : gifts which give us most pleasure to give are usually those which represent a "sacrifice" on our part; if things involve effort we tend to enjoy them more (compare a football match where we try hard and win in the last minute with one which goes our way all the time without effort—which is the more enjoyable game?); gifts are symbols of what we feel for another person; they are symbols of our friendship, care and willingness to give something of ourself to another person. Gifts have to be "freely given" if they deserve to be called "gifts"—we shouldn't give them in order to get something in return.

Activities might include arranging a party (another symbol— of what?), drawing up a list of people to invite. Would you only invite your friends? Would it matter if someone came without bringing a present? What party games (another symbol—of what?) would you play? What makes the games enjoyable? Does it matter about the food? The cake? (Do these symbolise anything?) Make a list of symbols we use in everyday life. Which ones are concerned with telling someone how you feel? (a hand-shake, a kiss, a hug, a wave, a smile, a clenched fist, turning your back and so on).

Stage Three
Abstract or "spiritual" gifts

The following "gifts" may be illustrated by either *secular* stories or by stories from the New Testament.

1 *The gift of friendship.* Luke 19 : 1-10; the story of Zacchaeus. Ideal for dramatisation and for placing in a modern setting. See B.B.C. L.P. record, *Johnny Morris tells Stories for Assembly* (RESR 14), side two, track three, "The Children".

2 *The gift of helpfulness.* John 6 : 1-15; the feeding of the 5,000 with an emphasis on the boy who was willing to share his lunch when 5,000 others were not. The boy helped Jesus to help the others to help each other. (Not an orthodox interpretation but one which shows how Jesus had a way of bringing out the best in people—compare his effect on Zacchaeus.)

3 *The gift of happiness.* Jesus causes happiness in Mark 1 : 40-45; 5 : 1-20; 5 : 21-43. The parables of the lost sheep, the lost coin and the (lost) Prodigal son (Luke 15) all contain joy and happiness which people feel the need to share with others.

4 *The gift of understanding.* Mark 10 : 17-22 (the rich young man); Mark 14 : 3-9 (the woman at Bethany) and John 13 : 21-30 (Jesus understands Judas).

5 *The gift of sympathy.* Luke 7 : 11-17 (the widow of Nain and her son); Luke 25 : 39-43 (Jesus's sympathy for the thief on the cross).

6 *The gift of caring.* Luke 10 : 30-37 (The Good Samaritan).

7 *The gift of forgiveness.* Luke 7 : 40-47 (the parable of the two debtors); Luke 15 : 12-32 (the parable of the Prodigal son); Luke 23 : 32-34 (Jesus forgives those who crucify him); Matthew 5 : 21-26 (teaching on reconciliation); Matthew 5 : 38-42 (teaching on non-retaliation); Matthew 5 : 43-45 (teaching on forgiving enemies); Matthew 7 : 1-5 (teaching on fault-finding); Matthew 18 : 21-35 (Peter's question concerning forgiveness and the parable of the unmerciful servant).

8 *The gift of love.* This should be seen as a gift which includes all the other gifts. You can't give the gift of love without also giving help, happiness, understanding, sympathy, care and forgiveness. John 13, Jesus washes the disciples' feet as a symbol of his love for them. His death on the cross is also a symbol of his love.

Stage Four
The gift of life

This section is concerned to provide an opportunity for children to reflect on the wonder and mystery of life and on the importance of having respect for life—their own and other people's. This may be done through work on reproduction, the birth of a child, its dependence upon its parents, its need for love, care, warmth and so on, its inheritance of the features of its parents but also its uniqueness as an individual. Every birth has special significance to someone. Stories of births which have had special significance for mankind might be told, e.g. the birth of Jesus, Muhammad, the Buddha, great artists, musicians, poets, statesmen, thinkers and so on.

Stage Five

The scheme might end with a lesson devoted to "What Christians believe about Jesus". Here the concern should be to show how the "gifts" of Jesus to Mary and Joseph was also a "gift" to the rest of mankind. It is a gift that symbolised God's love for man. At the same time it is a gift which tells man much about God—

it is his gift of himself. All that we have said about giving and the types of gifts that we should give, especially those like friendship and love, is symbolised in the person and life of Jesus. In giving his gift, God, according to Christians, shows us how and what we should give to others. What sort of "gifts", then, would you expect Christians to give to each other?

An example of background work on symbols and language for use with pupils from nine years onwards.

A crucial pre-requisite to understanding religious language is a wide experience of using imagery. With the exception of work in English, the school curriculum is heavily biased towards thinking and writing in "descriptive" terms. Not surprisingly, children's spoken and written language (and the thinking which lies behind it) is becoming increasingly stereotyped and devoid of metaphor, simile, image and symbol. If we are to restore the balance between "descriptive" and "evocative" language we must seek to make children more *conscious* of the images and symbols which surround them and then help them to transfer these to their thinking and writing. It is only when children are conscious of a metaphor or an image and are conscious of why they are using it that they will be able to approach religious language intelligently and with understanding of the type of language that it is. Set out below are some suggestions as to how teachers might contribute to this process of creating an awareness of images at a conscious level. The work should begin in the Late Junior school and proceed throughout the secondary school.

Objectives: To provide children with an opportunity to :

1   become conscious of the images and symbols provided by their immediate environment;

2   express their own ideas, thoughts and feelings in appropriate symbols and language;

3   become familiar with language which is evocative, poetic, metaphorical and dramatic.

191

Stage One
Making Connections

The task here is to help children to associate certain feelings with particular objects and then to use the objects as a symbol of the feelings. The work might be done orally or by using two sets of cards—one set having an object or image, the other a verbal description or a single word. Children are required to connect the ideas by matching the cards.

E.g. a picture of a Christmas tree, a yellow balloon, someone scoring a goal at football, someone smiling, a sandcastle, a bucket and spade and so on.

These cards should be matched with a card with the words, "Happiness is . . .". e.g. "Happiness is a yellow balloon", "Happiness is a smile in the street" and so on.

It may be necessary to explain the connection, i.e. yellow balloons are things we have at parties; we are usually happy when we are at a party; we can talk about our feeling of happiness by using a yellow balloon as a symbol of how we feel.

Further possibilities :

Loneliness (or "being left out") is an empty room, a tree standing in a field, a bar of chocolate with no-one to share it, "an empty space where there should be love". With young children a game might be played in which certain people are "out". How do you feel when you're out? What sort of words could you use to describe those feelings? Could you use words which don't describe anything but which help us to know how you feel? e.g. "like a tree in a field", "like a forgotten toy".

Sadness is a man who has lost his dog (note that the strength of the image is increased if it is an "old" man who has lost his dog. Why?), a broken toy, a nest that has been robbed, a willow-tree, an empty chair.

Blindness is a turned out light, a man in a blizzard, a bottomless hole, a fog at sea, a white stick, a back that is turned away, a man who sees only himself, ignorance.

Hope is a knock at the door, a letter from a friend, a distant light in the dark, the dawn.

Disappointment is a wrongly delivered letter, a forgotten birthday, an unsaid "Thankyou", an empty chair, a failed examination, harsh words from a friend.

Wonder is a new born child, a snowflake, a butterfly, a flower, a frosted windowpane, a snow-covered tree, a growing seed.

Stage Two
Similes

In examining and using similes the intention should be to focus attention on the image at a conscious level and then to extend it through further images, e.g. "He is as hard as nails". What sort of person is he? What might he look like? How might he behave? What other images might we use to give an impression of the sort of person he is? e.g. "His eyes were as cold as ice—they pierced right into your mind". (Note the ideas evoked by the image of "piercing". Why is it a strong image? What sort of associations does this word have?) "His fingers were like iron talons." "He had a heart of stone." Work of this nature might lead to the children writing a poem about this man using the images that have been discussed and introducing other images of their own. It is unnecessary to make a rigid distinction between similes and metaphors. In both cases children should be helped to gain insight into the different ideas and feelings which are "disclosed" by the image.

Stage Three
Poetry

There are many poems available which can be used to deepen a child's awareness of images and symbols and help him to gain insight into their function. Most classroom anthologies can supply the teacher with material for use within this scheme. Take, for example, the following poem by Carl Sandburg:

Fog

The fog comes
on little cat feet.
It sits looking
over harbor and city
on silent haunches
and then moves on.

(From *Chicago Poems,* published by Holt, Rinehart and Winston Inc.)

Initially, children will need to be helped to make the connection between the subject (fog) and the image (a cat). Indeed, many children are likely to say that this is a poem about fog settling on 'a little cat's feet. This mistake is precisely the same as that of imposing a literal interpretation upon such a Biblical passage as

Isaiah 6 : 1-8. Work on modern poetry—including the writing of poems—would appear to be an obvious pre-requisite to work on Biblical passages involving imagery.

Stage Four
Proverbs

There is a decrease in the use of proverbs in conversation and writing today which is, perhaps, another symptom of the current bias towards "descriptive" or factual language. Proverbs, however, are useful as a way of introducing children to the type of short, pithy, gnomic statements which appear in Sacred Scriptures. With proverbs children need to look at the image and then to look beyond it in order to see the proverb's point. Thus, like religious statements couched in symbolic terms, proverbs "disclose" a truth which transcends the boundary of their "local" language. It is unlikely that the Book of Proverbs in the Old Testament, despite its title, is an appropriate choice for use within the classroom although some Biblical proverbs might be included (e.g. some of Christ's words from the Sermon on the Mount). Most examples will be secular proverbs, e.g. Half a loaf is better than no bread. The wish is father to the thought. All that glitters is not gold and so on. Riddles and fables might also be used.

Stage Five
Parables

A logical development of the scheme would be to examine some of the New Testament parables. Here the images used would need to be filled out by reference to their Palestinian background and the image then related to the single point of the parable. This work might be either preceded or followed by encouraging children to write their own parables using images from everyday life.

194

An example of a Symbol and Language Theme for use with children aged eleven-thirteen.

Aim: To initiate children into Religion as a unique mode of thought and awareness by providing them with an opportunity to :

1 express their own ideas, thoughts and feelings in appropriate symbols and language.

Theme: Darkness and Light.

Objectives: To provide children with an opportunity to :

1 become conscious of the feelings and ideas which they associate with darkness and light;

2 explore the connections between light and the concepts of joy, happiness, hope, safety, security, presence, understanding and truth;

3 gain insight into two of the central symbols of religion prior to examining feasts and festivals in which they feature.

Content and Learning Experiences

Stage One
Being in the dark and being in the light

It's difficult for us to imagine being in *total* darkness. Why? (There are chinks of light even on the darkest night.) Most of us have had the experience of being in darkness at some time—e.g. during an electricity failure. What are your first feelings when the light suddenly goes off? (Surprise, annoyance, excitement, fear.) What is the first thing that happens in the home? (Someone lights a candle, lamp or torch.) Why is it that our first reaction to darkness is to get rid of it with light? Why don't we just sit in the dark? Imagine that you did choose to sit in the dark; how would you feel? (Bored, frustrated, sleepy, powerless, uncomfortable, nervous.) Imagine that someone in your family started talking about ghosts, witches, demons or even about burglars. How would you feel? Even if we don't believe in ghosts and even if we have a fierce Alsatian dog to take care of burglars, we tend to find this sort of talk disturbing if we're in the dark. Why? (Darkness is associated in our minds with evil. Things which happen in the dark seem to be outside our control. In the dark we feel defenceless.) Darkness makes us feel uncertain of things. We could say that darkness represents "the unknown"—things that we are not sure about, things that we are afraid of, things that we don't "know" about. When someone says, "I'm in the dark!" they often mean that they don't under-

195

stand something or don't know about something. When they say, "I see it now!" they often mean that they now "understand" something. Some people say, "Oh! the light has just dawned!" or "I've seen the light!"; these expressions also tell us that the person now "understands" something. We can say, then, that whereas darkness is associated with fear, discomfort, uncertainty and ignorance, light is associated with peace of mind, security, certainty and understanding. Light is also associated with joy and happiness because we feel joyful and happy when we have peace of mind, security, certainty and understanding.

Activities might include writing two poems, one on "Darkness" the other on "Light". The children could be asked to imagine being alone on a windswept moor in total darkness and that after a time they see a light in the distance. They could act out the situation or write about it. A dance on "Darkness and Light" could be devised.

Stage Two
Light as a symbol

(Further development of symbolism in Stage One.)

(a) Light as a symbol of joy and happiness, e.g. the use of lights at Christmas (streets, shops and homes are made bright and gay with decorations and lights), birthday candles, fireworks and so on. (Despite its historical background it is appropriate that "Bonfire night" falls in November. Why?) Note phrases like "Their faces lit up when they saw . . ." and "Her eyes shone when she saw . . .".

(b) Light as a symbol of hope, e.g. a pin-prick of light in the distance gives lost travellers, sailors and hikers hope. (Note the practice of people living near the Berlin Wall placing a lighted candle in their window at Christmas—a sign of hope rather than a sign of joy.)

(c) Light as a symbol of safety and security, e.g. runway lights on an airfield—lights which "guide" the pilot to safety; harbour lights, lighthouse beams, and so on.

(d) Light as a symbol of presence, e.g. the porch light or the light outside the front door, lights on in the house, and so on.

(e) Light as a symbol of understanding. Expressions using the word "light" as a synonym for "understanding". This might be linked with the idea of light as a symbol of "truth". The word "enlightenment" draws understanding, truth and light together into a single concept. Activities might include devising a way in which these symbols can be expressed through poetry, drama, dance and painting.

For an example of how this theme may be related to work within the *Dimensional Approach* see pp 215-225.

An example of a Symbol and Language Theme for use with children aged fourteen-sixteen.

Aim: To initiate children into Religion as a unique mode of thought and awareness by providing them with an opportunity to recognise the special characteristics of religious language and symbolism by :

1 acquainting them with language which is evocative, poetic, metaphorical and dramatic (especially within a religious context) and educating them in its use;

2 acquainting them with the context (country, life and customs) out of which the traditional language and symbols of religion have grown.

Theme: Words about God.

Objectives: To provide children with an opportunity to :

1 discern how human situations provide models or images for talking about God;

2 discern how man's ideas of God and the images he uses to talk about God are relative to his level of religious experience;

3 relate the images used of God in the Old Testament to the occupational, institutional and family life of Israel.

Content and Learning Experiences:

Stage One
Experience of people

How do we get to know a person? What sort of "clues" do we use in order to find out about the sort of person they are?

1 *We notice what they look like.*
e.g. whether they are tall or short, fat or thin, dark or fair, the length of their nose, the colour of their eyes and so on. Some psychologists (e.g. Kretschmer, Sheldon) have argued that a certain type of body "build" is related to a particular type of personality (e.g. someone who is short, fat and round is often jolly whereas someone who is tall, thin and gaunt is often the opposite. Compare pictures of Sancho Panza and Don Quixote, John Bull and Mrs Grundy and so on). Do you think there is any truth in this? We also notice the sort of clothes a person wears. They too have been said to be a reflection of personality. What arguments are there against this?

197

2   *We notice where they live and what they do for a living.*
Certain jobs require a certain type of person. Think of some
examples. We have certain expectations of persons in particular jobs. What sort of person do you imagine when you are told
they are a nurse, an army officer, a judge, a farmer, a fisherman,
a doctor, a teacher, a king?

3   *We notice their interests, hobbies and achievements.*
We learn about these either from other people or from the person himself. Would your view of a person be any different if (a)
someone told you he had won the Nobel Peace prize, and (b) he
told you himself when you first met?

4   *We notice what they say.*
What conclusions do you draw about a man who spends all
the time talking about himself? Consider this Spanish saying:
"Tell me what you are and I will be able to tell you what you
are not!" What do you think this means? We can learn a great
deal about a person's attitudes and values by listening to what
they say. Give some examples.

5   *We notice what they do.*
"Actions speak louder than words." Does the person put his
ideas and ideals into practice? How does he behave towards
people? Is he truthful? Does he keep his word? Does he show
that he cares about others or only about himself? Is he consistent? Is he reliable?

6   *We find out most about a person through our own relationship
with him.*
Once we have established a close relationship with a person we
no longer give much importance to what they happen to look
like, where they live, the job they do or even what their interests,
hobbies and achievements are. For example, someone might
describe a person as, "A man of medium height, dark, well-
dressed, living in a detached house, practising as a solicitor,
having an interest in country dancing, natural history and
detective stories. . . ." We might recognise that this description
is of a friend of ours, but we would probably say, "That does
describe John to some extent, but he's much more than that.
You've left out his tremendous sense of humour, his love of
children, his kindness and thoughtfulness, and lots of other
things too. If you get to know John yourself you'll see what I
mean." Descriptions, then, can point us towards a person but
they can never actually present that person totally. Every person has many sides to him and these may even be contradictory.
But there is always a part of him which eludes description. It is
a part which can be sensed but never described. It is unique
to each individual. We sometimes refer to it as the "self". Try
writing a description of your "self" and see if you are satisfied

with the result. Start with your physical features and eventually move on to describing your feelings. Notice how your name eventually comes to represent your "self". Is it possible to get to know a person without using their name or without even knowing their name? Imagine that you got to know a person as "Richard" and, after a year, they informed you that their name was "Andrew". Why would you find it difficult to begin thinking of them as "Andrew"? Some people often say that they would like to change their name. Why?

Stage Two
Experience of God

Early man came to associate God with the elements. Why? Not surprisingly he used the images of the elements as a way of talking about God. In other words, he drew conclusions about God's nature from the images he used. Let us look at some examples.

(a) *The gods of the Hindu Vedas.*

Dyaus Pitar, the bright sky, the "Sky who knows all", the "Sky Father".
Varuna and Mitra—"the two powerful and sublime masters of the sky". Varuna "darkening the clouds he shows himself at the first growl of thunder and makes the sky rain by a divine miracle". He is "thousand-eyed" (an image of the stars) and the guardian of the laws of the universe, physical and moral. He guarantees the contracts of men, "binding" them by their oaths. He holds the power of the universe and is the universal king.
Parjani, the god of hurricanes, the son of Dyaus. The whole universe trembles when he unleashes his storms.
Indra, the national god of the Aryans, a god of war, he covers the sky, is greater than the earth and wears heaven as his crown. He makes sap and blood circulate, puts the life into seeds, gives free play to rivers and seas, and bursts open the clouds. A thunderbolt is his weapon. He is compared to a bull and a ram.
Vayu, the wind god, the bearer of perfumes.
Surya or Sivitri, the sun god, god of night and day, "the spy" over all the world.
Agni, the god of fire.
These gods were depicted in elemental images and often spoken of in terms of their actions. For example, Indra is seen as the ally of the Aryans in their invasion of northwest India. He is a gigantic figure, with long flowing hair and a wind-tossed beard through which he shouts and roars with a loud voice. He "slew the drought

199

dragon, Vritra" (the Dravidian's irrigation system) which was holding back the waters, so that they flowed swiftly to the ocean. Rudra, the mountain god, on the other hand, was the enemy of the Aryans for he destroyed their goods and persons. They prayed that he would ". . . kill not our great or our small, our growing one or our full-grown man, our father or our mother. Injure not, O Rudra, our dear selves. Injure not our cattle or horses. In thy wrath, O Rudra, slay not our heroes. We invoke thee ever with sacrifices". Ushas, the Dawn, is a "young maid in white robes" shining afar in her chariot drawn by red spotted horses. Surya, the sun god, is often depicted riding his chariot, his head surrounded by a halo of sun rays.

(b) Yahweh, the God of Israel.

Some of the earliest parts of the Old Testament make a great deal of use of elemental imagery to evoke an idea of Yahweh. For example, he displays his power by means of storms; thunder is his voice and lightning is his "fire" or his "arrows". ". . . thunders began to be heard and lightning to flash, and a very thick cloud to cover the mountain" while he was transmitting the Law to Moses. "And all Mount Sinai was wrapped in smoke, because the Lord descended upon it in fire; and the smoke of it went up like the smoke of a kiln, and the whole mountain quaked greatly." (Exodus 19 : 18.) Yahweh is seen also through his actions, especially his saving act of delivering Israel from the Egyptians. He leads them by a cloud by day and a pillar of fire by night. He is Israel's ally in conquering Canaan. He warns Elijah of his approach by "a great and strong wind . . . renting the mountains, and breaking the rocks into pieces . . ." (1 Kings 19 : 11). See Job Chapter 36 : 26—40 : 2 for a dramatic account of God in terms of elemental imagery. Also Psalm 18 : 6-19.

Points of focus

Why did early man see God in these elemental terms? What sort of character do these images give God? If God is thought of in this way, what sort of relationship would man feel that he should have with God? Nearly all religions have moved beyond this type of view of God. Why?

Activities might include writing psalms using elemental imagery, devising a dance drama based on some of these images, doing some research into the gods of the Vedas and finding out more about the Aryans and the early Hebrews.

Stage Three
Talking about God through the images of men's work, crafts and professions

We have seen how early man used elemental imagery to talk about his awareness of God. This imagery gave a very restricted view of God because it only tended to present one side of his nature —that of his terrible power over man. As a consequence God seemed remote, severe and even capricious. The only attitude for man to adopt towards God was one of fear. It fell to the prophets to disclose to Israel other sides of Yahweh's character—sides which they had come to recognise through their own experience of God. To do this, they used images taken from the familiar figures and activities of Israel's everyday life. Some of the images they used were :

1   The shepherd. Psalm 23; Ezekiel 34 : 31.
2   The farmer. Amos 9 : 9.
3   The dairymaid. Job 10 : 10.
4   The fuller—the laundress. Malachi 3 : 2; Isaiah 4 : 4.
5   The builder. Amos 7 : 7.
6   The potter. Jeremiah 18 : 6; Isaiah 64 : 8.
7   The fisherman. Habakkuk 1 : 14-15.
8   The tradesman. Isaiah 55 : 1.
9   The physician. Jeremiah 30 : 17.
10   The teacher. Jeremiah 31 : 33.
11   The nurse. Isaiah 1 : 2.
12   The metal worker. Malachi 3 : 2-3.

Points of focus

What does each of these images contribute to the character or nature of Yahweh? What is the effect of using "human models" rather than "elemental models" to talk about God? Why is it necessary to have so many different images? What does each image suggest about the sort of relationship that man can have with God?

Activities might include looking more deeply into the occupations listed, relating them to life in Israel before the Exile, considering the relevance of these images as ways of talking about God in the 20th century, and examining the "call experience" and message of one of the prophets (e.g. Amos or Jeremiah).

201

Stage Four
Talking about God through images taken from Israel's national institutions

1 The King. Jeremiah 10 : 7; Psalms 10 : 16; 29 : 10.
2 The warrior and soldier. Isaiah 63 : 1; Psalm 68.
3 The judge. Isaiah 33 : 22; Psalms 7 : 8-11; 58 : 11; 135 : 14.

Points of focus

What made national institutions appropriate as a way of talking about God for the Israelites? Consider the part played by the king in Israel's national life. Look at the events leading to the establishment of the monarchy in Israel. Why did some people oppose it? Why are there so many references in the Old Testament to God as Judge? What are the particular characteristics of a judge? Look at Amos's experience and see what aspect of God's character is stressed in his teaching.

Stage Five
Talking about God through the images of home, family and friends

1 Father. Jeremiah 3 : 19.
2 Mother. Deuteronomy 32 : 18; Isaiah 66 : 13.
3 Husband. The Book of Hosea.
4 Friend. Jeremiah 3 : 4.

Points of focus

These images gain their strength from the sort of relationship to which they point—relationships of love, trust and faithfulness. They represent or "sum up" man's deepest experiences, the ones that he values most. It is very natural, therefore, that he should use these images to illuminate the nature of God and to "disclose" the sort of relationship which man may have with God.

Activities might include a consideration of Hosea's experience and what it taught him about God.

Stage Six

The scheme may be extended in a number of ways :
1 A consideration of some of the images used in talking about God in the New Testament, e.g. Abba, Father, Spirit, Light, Love.

2 A consideration of some of the images used in talking about Christ, e.g. Lamb of God, Son of Man, Messiah, Servant, Bread of Life, Resurrection and the Life, Saviour.

3 A consideration of Symbols used in religion, especially in the Christian Church. (A set of six film strips with taped commentaries are available from *Concordia Films* on the subject of symbols.)

4 A consideration of the names and symbols of God in other faiths (e.g. Islam, Hinduism and Zoroastrianism).

3 SITUATION THEMES

Aims:

1 To promote moral insight and moral development by providing an opportunity for children to :

    (a) explore, examine and discuss situations which call for a moral choice or judgment to be made about the situation or/and about the attitudes and actions of persons involved in it;

    (b) learn how to assess situations in terms of the consequences of attitudes and actions;

    (c) perceive the need for principles which can provide guidelines for moral decision-making;

    (d) formulate principles which can provide guidelines for moral decision-making;

    (e) perceive the connection between beliefs, values, attitudes and behaviour;

    (f) introject attitudes and values through identifying with characters displaying moral sensitivity;

    (g) accept or admit to their own emotional experiences and come to some conclusions about the sort of responses they might reasonably adopt towards them.

2 To initiate children into Religion as a unique mode of thought and awareness by providing them with an opportunity to :

    (a) explore, examine and discuss situations in which a religious belief is seen to provide the rationale underlying a person's attitudes, values and actions;

    (b) recognise that religious beliefs and attitudes reflect a particular type of response to certain emotional experiences;

    (c) gain insight into the "implicit" or feeling side of religion by examining the ways in which it deals with emotions, especially those particularly characteristic of the religious attitude, that is, awe, reverence and worship.

An example of a Situation Theme for use with children aged eleven-thirteen.

Aim: To initiate children into Religion as a unique mode of thought and awareness by providing them with an opportunity to explore, examine and discuss situations in which a religious belief is seen to provide the rationale underlying a person's attitudes, values and actions.

Theme: The Events of Holy Week.

Objectives: To provide children with an opportunity to :

1 compare Jesus's behaviour with that of the other characters in the account;

2 relate behaviour to attitudes and attitudes to beliefs;

3 compare the concepts of determination, dedication, courage, humility, compassion, forgiveness, self-sacrifice and love with the concepts of cowardliness, fear, avarice, cruelty, malice, selfishness, gullibility and betrayal;

4 engage in elementary Biblical research and "Biblical criticism" and to draw conclusions in accordance with their findings.

Content and Learning Experiences:

Stage One
Sunday: Jesus rides into Jerusalem

Teacher written/told account based on Matthew 21 : 1-11; Mark 11 : 1-10; Luke 19 : 28-42; John 12 : 12-19. A plan of this lesson is given at the end of the scheme.

Stage Two
Monday: Jesus clears up the Temple

Matthew 21 : 12-16; Mark 11 : 15-19; Luke 19 : 45-48; John 2 :13-16.

Do Jesus's actions here fit in with our picture of a gentle, tolerant person? Why did he act in this way? What did his actions "say" to those who witnessed the incident? (Some reference to Temple practices is needed here.) How did the chief priests react? Why? Was it this action more than any other which led to Jesus's death?

205

Stage Three
Tuesday: Jesus fights a duel with words

(a) The question of Jesus's authority. Matthew 21 : 23-27; Mark 11 : 27-33; Luke 20 : 1-8. What do we mean by "authority"? Where is the "catch" in the question? (Possible use of Luke 20 : 9-20, a parable formed into an allegory.)

(b) The question of paying taxes to Caesar. Matthew 12 : 13-17; Mark 12 : 13-17; Luke 20 : 19-26. Where is the "catch" in the question?

(c) The question of the greatest commandment. Mark 12 : 28-34. Was the scribe still trying to catch Jesus out or did he really want to know? What sort of effect does Jesus have on this man? Why? Look at Luke 20 : 46-47 and Matthew 23 for what Jesus said about the scribes. Do you think they were all like this?

Stage Four
Wednesday: A friend found and a friend lost

Matthew 26 : 1-16.

While the chief priests plot to arrest and kill Jesus, Jesus is honoured by a woman at Simon's house. Note that both the woman and Simon are social outcastes. Why? What did her action mean? What made her do it? Note the reactions of the disciples and see John 12 : 4-6 for a comment about Judas. Does this comment help us to see why he agreed to betray Jesus? ("Betray" here refers to telling the chief priests where they can arrest Jesus quietly.) Do you think Judas had other motives for betraying Jesus than the motive of money? (He was impatient and wanted to goad Jesus into action? He was a Zealot and had grown tired of Jesus's talk? He no longer thought he was the Messiah?)

Stage Five
Thursday: A lesson in friendship

Matthew 26 : 17-35.

Secret preparations for the Passover meal (background details required). The Last Supper. Attempts should be made to explore the wealth of symbolism in this incident, e.g. the significance of taking a meal together; the special significance of this meal; what was Jesus trying to teach his disciples through the meal and when he washed their feet? How do you think they felt about this? Note how they pledge their friendship and loyalty to Jesus—especially Peter.

Stage Six
Thursday cont.: The plot is put into operation

Matthew 26 : 36-75.

What sort of feelings does Jesus have here? Note that while Jesus prays the disciples sleep. When Judas and the mob come Jesus does not resist them but the disciples run away. Is there a connection between sleeping and running away? What gives Jesus the strength to face certain death? Jesus is given a "rigged" trial before Caiaphas, the High Priest, in the middle of the night and is beaten up. Do you think that the fact that the trial took place at night, during darkness, is important? Who is more afraid and has more to lose? Caiaphas or Jesus? Note what happened to Peter. What sort of thoughts do you think he was having during the trial?

Stage Seven
Friday: Jesus is tried by Pilate and executed

Teacher written/told account based on Matthew 27 : 11-61; Mark 15 : 1-47; Luke 23 : 1-56; John 18 : 29-42.

(The focus should be on the events of the trial rather than on the crucifixion, although pupils of this age should not be shielded from the brutality of the latter.)

What happened to Judas? (Matthew 27 : 3-10.) Was there any other way open to him other than suicide?

Possible ways of developing aspects of the trial:

(a) The behaviour of the chief priests and scribes; their ruthless insistence on Jesus's death; their false political charges (Luke 23 : 1-5); their bribery of the people to demand Jesus's death; their attitude to Judas (Matthew 27 : 4). What did they want most out of life?

(b) The behaviour of Pilate; his precarious political position in view of earlier disturbances (Luke 13 : 1); his unwillingness to follow his apparent belief in Jesus's innocence because he might provoke a riot and so jeopardise his own political career; his abdication of responsibility through fear (John 19 : 8; Matthew 27 : 24). What did he want most out of life?

(c) The behaviour of the crowd; their gullibility and willingness to be manipulated by the priests; their sadistic enjoyment of the spectacle; why had they changed their minds about Jesus? Was it because he had not turned out to be a political Messiah willing to rid Palestine of the Romans? Did they see in Barabbas a potential revolutionary leader who would fulfil their hopes? Whatever they thought, they were willing to assume responsibility for Jesus's death (Matthew 27 : 25). What did they want most out of life?

(d) The behaviour of the soldiers; tense in the face of an angry mob; not understanding the issues involved; welcoming an opportunity to taunt and mock Jesus (Matthew 27 :27-31) as light relief from their military duties; willing to crucify a man for the drink and extra pay and for the chance of obtaining his clothes. What did they want most out of life? (Note Mark 15 : 39 and Matthew 27 : 54 : these passages suggest that their fault, unlike that of the priests, was indifference to Jesus and that could change whereas fanatical hatred could not.)

(e) The behaviour of the women; (See Matthew 27 : 55-56 and 61; Luke 23 : 49; John 19 : 25-27.) they were numbed with horror and full of misery. What did they want most out of life?

(f) The behaviour of Jesus; calm, dignified, patient, without malice, rarely speaking—a stunning contrast to those around him. What did he want most out of life?

Stage Eight
Saturday: The Silent Sabbath

For the Jew the Sabbath begins at dusk on Friday and continues until dusk on Saturday. It is a day of rest. There was only just enough time for Joseph of Arimathea (what were his motives?) to place Jesus's body in his tomb before it was the Sabbath and all activity had to cease. The customary anointing was left undone. During the "silent Sabbath" what sort of thoughts would pass through the minds of the disciples, of the women, of the chief priests, the soldiers, Pilate and the crowd? Matthew 28 : 62-66 shows what sort of thoughts the enemies of Jesus had and what sort of actions they prompted.

Stage Nine
Sunday: New Life

Make a chart (with five parallel columns) of the New Testament accounts of the Resurrection appearances, i.e. 1 Corinthians 15 : 3-8; Mark 16 : 8 (and 9-19); Matthew 28 : 1-20; Luke 24 : 1-53; John 20 : 1-29 and Chapters 21.

Discussion of the differences and similarities; does it really matter if all the accounts do not seem to fit? What do you think the Early Church is trying to say about Jesus through these accounts?

Stage Ten
Everyday: Jesus and the 20th Century

What have we learned? An evaluation of the scheme through a consideration of the effects that Jesus's beliefs, attitudes and actions have had on people since his death. In what ways does the Christian faith find expression today? (Individual commitment demonstrated in various ways—through attitudes and actions and through involvement in helping people; through the work of Christian agencies, through the work of the Church and so on.) The emphasis should be on translating the first century happenings into terms relevant to the 20th century.

A lesson plan for the first lesson in this scheme—Sunday: "Jesus rides into Jerusalem".

CLASS: 3X. AGE RANGE: 13+. DEVELOPMENTAL STAGES: Formal. TIME AVAILABLE: 90 mins. NUMBER OF CHILDREN: 35. THEME TITLE OR SUBJECT: The Events of Holy Week. NUMBER OF LESSON IN THE SCHEME: Lesson 1. Sunday: Jesus rides into Jerusalem. Used as a Situation Theme.

PART 1: Specific Objectives

The children will:

1 distinguish in writing between the beliefs, attitudes and actions of Jesus and the beliefs, attitudes and actions of the crowd;

2 compare the behaviour of the crowd in the story with the behaviour of a crowd in their own experience and draw conclusions about the effects on the individual of being in a crowd.

Preparation   Reading of Matthew 21: 1-11; Mark 11: 1-10; Luke 19: 28-42; John 12: 12-19. Reference to these passages in the *Pelican Gospel Commentaries*. Amalgamation of the accounts into a single narrative to be told or read to the class. Blackboard to be used in the Development for a summary of points.

Organisation   No special organisation required.

209

SUBJECT MATTER	METHOD
Introduction	Exposition interspersed with questions.
A brief background account of Jewish Feasts of pilgrimage in order to set the scene for Jesus's entry into Jerusalem on Palm Sunday. N.B. The N.T. accounts imply that the event was connected with Passover. The event may, however, have occurred at the Feast of Hannukah. This is especially appropriate as Jesus "re-dedicates" the Temple.	1 The Temple—the centre of Jewish national and religious life. 2 The custom of making pilgrimages to Jerusalem for principal feasts. 3 Feast of Hannukah or the Dedication of the Temple. A joyful feast. Green branches and palms were carried and hymns (Psalms 113-118) were sung.

Development

Let us look at what happened to Jesus—by now a well-known figure in the community—when he joined the pilgrims on their way to this Feast of Dedication of the Temple.

The following points and observations to be made:

Speculation on the part of the chief priests about whether Jesus will dare to come to the celebrations in Jerusalem. Jesus *determines* to go, even though he recognises the danger. He requests his disciples to go into a nearby village where they will find a colt; they are to untie it and bring it back; if anyone says anything they are to use the pass-phrase, "The Lord needs it". Despite the strangeness of the request the disciples obey without question. They place their coats on the colt's back and Jesus mounts. As they make their way towards Jerusalem they meet up with other pilgrims on their way to the feast. (Focus on the crowd.) They are excited, enjoying not having to work, looking forward to meeting old friends at the feast; they are in high spirits, talkative and ready to share the traditional blessing with anyone approaching the holy city— "Hosanna" from Psalm 118 : 25—"Blessed in the name of the Lord be he who comes!" For the Feast of Dedication they are taking green branches and palms to decorate the Temple. They wave them gaily as they walk. In their excitement they have forgotten that they are an oppressed people whose country is occupied by the Romans.

On seeing Jesus approach, their excitement mounts. He is well known for his teaching and, as well as being called a "prophet", some people have said that he is the long-awaited Messiah. ("Messiah" being equated with a "true son of King David", a soldier and king who would bring back the Golden Age of Israel just as it had been in David's Day.) No doubt someone reminds another person of this and, *because it is a crowd,* the idea spreads like wildfire. Further support is lent by a man who remembers what the prophet Zechariah (9 : 9) had said about the Messiah— he would come like a king, riding on a colt! The crowd erupts into shouts and cheers. Can it be, at last, the time for their troubles to come to an end? Is Jesus going to lead them against the Romans and make them free again? What will he do in Jerusalem? How will he go about bringing in "The Kingdom of God" to replace the hated "Kingdom of Caesar"? They do not know the answer to these questions. Indeed, they do not want to bother their heads with such technicalities! Something is in the wind and anything is better than nothing! The natural reaction is to cheer and shout and help it along. It is little wonder that when Jesus reaches Jerusalem, everyone is talking excitedly about him, especially about what they think he will do. And that includes the Romans and chief priests, but for very different reasons.

Questioning and discussion. (Blackboard summary of points.)

What does the incident show about Jesus?
1 He had "authority". Meaning? He had "power"? No. Why did the disciples do as he asked? Fear? No. They respected him because of the sort of person he was. Note that a person shows what he is like by the way he lives and the things he does. Actions result from what a man believes—about himself and about others. So :
2 He had beliefs which resulted in actions—positive actions. What did he believe? His beliefs about himself and about others came from what he believed about God. He believed that God wishes to be served not just externally through prayer and ceremony (or even through going on a pilgrimage) but through loving people and thinking less of oneself. What is there in this incident which shows this very well? His decision to go to Jerusalem in the face of danger. So :
3 He was dedicated and determined. He was also courageous. He had thought things out carefully and was prepared to see things through, even if it meant losing his life. He did not boast about this; on the contrary, he did not speak about it. He showed it in his actions though. For example, even though he knew people were saying that he was the Messiah he

211

wanted to show them that a strong military leader would never help them to a better and happier life. He showed them that there is something much more powerful than military strength. How? What? He rode on a donkey—a symbol of service, humility and peace. A horse would have been seen as the symbol of a warrior and earthly king. Through his actions Jesus expressed his belief to the people that they would only find a better life if they dedicated their lives to God and showed this in their behaviour with other people.

How did the crowd react to this message? What does the incident show about the crowd?

1   They were a crowd of pilgrims going to a feast of *dedication*. But had they thought about *why* they were going and what it implied for themselves (e.g. their own dedication)? Hardly. They were going to *take* rather than to *give*—take the fun, the laughter, the enjoyment of being part of a happy crowd and a colourful ceremony. These things are not bad in themselves; it is just that they are not enough in themselves. But would this be true of *all* the pilgrims? We cannot tell and we will never know. The individual, with his thoughts and beliefs, was swallowed up by the crowd. Their excited behaviour was "contagious"—individuals did not have either time or inclination to think for themselves. So :

2   They were a crowd whose thoughts and actions influenced each other. We see this best by the way that they all began to cheer and shout, throw down their coats and wave palm branches when Jesus came along. Would a person have done this if he had been alone? (Compare crowd behaviour at football matches.) Once the idea of Jesus as the Davidic Messiah occurred it was believed by all, and that prevented individuals from thinking for themselves and seeing the real significance of Jesus on the colt. So :

3   They were a crowd who only saw what they wanted to see. They were not open to new ideas. And what they saw they made to fit their selfish desires—a man willing to lose his life getting them a better life. This was their belief and their actions stem from it. Now they cheer and shout in Jesus's support—an easy thing to do while Jesus was asking them to do something much more difficult, i.e. to dedicate themselves to God and start loving each other. Soon (on Friday) they will cheer and shout against him and ask for his death (another easy thing to do). The crowd, then, acts without thinking carefully; its beliefs are shallow and stem solely from selfishness.

Conclusion

Evaluation of the lesson in terms of the Specific Objectives.

1 Write two short scenes such as might appear in a play:
   (a) a conversation between Jesus and his disciples about the events of the day;
   (b) a conversation between several pilgrims who had been in the crowd and had seen Jesus.

or 2 Give an account from your own experience of a time when you have been influenced by being a member of a crowd or gang. Why, do you think, were the people in the crowd that cheered Jesus unable to think for themselves?

PART 3: Evaluation
Were the Specific Objectives achieved?

PART 4: Self Criticism
How do you account for your success or failure?

An example of a Situation Theme for use with children aged fifteen-sixteen.

Aim: To provide children with an opportunity to explore, examine and discuss situations which call for a moral choice or judgment to be made about the situation and/or about the attitudes and actions of persons involved in it.

Theme: Family and Racial Conflict.

Objectives: To provide children with an opportunity to :—
1 practise the skill of synthesising evidence, experience and observation with religious and moral beliefs and coming to rational conclusions in particular situations.

Content:
"Mr and Mrs Smith and their 17-year-old daughter Jean are a 'white' Christian family living in the 'respectable' suburbs of

213

a large industrial city. There is a large minority of 'coloured' West Indian immigrants in the city, mostly living in slums near the city centre. There is considerable racial ill-feeling between the immigrants and other citizens, and the two mix very little. Jean Smith wants to leave home and go to live with Jim Jones who is West Indian, lives in the slums and is an atheist. Jean and Jim wish to marry but cannot do so yet since Jim is already married, his wife having left him 18 months ago."

(D. McIntyre and A. Wainwright, *Curriculum and Examinations in R.E.*, Moray House College of Education, Oliver and Boyd, 1968.)

Consider how Mr and Mrs Smith might react to this problem and come to some conclusions about the way in which it might be resolved.

The *Man and Religion Series* (Ronald Dingwall, Religious Education Press), Part 6, "Facing up to Life", provides useful material for Situation Themes. Each of the books (e.g. *Work, Relationships, Leisure*) is accompanied by a wallet containing 12 "Drama Cards" and 12 "Identi-Cards" for introducing discussion and role-play.

Case-Studies in Adolescence by George and Pauline Perry (Pitman, 1970) is another useful source of material for use with older secondary school pupils. The book contains 24 situations involving adolescents and each situation is followed by questions for discussion.

Appendix Two

Practical Examples of the Dimensional Approach

1 Using Experiential, Mythological and Ritual material
    pp 215-225
2 Using Social and Ethical material   pp 226-234
3 Using Doctrinal material   pp 235-240

THE DIMENSIONAL APPROACH

As outlined in Chapter 6, the intention of this approach is to present selected religious concepts by way of the six dimensions of religion—experiential, mythological, ritual, social, ethical and doctrinal. The teacher's task is to help children to build conceptual bridges between their own experiences and what they recognise to be the central concepts of religion. Accordingly, work undertaken within the *Dimensional Approach* should be related to work undertaken within the *Existential Approach*.

1 USING EXPERIENTIAL, MYTHOLOGICAL AND RITUAL MATERIAL

An example of experiential, mythological and ritual material for use with children aged eleven-thirteen.

Aim: To initiate children into Religion as a unique mode of thought and awareness by acquainting them with material illustrating its experiential, mythological and ritual dimensions.

Theme: Feasts and Festivals of Light.

Objectives: To provide children with an opportunity to :
 1 relate their own experience and understanding of the symbols of darkness and light to the use of these symbols in religion;

215

2   examine three different festivals of light from three different religions and to discern the way in which the symbol of light is used to illuminate key concepts within those religions;

3   discern the relationship between myth and ritual and the experiential dimension of religion;

4   become sensitive to the need to examine religion from the point of view of its adherents.

(This scheme is intended to be a continuation of the Symbol and Language Theme on "Darkness and Light", given on pp 195-196.)

Content and Learning Experiences:

Stage One
The Jewish Festival of Hannukah
(or "Chanucah" or "Chanukkoh")

Date of festival: the 25th day of the month of Kislev, continuing for eight days (approximately the first or second week in December).

Background to the festival:

From the time of the Babylonian Exile (586 B.C.) until the Maccabean revolt in 164 B.C., the Jews had no independent kingdom in Palestine and were continually subject to the rule of other countries. For 200 years they were under Persian rule. At the end of the fourth century B.C. they were ruled by Alexander the Great, a Greek. Under Alexander many Greek ideas were introduced to the Jews; some Jews began to speak Greek and to forget their own language and religion. When Alexander died his empire was broken into many kingdoms. The Jews in Palestine were wedged in between two separate kingdoms who were continually at war with each other—Syria, ruled by the Seleucids, and Egypt, ruled by the Ptolemies. The Jews were pinioned between "the hammer and the anvil". For 100 years (the third century B.C.) the Jews were ruled by Syria (the Seleucids) who were very interested in Greek ideas. Then Egypt (the Ptolemies) captured Palestine and they were less interested in Greek ideas. Often the Jews were unable to tell to which kingdom their country belonged. Some Jews were in favour of Egypt and others were in favour of Syria. Suddenly, Antiochus Epiphanes became King of Syria. He showed favouritism to those Jews who supported Syria and liked Greek ideas. He made one of these Jews High Priest (Jason) but he did not trust him so he made another Jew, named Menelaus, the High Priest. Menelaus was the leader of all those Jews who supported Syria. There was a terrible fight between Jason and Menelaus and Antiochus came with his army and killed hundreds of Jews who did not like Menelaus. Antiochus went into the Temple and wrecked it and took all the golden and silver utensils. Antiochus issued an order that all the peoples of his empire were to worship Greek gods and become Greeks. All the peoples of the empire obeyed except the Jews. Antiochus sent an army to Jerusalem, went into the Temple and turned it into a place for the worship of Greek gods. The Jews were forbidden, under penalty of death, to practise their own religion. Many Jews died as martyrs. A man called Judas Maccabee organised a resistance movement with the help of his brothers—the Hasmonean family. One of the first things they did was to hold a Jewish service in the Temple—which had not been worshipped in for three years. On the 25th day of the month of Kislev they re-dedicated the altar in the Temple with a great ceremony, and decreed that an eight-day festival, commencing on that day, be observed every year. This Festival is called "The Festival of Hannukah" or "The Feast of Dedication".

In time, through Judas Maccabee, the Jews were able to have their own kingdom for about 100 years—a kingdom in which they were able to worship their own god, Yahweh, without fear. When they were conquered by the Romans they often remembered this period because it gave them hope that one day they would be able to be free again.

The festival:

There is a legend associated with the festival which Jews still remember today. When Judas went into the Temple he wanted to light a lamp to symbolise the presence of God. He also wanted it to be a symbol of hope, of goodness and of joy. All the lamps had been spoiled by the Syrians except one and that lamp only had enough oil in it to last one day. He lit it but to his amazement it burned for eight days. The Jews saw this as a great miracle. It also showed them that God had helped them to defeat the evil of the Syrians.

On the 25th day of Kislev, Jews all over the world still celebrate the Festival of Hannukah. As soon as it becomes dusk, they place a Hannukah Lamp or a Hannukah Menorah (candelabrum) having eight candles or lamps, in their window. After saying prayers of thanksgiving for God's help to Judas Maccabee, they light the first candle or lamp on the far side of the Hannukah Lamp. Each night one more candle is lit until by the eighth night all eight candles are burning brightly. They sing a number of hymns, one of which is "Rock of Ages".

There are other customs associated with Hannukah. There is the custom of eating cheese and pancakes and of playing with a spinning top called a "dreidel". The top has four wings and each one bears a letter—N, G, H and SH. These are the first letters of the words which make up the sentence "Nes Godol Hoyoh Shom" which means, "A great miracle happened there". What miracle does this refer to? There is also a custom of playing cards on Hannukah evenings. It is said that this custom originated when the Jews wanted to get used to staying up late without falling asleep so that they could read the Torah longer!

The Festival of Hannukah is often called "The Festival of Lights". What do the lights symbolise?

1 The victory of goodness over evil.
2 The victory of the weak over the strong.
3 Hope. (Relate this to the present position of the Jewish people.)
4 Joy and Thanksgiving.
5 The presence of God.
6 The unity of the Jewish people. (They are all doing the same thing at the same time.)

We might also say that the lights symbolise the victory of the spirit of Judaism.

It is important that the scheme is augmented by pictures, films, and, if possible, a Hannukah Lamp or Menorah and dreidel tops.

Stage Two
The Christian Festival of Easter

Date of the festival: determined by the Paschal Full Moon, its extreme limits being 21 March and 25 April.

Background to the festival:

The scheme of work may be approached by way of an examination of the events of Holy Week as given in the Gospels, or by way of an examination of the liturgical life of the Christian Church from Ash Wednesday until Easter Day. Both approaches should culminate in an examination of how the Christian Church celebrates Christ's Resurrection. Taking the second approach, we should note that the importance of Easter, "The Feast of the Resurrection of Christ", is emphasised liturgically by the long preparation of Lent and Passiontide (the latter being the last two weeks of Lent, extending from Passion Sunday until Holy Saturday), by the special ceremonies of Holy Week (the last week of Lent) and by the following Paschaltide (lasting the 50 days until the Saturday before

218

Trinity Sunday). Through these observances and ceremonies the Christian Church both prepares its members to celebrate Christ's Resurrection and teaches them of its significance. The contrast between the "darkness" and sorrow of Passiontide and the "light" and joy of Easter is vividly displayed by the use of contrasting liturgical colours—the purple (and the black of Good Friday) giving way to white. It is during the Easter Vigil on Holy Saturday that the transition from darkness to light occurs.

The festival:

For Christians, "Good Friday" is the saddest day of the year. It is the day when they remember the suffering and death of Jesus on the cross and his burial in Joseph of Arimathaea's tomb. Many Christians fast during this day and go to church in the afternoon. The services they attend at church vary according to the different denominations, but all have the same intention—to remember Jesus's death. Protestants often do this by listening to readings from the Gospels and, perhaps, by singing a special musical setting of the events of Jesus's last days on earth. It is common practice for a three-hour devotional service to be held during the afternoon. In this service the priest or the minister helps the people to think about Jesus's life and teaching and to relate it to their daily lives. In Roman Catholic and some Anglican churches very ancient ceremonies going back hundreds of years are held. These ceremonies are also designed to help the people to think about Jesus's life and teaching and to give them an opportunity to show their sorrow at his death. We are going to look at some parts of these ceremonies.

When Catholics arrive at church they find it completely bare; the altar is without cloths, candles and a cross. Why do you think this is? The priest wears red vestments or robes—they are red to help the people to remember the blood that Jesus lost on the cross. They also remind them of the martyrs who have died for the Christian faith. They read together a passage from Isaiah Chapter 52 about an innocent man who, without complaining, suffered on behalf of other people. Originally this passage may have referred to the whole nation of Israel who suffered Exile in Babylon, but the Early Christian Church thought that it fitted Jesus so exactly that it must have referred to him. The person in the passage is known as "The Suffering Servant". Why did Christians think that this was a good title for Jesus? Psalm 22 deals with a similar situation of a man who suffered. Perhaps Jesus was thinking of this psalm when he said "My God, my God, why have you forsaken me?" (Mark 15 : 34). Some have said that this shows that Jesus lost his faith in God when he was on the cross. But if we look at the ending of Psalm

219

22 we see that the man does not lose his faith. Jesus perhaps was thinking of this—the whole psalm rather than the first verse.

After reading the story of Jesus's arrest, trial and death, the people then say prayers for the Church and its clergy and people, for the unity of all Christians, for the Jews, for those who are not Christians, for those who do not believe in God and for those who are in special need, especially people who are ill, hungry and sad.

After this a very ancient ceremony is observed which is called "The Veneration of the Cross". The priest holds up a crucifix for people to look at to help them remember Jesus's suffering. Some people like to show their love for Jesus by going to the cross and kneeling before it and saying a special prayer. After this the people take communion.

Historically, Jesus's body was taken down from the cross and placed in the tomb before six o'clock on the Friday evening as this was when the Jewish Sabbath began. In some churches an Easter garden with a tomb is made. People may come into the church on Friday evening and throughout Saturday to say a prayer in front of the model of the tomb and to think about Jesus's death. When it is dark on Saturday evening, many churches hold a special service called "The Easter Vigil". The Vigil may continue until midnight. Before midnight, however, another ancient ceremony takes place. All the lights in the church are put out—everywhere is in complete darkness. What do you think this is meant to symbolise? People come into the darkened church and take their places while the priest and his assistants go outside where a fire has been prepared. One of the assistants takes with him a very large candle called "The Paschal Candle" or "The Easter Candle". The priest blesses the fire and then cuts a cross in the candle with the date of the current year. Five grains of incense are inserted into the candle in the form of a cross. The priest then lights the candle from the fire and says, "May the light of Christ, rising in glory, dispel the darkness of our hearts and minds". He then lifts the lighted candle high and sings the words, "Christ our light" and his assistants reply, "Thanks be to God". The priest and his assistants then enter the darkened church and, at the church door, the words "Christ our light" are repeated and all the people reply, "Thanks be to God". The people, who have been given unlighted candles, then light their candles from the Easter Candle and follow in procession to the altar where the words, "Christ our light" are sung a third and final time. The whole of the church is now bright with candle light and the Easter Candle is placed near the lectern where it will remain until Ascension Day. With everyone holding lighted candles the "Easter Proclamation" is then said or sung. If we look at some of the words we will see what the Easter Candle and the words "Christ our light" mean :

220

Rejoice, heavenly powers! Sing, choirs of angels!
Exult, all creation around God's throne!
Jesus Christ, our King, is risen!
Sound the trumpet of salvation!
Rejoice, O earth, in shining splendour,
radiant in the brightness of your King!
Christ has conquered! Glory fills you!
Darkness vanishes for ever!
Rejoice, O Mother Church! Exult in glory!
The risen Saviour shines upon you!
Let this place resound with joy,
echoing the mighty song of all God's people!

The proclamation ends:

Accept this Easter candle,
a flame divided but undimmed,
a pillar of fire that glows to the honour of God.
Let it mingle with the lights of heaven
and continue bravely burning
to dispel the darkness of this night!
May the Morning Star which never sets find this flame still burning:
Christ, that Morning Star, who came back from the dead,
and shed his peaceful light on all mankind,
your Son who lives and reigns for ever and ever.
Amen.

A list might be made of all the different ideas which are symbolised in this festival by darkness, light and the Easter Candle. Further work might be undertaken on the symbolism involved in the "Liturgy of Baptism" which occurs during the Easter Vigil.

It is important that the scheme is augmented by pictures and films and, if possible, a visit to a church for the Holy Saturday and Easter Day ceremonies. Occasionally this service is televised and could be videotaped by schools possessing the necessary equipment.

Work might also be undertaken on the Christian Festival of Candlemas—the ceremonies being related to Luke 2: 22-40 and seen as "dramatised theology".

Stage Three
"The Hindu Festival of Diwali"
(or "Divali", "Dipavali", "Kali Puja" or "Tihar")

Date of festival: in October or November at the end of autumn and the beginning of winter.

221

Background to the festival:

("The Festival of Diwali" is celebrated in a number of different ways by Hindus, Sikhs, Jains and Buddhists. For some it is a New Year Festival. Practices vary according to the locality, e.g. there is a contrast between the Nepalese Festival of Tihar and the Indian Festival of Diwali. (See M. M. Anderson, *The Festivals of Nepal,* George Allen & Unwin Ltd, 1971, pp 164-174 for an account of Tihar.) Some initial explanation of the Hindu *trimurti* (trinity) and the place given to *avataras* (descents of God to earth) helps to bring out the significance of this festival for Hindus.)

Hindus believe that the One God, the Universal Divine Spirit called Brahman, is expressed through many different gods. The three most important gods (which depict the three primary activities of Brahman) are *Brahma,* the Creator, *Vishnu,* the Preserver or Sustainer, and *Siva* (or *Shiva*) the Destroyer who brings the old to an end so that new may be born. These three gods form the Hindu *trimurti* or trinity. (Pictures of the three gods might be shown, e.g. Brahma a bearded man with four heads and four arms, riding a goose and carrying the Vedas, a sceptre and other insignia which show him to be the god of wisdom and creation.) Vishnu, whom many worshippers say is the one god, is the good, kind and merciful god and he and Siva are far more important and popular today than Brahma.

The people of India love to tell stories about their gods. These stories, some of which are very old, are meant to teach people about the character of the gods and to show the difference between good and evil and right and wrong. Both Vishnu and Siva have wives or "consorts" and these are goddesses. The name of Vishnu's wife is *Lakshmi* (or *Sri*) and Siva's wife is called *Devi* (or *Uma, Parvati, Durga* or *Kali*). Lakshmi, Vishnu's wife, is the goddess of good fortune, wealth and happiness. She is often represented as a beautiful golden woman, usually sitting or standing on a lotus, her symbol. She is devoted to her husband, Vishnu, and is often shown in pictures and statues massaging his feet. Hindus believe that life is a constant struggle between good and evil. In the normal course of events, good and evil are evenly matched in the world; at times, however, the balance is destroyed and evil gains the upper hand. Such a situation is considered unfair to men and so at such times it is Vishnu, the Preserver, who intervenes by descending to earth in an "incarnation" or "avatar" ("avatar" means "descent"). Vishnu's descents are therefore designed to provide man with protection and guidance. According to Hindu mythology, Vishnu has descended to earth nine times, each time being accompanied by his devoted wife, Lakshmi. The outward form of Vishnu and Lakshmi have

222

sometimes been human and sometimes animal. Each time they have descended they have had different names.

Vishnu's "avatars" are :
1 *Matsya,* a fish. (In the Hindu Deluge Myth.)
2 *Kurma,* a tortoise.
3 *Varaha,* a boar.
4 *Narasinha,* half-man and half-lion.
5 *Vamana,* a dwarf.
6 *Parasurama,* the son of a Brahmin (priest).
7 *Ramachandra* or *Rama,* a prince who became a king.
8 *Krishna,* a handsome cowherd.
9 *Buddha,* a teacher.

Vishnu's tenth avatar is still to come. According to Hindu belief, he will come to earth riding a white horse, *Kalki,* when evil has completely overcome goodness.

Vishnu's most important avatars are Rama and Krishna. He is worshipped through these two forms throughout India today. When he descended as Rama, his wife, Lakshmi, descended as the princess *Sita.* When he descended as Krishna, Lakshmi became both *Radha,* a cow-girl who falls in love with Krishna, and *Rukmini,* Krishna's wife.

The story of Krishna is told in a book called the *Bhagavad-Gita* or "the Song of the Lord" and the story of Rama and Sita in *"The Ramayana"* or "the Career of Rama". These stories were composed between 200 B.C. and 22 A.D. and they are the best known and most loved stories in India. Many Hindus know the *Bhagavad-Gita* by heart, although it is about the length of the Christian New Testament.

(At this point the story of Rama and Sita and their victory over Ravana, the powerful demon king from Ceylon, might be told in simple terms. It is a story of the victory of goodness and faithfulness over evil and treachery. A useful account is provided in *A Hindu Family in Britain* by Peter Bridger, R.E.P., 1969. For a more detailed account for use with older children see Veronica Ions, *Indian Mythology,* Paul Hamlyn, 1967.)

The festival:

"The Festival of Diwali" is a festival of lights in honour of Lakshmi, the goddess of good fortune, wealth and happiness who loves light. (Bengalis worship Kali, the wife of Siva, instead.) For months before the actual festival Hindu women and girls make hundreds of candles and lamps to decorate their homes on the three nights of the festival (five in Nepal). For the actual festival candles and lamps burn at every window, verandah, doorway, courtyard wall and rooftop. Temples, such as the Lakshminarain Temple at New Delhi, are decorated with strings of lights. According to tradition, the goddess Lakshmi circles the earth on an owl on the third night of the festival (sometimes called "Lakshmi Puja"), inspecting the homes to see that they have been scrupulously cleansed and a light left burning in her honour. Sometimes people illuminate the path to their house so that the goddess may find her way. If she is pleased with what she sees she will grant the family prosperity throughout the coming year. Many families display a flower-decked statue or picture of Lakshmi during the festival.

As well as being a time to give honour to Lakshmi, Diwali is a time for changing old clothes for new ones, for the closing of old accounts and the opening of new ones, and for renewing family vows. It is appropriate that this should be done at the end of the old year and at the beginning of the New Year. In many ways these practices are similar to our custom of making "New Year Resolutions" and wishing everyone "A Happy and Prosperous New Year". The Nepalese people have a special ceremony in which sisters honour their brothers by kneeling before them and offering them flowers, nuts, fruits and rice and bestowing a "Bhai Tika" upon their foreheads. This is a line of yellow paint drawn with the little finger. The sister then says, "May your life be as long as the nut-flower remains unfading, your body hard as a walnut, and your heart as soft as butter". In some parts of India honour is also paid to cows because they have always been regarded as the visible form of Lakshmi and the "Earth Mother" who provides the essentials of life—milk, curds and butter. The cows are bathed, red paint is dabbed on their foreheads and garlands are hung round their necks.

But above all, Diwali is a time to remember that evil must be overcome by goodness, just as the darkness is overcome by light. The story of the victory of Rama and Sita over Ravana is told and sometimes danced, and people are encouraged to be like Rama and Sita. The light, therefore, is a symbol of goodness and truth —something to remind Hindus of their duty to fight against evil and ignorance and so eventually overcome death itself. This idea is to be found in an ancient Hindu prayer which is repeated every night at twilight :

O God, lead me from darkness to light,
from the unreal to the real,
from death to immortality.

It is important that the scheme is augmented by pictures and films of Hindu practices and ceremonies, including the Festival of Diwali.

(The scheme might be extended by reference to Zoroastrianism

(Parsee) in which Ahura Mazda, "Lord Wisdom", is the God of Light and Goodness in opposition to the dark and evil Ahriman. Where teachers prefer to remain within the Judaeo-Christian tradition an examination of the symbolism of light in the Old and New Testaments might be undertaken (e.g. Creation, Moses and the burning bush and the giving of the Law, the Incarnation (John 1 : 1-14), the Epiphany (Luke 2 : 9 and Matthew 2 : 9), the Transfiguration (Mark 9 : 2-9; Mattthew 17 : 1-8; Luke 9 : 28-36), "God is Light" (1 John). Other festivals in which light is featured include the Chinese Lantern Festival, the Buddhist Full Moon Festival of Vesakha-Puja, and the Japanese Buddhist festival of lanterns called "Obon".)

Work of this nature might culminate in pupils devising their own "Festival of Light" as a basis for a school Assembly. In addition to including symbolism from the different religions examined in this scheme, the Festival might contain their own poems and prayers using the symbols of darkness and light.

2 USING SOCIAL AND ETHICAL MATERIAL

It is essential that work on material illustrating the social and ethical dimensions of religion is preceded by Depth and Situation Themes which provide children with an opportunity to become more aware of the social and ethical dimensions in their *own* experiences. Depth Themes such as "Rules and Fair Play", "Leading and Following", "Groups we belong to" and "Working Together" may be introduced in the Late Junior school and developed throughout the secondary school. Similarly, sensitivity to the need for the individual to regulate his behaviour in accordance with the needs of others and to formulate principles for moral decision-making may be developed by the use of "situations" such as those used by Piaget and Kohlberg in their research into children's moral development. The sort of situations presented by J. Fletcher in *Situation Ethics* (SCM Press Ltd, 1966) may also be valuable as a basis for work with older secondary pupils. Work of this nature has as its intention the development of what Piaget has called the "morality of cooperation or reciprocity", the basic elements of which are awareness of other people's points of view, realisation that moral rules grow out of human relationships, and the individual's incipient moral autonomy. Unfortunately, religion is usually associated with the imposition of a set of rules upon the individual which not only deprives him of his own moral autonomy but serves to reinforce and perpetuate "moral realism", the basic elements of which are acceptance of rules as moral absolutes issuing from an authority which is to be respected and feared, namely God. In order to offset this effect it is important that work on the ethical dimension of religion is approached "phenomenologically"—i.e. examined in terms of the beliefs and intentions of the adherents to a particular faith so that the observance of ethical teaching is seen as a way in which a person expresses his religious commitment. Consequently material should be taken from a variety of faiths rather than from a single faith such as Christianity. Furthermore, those elements in the ethical teaching of a faith which actively foster personal moral autonomy should be given special attention. For example : Jesus's independent attitude and refusal to subscribe to laws, rules and opinions which debased man's freedom, integrity and dignity; the emphasis in Buddhism and Christian mysticism on personality transformation through a process in which anxiety, guilt, personal ambition and envy are replaced by serenity and compassion and by a profound freedom from psychological dependence on others.

An example of social and ethical material for use with children from eleven onwards.

Aim: To initiate children into Religion as a unique mode of thought and awareness by acquainting them with material illustrating its social and ethical dimensions.

Theme: Communities of Faith.

Objectives: To provide children with an opportunity to :
1   gain elementary knowledge of the distinctive beliefs, practices and forms of organisation of five communities of faith—Jewish, Christian, Muslim, Hindu and Sikh;
2   discern how acceptance of particular ethical teaching follows from commitment to a particular religious belief or a religious perspective;
3   discern the relationship between religious belief and conduct;
4   compare and contrast the different bases of religious belief and practice;
5   discern common elements in the ethical teaching of five major religions;
6   become sensitive to the need to examine religion from the point of view of its adherents.

Content and Learning Experiences:

Stage One
The Jewish community

(a) *The birth of the Jewish nation*

Semites scattered throughout the Middle East from 15th-13th centuries B.C. Some in Palestine (Canaan), some in Egypt. Related to the Hyksos who controlled Egypt until c. 1580 B.C. When the Egyptians re-conquered Egypt (XVIII and XIX Dynasties) those Hebrews who were in Egypt became slaves. Exodus from Egypt under the leadership of Moses who acted as a mediator between Yahweh and the Hebrews. Exodus seen as Yahweh's intervention into history on behalf of the Hebrews. Yahweh "saved" the Hebrews and made them his Chosen People—central to the faith of the Jews. The scattered Hebrew people now given unity through their faith in Yahweh. Solemn ratification of a covenant between Yahweh and the Hebrews of the Exodus on Mount Sinai. Duty to one's neighbour expressed as a duty to God. Decalogue (Exodus 20) designed to meet the needs of the time—provided a basis for com-

227

munity life and prevented fragmentation occurring through inter-marriage and the adoption of other gods. A theocracy. Hebrews no longer a tribal or racial group, but a religious community, the nation of Israel, committed to loyalty to God. The Decalogue (and the laws that were later added to it) became the treaty document between Yahweh and Israel—it is seen as binding on all the people. To break it is to commit a "sin" against God. Early community life centred round the Ark and the Tabernacle. Development of the "cult" and the worship of God through sacrifice, prayer, fasting and the fulfilment of religious/ethical duties. Development of scripture showing how Yahweh acted to fulfil his purpose through Israel. Institution of feasts and festivals to remind Jews of their duty to Yahweh and to celebrate Yahweh's acts. Emphasis on the family. Religious and political life of Israel centred on the Temple. During and after the Exile (586 B.C.) it centred on the synagogue and the home. Development of extra-Biblical writings interpreting the Torah.

(b) *The Jewish community today*

Still remembering and honouring Yahweh's covenant with Israel at Sinai through the observance of the Law and the preservation of customs, feasts and festivals. Unity maintained through this despite the present fragmented nature of the Jewish people. Continuation of policy of particularism or exclusivism introduced during the Exile; e.g. still opposed to intermarriage. Three branches of Judaism—Orthodox, Conservative and Reform.

Activities might include reading the Ten Commandments and discussing their relevance to man in the 20th century. Reference might also be made to Micah 6 : 8; Ecclesiastes 12; and to such statements as, "He that loves his neighbour has fulfilled the law"; "Loving-kindness is greater than law; and the charities of life are more than all ceremonies".

A Rabbi might be invited to school to talk about the local Jewish community and to answer questions about Jewish belief and practice.

Stage Two
The Christian community

(a) *The birth of the Christian community*

Early Christians united by their commitment to Jesus as Son of God, Lord and God Incarnate. Commitment the result of the preaching of the Gospel that Jesus rose from the dead and that

228

through his death men's sins are forgiven by God. Emphasis on belief in Jesus as "Saviour". Just as his death established a new relationship (or covenant) between God and man, so his teaching established a new insight into God as loving and forgiving father. Because God is loving, man must be loving too. (Compare Jewish view, "You shall be holy, for I the Lord your God am holy", Leviticus 19 : 2.) Man learns to love God by learning to love man. Man is required also to be forgiving—"And forgive us our trespasses as we forgive them that trespass against us . . .". His love and forgiveness should extend to his enemies and those that harm him.

Early development of the Church—seen as the Body of Christ inspired and guided by the Holy Spirit. Not merely a voluntary association of disciples but the New Israel. Christ's teaching handed on by the Church partly through Tradition and partly through Scripture. Expression of Christian teaching through Christian doctrine—"that which is taught". Division of Christians over the question of "authority". Catholics hold that the Church's teaching has absolute authority over the individual; Protestants confine their authority to the Bible, guaranteed by its appeal to the individual conscience rather than by the consent of the Church. Different denominations adopt different forms of Church organisation and different attitudes to the Sacraments.

(b) *The Christian community today*

Still proclaiming the Gospel of Christ as the basis of man's salvation from sin and judgment. Communal life sustained by the preaching of the Word and the taking of the Sacraments. Accepting the Ten Commandments but applying the Christian ethic of love to circumstances demanding a moral judgment.

Activities might include reading and discussing Jesus's ethical teaching and relating it to his view of God as Father of all men, e.g. Matthew 5-7; 1 Corinthians 13; Romans 12 : 14-21; 1 John 4 : 16, 20-21; James 2 : 14-17. Does Jesus's teaching provide us with useful guides for moral decision-making? Local clergy, representing different denominations, might be invited to talk about their church and to answer questions about their faith and its application to everyday life.

Stage Three
The Muslim community

(a) *The birth of Islam*

The revelation of Allah, the One God, to the prophet Muhammad

(570-632 A.D.)—the "seal" of the prophets. Acceptance of this revelation seen in terms of "submission" or total "surrender" to the will of Allah as laid down in the Qur'an. A "Muslim" is one who has "surrendered" his life to Allah. Belief and action bound together. Acceptance, therefore, of "iman" (doctrine), "ibadat" (religious duty) and "ihsan" (right conduct). These three are based on the Qur'an, on the Hadith (traditions) and on the "shari'ah" (traditional law). Belief that Allah revealed a total pattern for the life of man, not just a religion; Islam. No separation of religious duty and social duty. Strong emphasis on the "brotherhood" of Islam—united through their acceptance of common beliefs and practices. Comprehensive legislation for every act from birth to death. Unbelief the greatest sin. Social sense developed through compulsory almsgiving ("zakat"), pilgrimage, fasting (Ramadan), feasts and festivals (e.g. the birthday of Muhammad, the New Year of Hijra, Id-ul-Fitr and Id-ul-Adha) and prayer. Laws about marriage and divorce; prohibition of alcohol, eating the meat of dead or strangled animals, pork, lending money on interest, gambling, sex in all respects outside marriage, lying, stealing, cheating, murdering and committing suicide.

(b) *The Muslim community today*

The emphasis should be placed on the Muslim community in Britain. Most of the Muslim immigrants come from Pakistan; some come from East Africa and the West Indies. There is still a tendency for them to live apart from the rest of society. Men and boys appear to integrate into British society more quickly than the women and girls. Why? Islam is slowly adapting itself to the changed conditions of the 20th century. What sort of beliefs and attitudes are particularly incompatible with life today? What beliefs do Muslims hold in common with Christians and Jews? Compare and contrast the different forms of social organisation adopted by these three religions. Would you expect Jews, Christians and Muslims to adopt the same attitudes to ethical problems? e.g. stealing, killing, war, poverty, marriage and so on. Why is there so much hostility between Jews and Muslims at the present time?

Activities might include reading and discussing some of the passages from the Qur'an which deal with conduct (e.g. Sura 4.40; Sura 2.172). The local imam might be invited to talk about Islam and the way in which it affects the lives of Muslims.

Stage Four
The Hindu community

(a) *The Hindu community today*

(It is not advisable to attempt to trace the origins of Hinduism within this scheme.)

Most Hindus worship either Vishnu or Siva. Vishnu, the benevolent and merciful god who defends goodness against evil, is often worshipped in the form of Lord Rama and Lord Krishna—two of his nine "avataras" or "descents". Rama is seen as the ideal man, and his wife, Sita, the ideal woman. Many Hindus worship both Rama and Krishna as gods. They follow the way of devotion ("bhakti-yoga") as a means of salvation from the "round of births" to oneness with Brahman, the Universal Divine Spirit. The way of devotion is taught in the *Bhagavad-Gita,* the most popular scripture in India. Krishna, the incarnation of Vishnu, reveals to the warrior-prince Arjuna, that man should come to God in love, because man is dear to God. Consider the following passage :

Listen again to my supreme word, the most secret of all. Well beloved art thou of me, therefore I shall tell thee what is good for thee. Fix thy mind on me, be devoted to me, sacrifice to me, prostrate thyself to me, so that thou shalt come to me. I promise thee truly, for thou art dear to me. (*Bhagavad-Gita,* 18, 64f.)

Many Hindus use statues of Krishna, Rama and other gods as aids to devotion. They offer them flowers, scent, incense, lights and food. Many Hindus have a shrine to their god in their home and begin each day with bathing, performing rituals and prayers and reading passages from the Hindu Scriptures. Each person tries to make his own soul fit for God. Corporate acts of worship are not compulsory in Hinduism. Another way of salvation, "karma-yoga", is through doing good deeds and performing one's duties and responsibilities. These vary according to the Hindu's "caste" or class. Originally there were four castes—Brahmins (priests), Kshatriyas or Rajanyas (warriors), Vaishyas (merchants, farmers, artisans), and Shudras (servants). Members of the first three castes are "twice-born" and they wear a sacred thread over the left shoulder across the body to the waist, the colours of these threads are white, red and yellow respectively. Today there are many more classes, mostly determined by birth and occupation. Some people were called "Untouchables" and these performed menial or dirty tasks. Ghandi tried to improve their religious and social position by calling them "God's people" ("Harijans"). The caste system still divides the Hindu community;

231

there is little inter-marriage between the castes. Hindus are often vegetarian and teetotal; some may eat pork but none eat beef.

The family unit is very important within Hinduism and great respect is paid to parents, relatives and the elderly. The husband is the head of the family, the wife often regarding him as lord and even god.

The diversity of beliefs and practices embraced by Hinduism is often confusing to the Westerner. It is very easy to misrepresent Hinduism as a form of idolatry. The following ancient Hindu prayer reflects the tolerant attitude adopted by Hindus to the wide variety of views represented in this religion :

As different streams, having different sources, all find their way to the sea, so, O Lord, the different paths which men take all lead to Thee.

Activities might involve reading and discussing such a passage as the following :

Those who are of good conduct here—the prospect is that they will come to a pleasant birth (i.e. rebirth), either the birth of a priest, or the birth of a warrior, or the birth of a merchant. But those who are of evil conduct here—the prospect is that they will come to an evil birth, either the birth of a dog, or the birth of a swine, or the birth of an outcaste.

(Chandogya Upanishad 5.10)

Consider if the doctrine of Rebirth provides a good basis for moral behaviour.

What difficulties do Hindus have in integrating with people of different faiths? Why, for example, has there always been a tension between Muslims and Hindus?

Consider the close relationship between belief and action in the following passage :

Thou, O Lord, dwellest in the hearts of those who have no lust, anger, infatuation, pride, delusion, avarice, excitement, affection or hatred, hypocrisy, vanity, deceitfulness; those who are dear to all, benevolent to all, equable in joy and sorrow, praise and blame, who speak the truthful and the pleasant and are endowed with discrimination, who, while awake or asleep, have taken shelter under thee and indeed have no other resort but thyself.

(Tulsidas, Holy Lake of Rama 2.130)

Compare the above with Galatians 5 :16—6 :5.

Where possible, a Hindu might be invited to talk about his faith and its application to everyday life.

(a) *The birth of Sikhism*

From the 11th century A.D. onwards Muslims began to invade India. By the 16th century the Turkish "Mogul Empire" was established in India and eventually this Muslim Empire comprised nearly all of the subcontinent. Relations between the Muslims and Hindus were often violent but eventually they came to exist side by side. Although they cooperated together over commercial and political matters they were divided on matters of religious belief and practice.

A poor Muslim weaver by the name of Kabir began to go about teaching that there is truth in both the Hindu and Muslim religions. He influenced a Hindu named Nanak Chand (1469-1538 A.D.) who found a similarity between the Hindu "bhakti-yoga", the way of devotion, and the emphasis on the need to love God being preached by Muslim mystics. These Muslim mystics, who recognised other religions also as ways to God, greatly attracted Nanak. Following a vision of God, he began to preach, "There is but one God, the true, the creator". He rejected the Hindu belief in "avataras" but continued to believe in rebirth after death. He said that caste divisions were wrong because all men and women are the children of God. He tried to break down the barriers between Hindus and Muslims by declaring, "There is no Hindu and no Muslim". He called God the Name (or "Nam"). Those who followed Nanak called him "Guru" (teacher) and he called them "Sikhs" (disciples). "Sikhism" was at first encouraged by Akbar, the Mogul Emperor, but on his death the Sikhs were persecuted. Nanak was followed by ten Gurus, all of whom were perfect and incarnated in his spirit. The fifth Guru, Arjun, brought together a collection of teachings of a number of people, Kabir, Nanak, Hindu teachers and others, and combined them with some of his own verses into a sacred book called the "Adi Granth" or "The Guru Granth Sahib". After the tenth Guru, Gobind Singh, the Sikhs said that from then onwards the Granth would be their only Guru. Thus they revere it as a living teacher who instructs and inspires them every day. The Granth is composed of hymns to God and these are sung every day in Sikh temples. No religious book in the world is shown such deep respect and veneration by its believers. It is written in Punjabi.

After the martyrdom of the ninth Guru, Guru Gobind Singh organised the Sikhs into a military community called the "Khalsa" ("God's Party"). Since the 18th century most male Sikhs have undergone an initiation ceremony called "amrit" and have received the name of "Singh" (Lion). Female members are given the name "Kaur" (Princess). Not all Sikhs are members of the khalsa but those men who are must vow to observe the "Five K's" (i.e. the *kesh,* uncut hair; the *kanga,* a wooden comb symbolising self-discipline; the *kachs,* short trousers giving greater mobility in battle; the *kara,* a steel bracelet worn on the right wrist symbolising the strength and unity of the khalsa and reminding the Sikh that God is one eternal; the *kirpan,* a small sword or knife, the symbol of authority reminding the Sikh of his duty to defend truth. The turban has also become a traditional part of the Sikh's dress.) Nearly all Sikhs are Punjabis.

(b) *The Sikh community today*

The emphasis should be placed on the Sikh community in Britain. (See W. Owen Cole, *A Sikh Family in Britain,* R.E.P., 1972.) The importance of the "gurdwara" (temple) as the focal point of the Sikh community. The emphasis on communal life and sharing through "Karah Parshad"—the sacred food—and the "guru ka langar"—the temple of bread or free kitchen.

What difficulties are Sikhs likely to encounter in adapting to life in Britain? Consideration might be given to the following examples of Sikh ethical teaching:

Regard all men as equal, since God's light is contained in the heart of each.

Fight with no weapon but the word of God; use no means but a pure faith.

Cruelty, worldly love, avarice and wrath are four streams of fire.

Let compassion be thy mosque, let faith be thy prayer-mat, let honest living be thy Qur'an, let modesty be the rules of observance, let piety be the fasts thou keepest.

Religion consisteth not in a patched coat, or a Yogi's staff, or in ashes smeared over the body; religion consisteth not in ear-rings worn on a shaven head, or in the blowing of horns. Abide pure amid the impurities of the world; thus thou shalt find the way of religion. Religion consisteth not in mere words; he who looketh on all men as equal is religious.

A member of the Sikh faith might be invited to talk about his religion and its application to everyday life.

3 USING DOCTRINAL MATERIAL

An example of doctrinal material for use with children from fourteen onwards.

Aim: To initiate children into religion as a unique mode of thought and awareness by acquainting them with material illustrating its doctrinal dimension.

Subject: The Three Jewels of Buddhism.

Objectives: To provide children with an opportunity to :
1 relate earlier work on material illustrating the mythological, ritual, social and ethical dimensions of Buddhism to the fundamental doctrine of which they are an expression;
2 gain insight into the key concepts of "enlightenment", "nibbána" and "Dhamma";
3 examine and discuss "The Four Noble Truths" and "The Eightfold Path";
4 relate the doctrine of Buddhism to the initial experiences of Gautama and the subsequent experiences of Buddhists, especially the Sangha;
5 establish an understanding of the fundamental doctrine of the Buddha prior to examining its development within Hinayana and Mahayana Buddhism;
6 consider the appeal of Buddhism as "religion without Theism" in the 20th century.

Content and Learning Experiences:

Stage One
The background to Buddhist doctrine

It is desirable that children are introduced to Buddhism first through an examination of its mythological and ritual dimensions and then through an examination of its social and ethical dimensions. This means that a child's first acquaintance with Buddhism may be in the Junior school through the stories and legends associated with Gautama. From these he could move on to become acquainted with some of the "external" features of the religion—its temples and shrines, images of the Buddha, ceremonies and rituals (e.g. pujas, marriage and funeral ceremonies and so on), the use of prayer wheels and flags, lights, incense, joss-sticks, bells, drums, the devotion shown to the Buddha by monks as well as laymen and so on. The social and ethical dimensions of Buddhism, introduced in the early secondary school, might be illustrated by reference to the life of Buddhist monks, their observance of the ten moral rules, their study of the Buddhist Scriptures, their teaching duties and their long periods of meditation. The life of a Buddhist layman may also be examined, e.g. his acceptance of five or eight of the moral rules, his careful choice of an occupation in keeping with Buddhist teaching, his charitable acts and his generosity to monks and neighbours and so on.

The Ten Precepts

The ten moral rules observed by Buddhist monks and novices are to refrain from :
1 taking the life of any living creature (the principle of "ahimsa" upheld by Jains);
2 stealing;
3 sexual misconduct;
4 lying and deceiving;
5 the use of alcohol and drugs;
6 eating after midday;
7 attending dancing, singing and dramatic spectacles;
8 using scents, garlands and ornaments;
9 sleeping on a raised and upholstered bed;
10 accepting gold and silver (i.e. money).

All Buddhist lay people undertake to observe the first five of these—"The Five Precepts". Some Buddhist lay-followers ("upásakas") also observe numbers six-nine on holy days.

It is important that Buddhism is related to the Indian social and religious culture from which it sprang. An understanding of Hinduism is, therefore, a pre-requisite to understanding Buddhist beliefs.

Where children have received none of this teaching it is advisable to postpone work on doctrine until the mythological, ritual, social and ethical dimensions of Buddhism have been covered.

Stage Two
The Middle Path

Gautama's search for "Enlightenment" (seen initially as "peace of mind", "Wisdom" or "Truth about Life" until the concept of "Nirvana" or "Nibbána" has been explained) led him first to Hindu sages who taught him philosophy and yoga, then to Hindu priests (whose blood sacrifices revulsed him) and afterwards to extreme mortification and asceticism. Finally he came to meditation which led to his "Enlightenment". He realised that if man places himself in the centre of his life, if all life is regarded from his own selfish standpoint, then he is doomed to suffer. The path to freedom and peace is the extinction of self for it is the self which makes man cling to his desires. And by having desires he suffers. Gautama thus became the "Enlightened One", the "Buddha" or the "Awakened One". He set out these truths in four sections—they are called "The Four Noble Truths":

1 All life is suffering ("duhkha").
2 Suffering is caused by man's desires ("trsna"). (Note that one man's cravings lead to other men suffering.)
3 To escape from suffering, one must rid oneself of these desires (e.g. the self-centred insistence upon "me" and "mine").
4 To be freed from desires, one must follow the Middle Path. (It is important to expand on these statements in order to assist understanding.)

Stage Three
The Eightfold Path

This is the Buddha's "prescription" for attaining "Nibbána"—the opposite to "duhkha"; the extinction of all greed, hatred and misunderstanding about life; the attainment of a state of mind characterised by generosity, love and clear insight.

1 Right understanding, views and beliefs.
(e.g. The Four Noble Truths.)
2 Right thought, aims or intentions.
(e.g. to renounce self and selfishness and ill will towards others.)
3 Right speech.
(e.g. to say what is kind and true; not to gossip or slander.)
4 Right action or behaviour.
(e.g. The Five Precepts given earlier.)
5 Right occupation or livelihood.
(e.g. choosing an occupation which helps others rather than harms them.)
6 Right mental effort.
(e.g. to be critical of oneself and to cultivate the right states of mind.)
7 Right mindfulness.
(e.g. keeping truth in mind and avoiding the temptation of feeling self-satisfied.)
8 Right concentration.
(e.g. to withdraw from external objects and turn to the realities of truth and love of mankind.)

Items one and two constitute Wisdom; items three, four and five constitute Morality; items six, seven and eight constitute Meditation. At the beginning, however, the attitudes given under one and two are only possible by way of faith—faith in the Buddha and in his teaching. When the attitude given under eight is reached, faith finds its proof in the wisdom gained. Thus, the ultimate purpose of "The Eightfold Path" is to enable the follower to perceive directly and immediately the reality of which the Buddha spoke and which is hidden from men who are immersed in ordinary existence. As indicated earlier, this reality is called "Nibbána".

(There is a tendency for people to equate the concept of nibbána with the Christian concept of "Heaven". This can be very misleading. The most useful approach with secondary pupils is to relate this word to another Pali word—"nibbuta"—a word describing the ideal man. This word was originally used to describe the state of a man who had recovered from a fever. The English equivalent is to say that the man is "cool". Buddhists adopted the word nibbuta to describe the condition of the man in whom the fever of evil desire had been cured, the man who was "cooled" from all passion and selfish craving. "Nibbána" is, then, a term used to describe the state of the nibbuta-man, the ideal man. The nibbuta-man is thus one who experiences the "real" itself and does not mistakenly regard "illusion" as real. In this sense, nibbána is ultimate reality. Any attempt to try and analyse nibbána's transcendental dimension is likely to lead to confusion. It can only be indicated by negatives—"unborn, unoriginated, uncreated, unformed and so on". As with the concept of "heaven", pupils should be discouraged from identifying it with a place to which people go after death. Rather it is a state of mind, a quality of existence attainable during life. Buddhists emphasise, however, that few people can attain nibbána in one lifetime. For this reason they accept the Hindu idea of rebirth (although it is not given the same interpretation as Hinduism gives to it). One who has attained nibbána is given the title of "Arhat" or "worthy one" and at the death of his body he attains the final nibbána called "Pari-nibbána", the nibbána of no return. This means that he will not be born again in the world. When Gautama achieved Enlightenment he declared, "this is my last existence, now there is no rebirth".)

Stage Four
"The Three Jewels" or "The Threefold Refuge"

Taken together, "The Four Noble Truths" and "The Eightfold Path" constitute the Buddha's doctrine. This is called "Dhamma". The word "Dhamma", however, has an even more specific meaning. It is "that which is self-subsistent, that which alone exists in its own right and without dependence on any prior reality". (T. Ling, *A History of Religion East and West*, Macmillan, 1968, p 87.) The Buddha taught the transient quality of all earthly experiences and the absence of a permanent enduring private "self" or "soul" within the human individual. He did not deny, however, that there was something eternal, something which was not subject to change. In the midst of a world in which nothing lasts and all things are in a state of flux, there is an enduring reality, changeless and eternal. This is "Dhamma". (Trevor Ling observes that it is strongly akin to the Greek notion of the Logos, that which upholds all things.) The immediate way of encountering the Dhamma is in that form of it which is the Buddha's doctrine of "The Eightfold Path". (Note that nibbána itself is also eternal and unchanging.) The Buddha and his Dhamma are seen, therefore, as man's means of salvation, man's *refuge* from meaningless existence characterised by suffering. Buddhists, therefore, turn to the Buddha and his teaching in faith that it is the way to reality, to nibbána. A man cannot, however, "travel" or "walk" the Eightfold Path unassisted. To help him he has the Buddha's teaching (as distinct from his doctrine) and this is set out in the Buddhist Scriptures. Northern Buddhists ("Mahayana Buddhists") and Southern Buddhists ("Hinayana Buddhists") have adopted different Scriptures and have developed the Buddha's teaching in different ways. The Scriptures of the Southern Buddhists are called "The Three Baskets" ("Tri-pitaka") —"The Vinaya-Pitaka" (monastic rules), "The Sutta-Pitaka" (discourses) and "The Abhidhamma-Pitaka" (supplements to the doctrines). The Northern Buddhists also accept the Tri-pitaka but add others of their own (e.g. "The Lotus Scripture" or "The Lotus of the Wonderful Law"). Although these Scriptures are read by lay-men, it is the monks who are expert in their interpretation and application. The monks are also expert in the art of meditation and concentration—something else which the lay-man finds difficult to learn and practise on his own. Thus, parallel in importance to the Buddha and the Dhamma is the "Sangha"—the monastic order founded by the Buddha and made up originally of the group of men who devoted themselves to the practice of meditation and the pursuit of transcendental wisdom under his guidance. The Sangha, therefore, is also a "refuge" for the man seeking truth. The fundamental "creed" of Buddhism, then, combines the Buddha, the Dhamma and the Sangha into a single formula uttered by millions of Buddhists each day :

I take refuge in the Buddha, our Lord,
I take refuge in the Teaching revealed by him,
I take refuge in the Order which he has founded.

Or :

> I go to the Buddha for refuge,
> I go to the Dhamma for refuge,
> I go to the Sangha for refuge.

Further Stages

In this scheme the fundamental doctrine of Buddhism has been developed in terms of a system of thought which is agnostic. In order to make a link between earlier work on the mythological, ritual, social and ethical dimensions of Buddhism, the scheme needs to be developed first by way of an examination of Hinayana beliefs and then by way of the more specifically "religious" interpretation of Mahayana Buddhism. Zen Buddhism is better left until the end.

Select Bibliography

(Completely Revised in 1978)

Part One of the bibliography (*Books for Pupils*, Sections A–H) consists of pupil's books and materials which might confidently be used, or adapted for use, within the Conceptual Framework for R.E. developed in Chapters 5 and 6.

The titles have been arranged in the following sections:

A. **The enrichment of experience.**
B. **Thematic approaches to religious, moral and social education.**
C. **The Bible and its background.**
D. **World Religions/Religious Studies.**
E. **Christian Studies.**
F. **Biography/Christian Lives/Heroes/Religious Leaders.**
G. **Children's literature in religious and moral education.**
H. **Discussion materials.**

Section **I.** consists of books and materials for use in **Worship and Assembly.**

Part Two of the bibliography (*Books for Teachers*, Sections J–Q) adds to and updates titles recommended in the text within the fields of religious education and religious and educational studies. Select lists of agencies serving the R.E. teacher have been added, including suppliers of audio-visual aids and resource materials together with the addresses of all publishers with titles listed in the bibliography.

This information has been arranged in the following sections:

J. **Reports, pamphlets and statements on Religious Education (1970-1978).**
K. **The Theory and Practice of Religious Education (1961-1978).**
L. **Agreed Syllabuses of Religious Instruction/Education (1966-1978).**
M. **Some useful books for the teacher:**
   (i) Religious and Theological Studies.
   (ii) Educational Studies.
N. **Journals and periodicals for the R.E. teacher.**
O. **Services to R.E. teachers.**
P. **Suppliers of audio-visual aids and resource materials.**
Q. **Publishers of titles listed in the select bibliography.**

A. The enrichment of experience

B. J. Bampton: *Living and Growing* (Macmillan, 1971)   (5–8's)
Alive; Babies; Growing Up; Homes; Protection; Plants.

P. Blakeley: *Make Up a Year* series (A & C Black, 1971)   (6–8's)
Suddenly it's Spring; Summer Sun; In the Autumn; Nip of Winter.

P. Blakeley: *Things I Like* series (A & C Black, 1971)   (5–8's)
Colours; Shapes; Sounds; First and Last; My Home and Yours; Rough and Smooth etc.

P. Egan (Ed.): *Benjamin Books* (Church Information Office, 1975)   (5–8's)
Here I am!; I was born; I'm special; I have a name; When I grow up; The day Grandma died; Who can I play with?; Can I cross the road?; Where are you, duck?; Who are you?; What shall I choose?; How can we help?.

M. Fergus: *Discovering* series (Lion Publishing, 1974)   (5–8's)
Discovering Everyday Things; Discovering Colours; Discovering Out of Doors; Discovering at the Zoo.

R. Jones (Ed.): *Preludes* series (Heinemann Ed., 1971)   (6–9's)
Poetry and photographs on: *Families; Work and Play; Five Senses; Weathers;* plus Teacher's Book

Ladybird Books: *People at Work* (Series 606B)   (6–9's)
The fireman; policeman; nurse; fisherman; farmer; builder; postman; miner; soldier; sailor; airman; roadmakers; car builders; shipbuilders; pottery makers; lifeboat men.

C. Milburn: *My Five Senses* series (Blackie, 1973)   (5–8's)
I Can Hear, See, Smell, Touch, Taste (plus a workbook).

K. A. Shoesmith: *Use Your Senses* series (Burke Books, 1973)   (5–8's)
Look and See; Listen and Hear; Scent and Smell; Taste and Flavour; Touch and Feel.

J. M. Taylor (Trans.): *The Who am I?* series (Blackwell, 1975)   (5–7's)
I am air; I am fire; I am a drop of water; I am sun.

242

D. Wrigley: *Query Books* series (Good Reading Ltd.,   (8–11's)
1977)
*What is a Person?; What is a Smile?; Do you
Fear?; Do you ever Wonder?; Do you see
Equal People?; Do you Understand?; Are
you Living?; Can you Choose?*

B. Thematic Approaches to Religious, Moral and Social Education

Basil Blackwell: *RE Theme Cards,* by D. Barlow and   (9–12's)
K. Harvey (1973)
16 workcards and a teacher's book on
*praying, courage, forgiving, thanking, com-
municating, living together, growing, creating, serving, caring, respecting, remembering,
building, discovering, being tested,* and
sharing.

Geoffrey Chapman: *Themes of Life,* by D. Byron   (9–13's)
Evans (1971)
News, Water, People of Courage, and *Man
the Discoverer.* Each theme has 8
workcards, cards 7 and 8 being concerned with moral and religious education.
The themes introduce World Religions.

Darton, Longman and Todd: *Eleven to Sixteen* series,   (11–16's)
edited by D. Lance (1970)
Topic booklets which include *Racial Pre-
judice; Attitudes to Adults; Conscience and
Sincerity; Commitment and Indifference;
Violence; Childhood; Loneliness and Solitude;
Making up our Minds; Belief; Poverty and
Wealth; the Individual and the State* etc.

Denholm House Press: *Search for Meaning* series,   (14–16's)
edited by C. Fletcher (1976)
6 pupils' books, 6 teachers' pamphlets, 3
cassette tapes and 5 slide folios.
1. *The One and Only Me* by I. Champer-
nowne; 2. *Something After Death?* by G.
Parrinder; 3. *Am I Free?* by C. Fletcher;
4. *Who is my Neighbour?* by R. Trudgian;
5. *Image and Imagination* by R. Rolls;
6. *Has Science exploded God?* by K.
Barnes

Through Children's Eyes series, by G. Duncan (1973–74) (6–8's)

Resource books to enable teachers of younger children to integrate R.E. into the curriculum.

1. *Discovering their World* (1973)

   Themes include: *Creation* (seasons, space, moon and stars, daytime and night-time, water, seaside); *Nature* (flowers, birds, trees, animals, colour); *All about Me* (seeing, hearing, touch, smell, taste); *Food* (bread, fish, parties, harvest).

2. *People in their World* (1974)

   Themes include: *Friends Everywhere* (my friends, we have fun together, caring for each other, we must try to share, friends in other lands): *Families and Homes* (me and my family, babies and young children, homes we know, homes in other lands, children without homes); *All About People* (people who care for us, people who provide for us, other important people, farms and farmers).

Evans Brothers Ltd: *Integrated Themes,* by J. Bainbridge and O. Aston (1972-3) (11–16's)

Air and Flight; Conservation; Fire and Flame; Man-Made; Time and Change; Water.

Rupert Hart-Davis Educational: *Readiness for Religion* series, edited by R. J. Goldman (1966–67) (9–11's)

A Diary for Teachers of Infants by F & P Cliff

About Myself by C. Parker (5 booklets)

What is the Bible? by E. Rolls *et al* (4 booklets)

The importance of Bread by M. Hughes (10 workcards)

Sheep and Shepherds by R. J. Goldman (12 workcards)

Symbols by N. J. Bull (4 booklets)

Light by W & I Bulman (6 booklets)

(All titles are neo-confessional in approach)

Frontiers of Enquiry series, by R. Richardson & J. Chapman (1971)   (15–18's)
4 books: *The Gods; In Love and War; Free for All; Heart and Mind.*

Journeys into Religion (1977–78)
The Schools Council Project on R.E. in Secondary Schools.
See page 255 for further details of pupil's materials.

Holmes McDougall Ltd: *Living Light,* by A. James,   (7–12's)
E. Penny, I. McDonald, I. Fairweather (1970–73)
An experience-based approach to R.E., predominantly Christian in outlook but with an introduction to world religions in Book 4.

Book 1	(7–8's)
Book 2	(8–9's)
Book 3	(9–10's)
Book 4	(11–12's)

Living Bible, by W. A. Shaw (1966–1970)   (13–16's)
An approach to the bible through contemporary themes and experiences.
Book 1 *Adventure in Religion;* Book 2 *Has Life a Purpose?;* Book 3 *Encounter with Love;* Book 4 *Commitment.*

Growing Christian, edited by A. Bullen   (7–11's)
(1970)
A series for use in Catholic primary schools.

Books 1 and 2 include: *We depend on*   (7–9's)
people; we care for people; the family grows up; people who are brave; the air above us; in touch with people.

Books 3 and 4 include: *homes; light;*   (9–11's)
water; communities; the bible; senses and sacraments; serving others.

Growing Faith, by T. McGurk, A. Purnell and D. Dodgson (1973)
A series for use in Catholic secondary schools.

Book 1	(12–13's)
Book 2	(13–14's)
Book 3	(14–15's)
Book 4 (in preparation)	(15–16's)

245

Exploring Your World series, edited by J. Dean (1973).   (9–13's)
A 64-book library about ourselves and the world, graded in difficulty.
Especially relevant are the 25 books on *Man* (A. *What is Man?* – 7 books: B. *Families and Communities* – 8 books).

This is Your World series, C. Garner *et al* (1970–72)   (7–12's)
Part of an Environmental Studies Project. Books 1–5.

Hulton: *Themes for Living,* by G. Parrinder (1973)   (14–18's)
4 books: *Man and God; Goal of Life; Right and Wrong; Society.*

Longman Group Ltd: *Aware,* edited by M. Curley (1978)
Materials for social, moral and religious awareness.
First Themes (for infants and lower juniors) *Hands* (4 books: *Hands can make; hands help; hands that talk; hands*)
Homes (4 books: *a home in Palestine; animal homes; building a house; house to home*).
Second Themes (for top juniors and lower middle) *I Share* (4 books: *sharing with others; I share at home; I share a neighbourhood; People together*) *I Care* (4 books: *man cares; man grows; man cares about the world; man cares about people*).

Startline (1978) (Schools Council Moral Education 8–13 Project)   (8–13's)
6 books on *Choosing* (1. *What Shall I Do?; Growing Up; Out and About; Getting it Right; Working Things Out; Friendship*.)
Photoplay 1 – 22 black and white posters
Photoplay 2 – 144 black and white cards
Setting the Scene – figurines
Making it Happen – 32 cards
How it Happens – 28 cards
Teachers' Handbook and notes.

Lifeline (1972) (Schools Council Moral Education Project for Secondary School pupils).   (13–16's)
3 sets of cards *In Other People's Shoes (Sensitivity; Consequences; Points of View)*

5 booklets on *Proving the Rule? (Rules and individuals; What do you expect?; Who do you think I am?; In whose interest?; Why should I?)*
6 booklets on *What would you have done? (Birthday, South Africa, 1904; Solitary Confinement, Lincolnshire, 1917; Arrest! Amsterdam, 1944; Street Scene, Los Angeles, 1965; Hard luck story, South Vietnam, 1966; Gale in Hospital, London, 1969)*
Teachers' Handbook: *ME in the secondary school. Our School* – handbook on the practice of democracy by secondary school pupils.

The Developing World series, edited by R. Pitcher (1971–75)   (11–15's)
Covers geography, history, religion and science.
Religion 1–4 by B. Wigley and R. Pitcher.
Book 1, *From Fear to Faith;* Book 2, *Paths to Faith;* Book 3, *Faith Looks Outwards;* Book 4, *The Extent of Faith.*
Christian viewpoint but dealing with other religions.

Way of Wisdom series, by N. J. Bull   (9–13's)
(1970–73)
A course in moral education.
5 books: *Living with Others; Myself and Others; Rulers; Drivers; Persons.*

Lutterworth Educational: *Understanding their World,*   (5–7's)
edited by M. Kitson (1971).
Develops the topics of *Homes and Families; Patterns; Looking through a window; Growing.*

Topic Books, edited by K. E. Hyde (1970).
Each topic has two books:
Book 1   (7–9's)
Book 2   (9–11's)
The Senses; Neighbours; Homes; Books; Food; Laws; Me.

Photopaks, by P. Longley and S. Kronen-   (11–16's)
berg (1971)
1. *Discovering Religion;* 2. *Discovering Religion in the Community;* 3. *Discovering*

247

Religion in Festivals; 4. *Discovering Religion in Life and Action.*

Vision 1 and *Vision 2,* compiled by I. Wragg (1977)   (11–16's)
2 packs of fifteen leaflets plus teachers' notes for use in RE with slow learning pupils

Macmillan Education Ltd: *Exploring God's World,*   (6–8's)
edited by C. Alves and M. Stanley (1971)
30 assignment cards, three story books, six picture reference books; one planning book. Covers the topics of *babies, the sea, movement, fire, presents, homes, growth, animals, touch and texture, healing.*

Themes in Religious Education for the 9–13's,   (9—13's)
by K. N. Smith (1969)
A Teachers' book containing a large number of activities but with a strongly confessional approach.
2 sets of large, black and white class pictures available: Set 1, *The Holy Land;* Set 2, *The World-Wide Church.*

Kevin Mayhew Ltd: *Christians Today,* by M. Grimmitt and G. Read (1977)
A thematic approach to teaching Christianity in R.E. 5 themes: *Christians Together; Christians Celebrating; Christians Telling; Christians Acting; Christians Choosing.*
2 sets of 32 black and white photographs of:
1. *Christians in their Homes and Churches*
2. *Christians in their Local Community and World Community*
Book of autobiographical and personal   (9–16's)
statements of Christian faith, *Christians Telling* (1979)

Thomas Nelson & Sons Ltd: *In Focus Books*   (14–16's)
(1970–75)
Illustrated books encouraging discussion, projects and investigations of social issues.
Focus on Faiths by R. Street; *Some People are Different* by P. Mathias; *Someone to Turn to* by D. Arthur; *Somewhere to Live*

by D. Church and B. Ford; *Crime and Punishment* by D. Church and B. Ford; *Looking after Yourself* by J. Lockett; *Focus on World Problems* by D. Church and B. Ford; *People in Towns* by D. Church and B. Ford; *People in Need* by M. W. Thomas; *The Developing Nations* by N. Dalgleish.

Living Plus series, by J. Clemson (1977–78)   (11–16's)
A five year course in R.E. for lower ability groups which links explicitly religious material with poetry, literature, photographs and drawings, and with human situations.
Book 1. *Living and Belonging;* Book 2. *Living and Sharing;* Book 3. *Living and Growing;* Book 4. *Living and Becoming;* Book 5. *Living and Believing.*

Religious Education Press: *Man and Religion* series, edited by R. Dingwall (1970–73)   (9–13's)
Part 3: *The Miracle of Man*
An R.E. and Integrated Studies approach to the question, 'What is Man?' 6 books; *Operation Man; Community Man; Man the Traveller; Man the Scientist; Man the Thinker; Man the Artist.*
(See page 252 for details of further titles in this series).

Wheaton Books for Integrated Studies series, by N. J. Bull (1977)   (9–14's)
Themes approached from historical, scientific, religious, social and moral perspectives.

Book 1. *Festivals and Customs;* Book 2. *Food and Drink;* Book 3. *You and Me;* Book 4. *Light and Darkness.*

C. The Bible and its background

Bible Society: *Jesus is Born; Jesus at the Wedding; The Good Samaritan; Jesus is Alive;* etc. (1975)   (5–7's)
Colourful books using original Dutch artwork with simple captions.

Bible Societies/Collins: *The Good News Bible* (1977)
Children's Colour Edition available.

M. Boys: *Life in the Time of Jesus* (U.L.P. 1973)   (11–15's)
Uses stories to give a vivid picture of the
world in which Jesus lived.

N. J. Bull: *A First Bible Dictionary* (Hulton, 1966)   (9–13's)

A Book of Bible Activities (Hulton, 1973)   (9–13's)

The Bible Data Book (Evans, 1975)   (9–16's)

Christian Education Movement: *Discovering the New*   (11–13's)
Testament (Dimension 2, 1978)
A workbook and/or set of 10 workcards
on *Background; People; Jerusalem; The
Gospels; The Church; Paul's Letters;
Hebrews; James* and *1 Peter*.

E. W. Crabb: *Living in New Testament Days* (E. J.   (8–11's)
Arnold, 1962)

M. Cox: *The Creation* and *The Family of Man* (Collins   (9–14's)
Liturgical, 1977) from the BBC TV
series: *In the Beginning.*

A. T. Dale: *Winding Quest* (OUP, 1972) (The heart of   (11–18's)
the OT in modern English)

Denholm House Press/BFBS/NBSS: *Good News for*   (9–12's)
Boys and Girls series (1974)
Selected passages from Today's English
Version of N.T.
1. *The Coming of Jesus;* 2. *The Friends Jesus
Made;* 3. *Jesus Wins the Battle;* 4. *Things
Jesus Said;* 5. *The First Jesus People.*

J. Edwards and M. Payne: *The Old Testament and its*   (11–14's)
background (Blandford) (1969–70)
Book 1. *They Heard God's Voice – Abraham
to Solomon.*
Book 2. *They were God's Messengers –
Solomon to the Exile.*
Book 3. *They were God's People – the Exile
to Herod*

J. Edwards: *The New Testament and its Background*   (11–14's)
series (Blandford, 1977)
For use with mixed ability classes
Book 1. *Jesus of Palestine – People, Work,
Customs*
Book 2, *Jesus, Son of God – The Messiah
and his message.*

250

Book 3. *Jesus Victor! – The Acts of the Apostles*

P. Egan/A. T. Dale: *Rainbow Books* series (CIO, 1975–77).   (6–9's)
Short bible stories delightfully illustrated in colour for children. 20 titles all highly recommended.

A. Farncombe: *Stories of Bible Times* (Lutterworth, 1977–78)   (5–7's)
Well-illustrated bible stories.
Danny's Picnic; Sarah and the Search; Philip visits the Temple; Reuben and the Olive Harvest; Matthew's Day with the Sheep; Hannah's Market Day; Ben, the Fisherman's Son; Seth Goes to School.

O. B. Gregory: *Read About It* series (Wheaton/REP 1968)   (7–9's)
Books 73–96: a collection of 24-page bible stories in full colour

R. Henderson and I. Gould: *Life in Bible Times* (Chambers, 1974)   (9–12's)

Holmes McDougall Ltd: *The New English Study Bible* (compiled by F. Meade and A. Zimmermann (1970)   (9–13's)
Book 1. *Eden – Joseph in Egypt*
Birth of Jesus and First Year of Ministry
Book 2. *Flight from Egypt – Settlement*
The Second Year of Jesus's Ministry
Book 3. *Early Kings of the O.T.*
The Death of Jesus
Book 4. *The Prophets – Exile – Return*
The Resurrection and Acts of the Apostles

C. J. Kitchell: *Radio Jerusalem* (Ginn and Company, 1972)   (11–13's)
8 radio scripts reporting on the Nativity, the beheading of John the Baptist, the events of Holy Week, Pentecost, the stoning of Stephen, and the conversion of Saul.

Ladybird Books Ltd: *Series 606A*
1. *Jesus the Helper;* 2. *Jesus the Friend;* 3. *Baby Jesus;* 4. *Children of the Bible;*   (5–7's)
6. *The Parable of the Sower;* 7. *The Parable of the two New Houses.*   (7–9's)

Series 522   (6–9's)
  1. *The Child of the Temple;* 2. *The Shepherd
Boy of Bethlehem;* 3. *The Little Lord Jesus;* 4.
The Story of Joseph; 5. *Moses, Prince and
Shepherd;* 6. *Two Stories Jesus told* (Good
Samaritan and Prodigal Son); 7. *The
Story of Daniel;* 8. *Jesus by the Sea of Galilee;*
9. *Jesus calls his disciples;* 10. *Naaman and
the Little Maid;* 11. *The Story of St. Paul;*
12. *Peter the Fisherman.*

A. J. McCallen: *Listen! – Themes from the Bible retold*   (5–11's)
for children (Collins Liturgical, 1976)

D. T. Prickett (Gen. Ed.): *Getting to Know About . . . . .*   (8–13's)
series (Denholm House Press, 1975–77)
A series showing how people lived in
Bible times.
1. *Houses and Homes;* 2. *Clothes;* 3. *Food;* 4.
Learning and Playing; 5. *Animals and Birds;*
6. *Trading and Transport;* 7. *Farming and
Fishing;* 8. *The Countryside;* 9. *Places of
Worship;* 10. *People;* 11. *Festivals;* 12.
Roman Life and Customs.

M. Putman: *Denholm Bible Story Books* (Denholm   (7–10's)
Press, 1973)
1. *Jesus Teaching People;* 2. *Jesus Meeting
People;* 3. *Jesus Helping People;* 4. *Stories
Jesus Heard.*

Religious Education Press: *Man and Religion* series
(14–16's)
Part 4: *The Old Testament Scene Festivals*
by G. Hood (1972)
Crown and Testimony by J. Thomas (1972)
Fire in my Bones by D. Stacey (1975)
The Common People of the OT by J. Stacey
(1977)
Part 5: *The New Testament Scene*
The Man from Nazareth by D. Stacey
(1969)
The New Superstition by J. Stacey (1970)
The Palestine Problem by J. Newton (1972)
(See page 249 for details of further titles
in this series)

M. Richardson: *The Boy Jesus Goes A-Walking; The*   (5–8's)
*Little Man in the Tree; Jesus and the Two
Blind Men; The King's Donkey; The Children
Go to Jesus; Jesus Meets the Fishermen.*

6 bible story books, 6 packs of 8 posters and 6 packs of 8 workcards for children. (Mayhew-McCrimmon,1977).

W. Spalding and H. Joanna: *Bible Alive!* (Kevin Mayhew Ltd., 1977) (5–8's)
Stories, quizzes, pictures to paint, games etc.

A. Wainwright: *Discovering the Bible* (Holmes McDougall, 1972) (12–15's)
Incorporates projects and activities.
1. *The Bible* (1972)
2. *The Book of the Christians* (1973)

H. W. Whanslaw: *Paper Reeds and Iron Pens* (REP, 1957) (9–13's)
A pictorial record of writing and printing developments and how they gave the bible to the world.

B. R. Youngman: *The New Outlook Scripture* (Nelson, 1972) (11–16's)
1. *The Challenge of the Gospels;* 2. *The Challenge of the Old Testament;* 3. *The Challenge through the Ages;* 4. *The Challenge Today;* 5. *The Challenge to Me.*
The first 4 books cover the work of the CSE syllabuses

The Challenge of the Prophets (Nelson, 1977) (14–16's)
Suitable for use with pupils preparing for 'O' level GCE.

D. World Religions/Religious Studies

M. Ballard: *Who am I?* (Hutchinson, 1971) (16–18's)
Introduction to 7 religions.

E. Bailey: *Belief* (Batsford 1974) (15–18's)
A title in the *World Wide* series which encourages pupils to explore the major religious and non-religious belief-systems.

M. Blakeley: *Nahda's Family* (A & C Black, 1977) (8–13's)
12 year old Muslim girl's life in the north of England. *Strands* series.

R. Boyce: *The Story of Islam* (REP, 1972) (9–12's)

B. Brett: *Mohammed* (Collins, 1972) (11–13's)

253

A lively account of the Prophet whom it, unfortunately, depicts visually.

P. Bridger: *A Hindu Family in Britain* (REP, 1969)　　(9–13's)
　　　　A West Indian Family in Britain (REP,　　(9–13's)
　　　　1972)

D. G. Butler: *Many Lights – World Religions: an*　　(11–18's)
　　　　anthology for young people (Chapman,
　　　　1975)

E. Carlton: *Patterns of Religion* series (Allen and　　(15–18's)
　　　　Unwin, 1973)
　　　　1. *Peoples and Religion;* 2. *Religions in*
　　　　Society.

Christian Education Movement: *Festivals* (1973)　　(9–13's)
　　　　Approaches festivals from several world
　　　　faiths through the theme of celebration

　　　　Ask About Religion series (1976–77)
　　　　Religious Dress　　(9–13's)
　　　　An illustrated booklet examining the
　　　　significance of dress in the world's reli-
　　　　gions.

　　　　Roundabout series (1976–77)
　　　　Religion Roundabout by R. Shepherd.　　(11–13's)
　　　　Planned with secondary slow learners in
　　　　mind. Collage of world religions.

G. Cleverley and B. Phillips: *Northbourne Tales of*　　(13–16's)
　　　　Belief and Understanding (McGraw Hill,
　　　　1975)
　　　　Real-life dialogue situations between
　　　　young members of different faiths.

J. L. Cohen: *Buddha* (Macdonald & Co.,　　(9–13's)

W. Owen Cole: *A Sikh Family in Britain* (REP, 1972)　　(9–13's)

　　　　Come Inside the Church (6 Religions)　　(8–10's)
　　　　(Studio Vista, 1974)
　　　　A delightfully illustrated introduction to
　　　　world religions.

P. W. Crittenden: *The Making of World History: Islam*　　(13–16's)
　　　　(Macmillan, 1972)
　　　　Three short books
　　　　1. *Muhammad and Islam;* 2. *Islam in the*
　　　　Middle Ages; 3. *Achievement of Islam.*

Denholm House Press: *Our Friends of Different Faiths*　　(9–13's)
　　　　series (1977–78)
　　　　32-page booklets

1. *Our Muslim Friends;* 2. *Our Christian Friends;* 3. *Our Hindu Friends;* 4. *Our Jewish Friends;* 5. *Our Sikh Friends;* 6. *Our Buddhist Friends.*

J. Duckworth: *Muhammad and the Arab Empire* (Harrap World History Programme: 1974)   (11–14's)

M. H. Grimmitt and G. T. Read: *Christians Today* (Kevin Mayhew Limited, 1977)   (9–16's)
A thematic approach to teaching Christianity as a world religion.
See page 260 for further details.

H. A. Guy: *Our Religions:* (Dent, 1973)   (14–16's)

Rupert Hart-Davis Educational: *Journeys into Religion (1977–78)*
(Schools Council Project on R.E. in Secondary Schools)
Teachers' Handbook A
Pupils' Materials
The Man from Nazareth; Religion in Britain Today; Signs and Symbols; The Muslim Way of Life; Pilgrimages.   (11–12's)
The Life of Man – The Family; How Others See Life; Exploring Belief; Science and Religion.   (13–14's)
Religion Through Culture – Judaism; Why Do Men Suffer?; The Hindu Way.   (15–16's)
Proposed additional materials:
Teachers' Handbook B
Who am I?; The Meaning is in the Story; The First Christian Writings.   (11–12's)
Making Sense; What is the Christian Church?; Worship; The Making and the Meaning of the Bible.   (13–14's)
Islam; Humanism; Buddhism; Work; Prejudice.

S. Hedges: *With One Voice* (REP, 1970)   (11–16's)

F. G. Herod: *What Men Believe* (Methuen, 1968)   (13–16's)

World Religions (Blond Education, 1970)   (13–16's)

F. G. Hilliard: *How Men Worship* (RKP, 1965)   (13–16's)

P. Holroyde: *East Comes West* (C.R.C., 1970)   (13–16's)
Short booklet on Hinduism, Islam and Sikhism

Hulton Press: *The Way* series (1972–77)   (9–13's)
    Simple 80-page books on the world's
    great religions.
    The Way of the Buddha, by C. A. Burland;
    The Way of the Jews, by L. Jacobs; *The*
    Way of the Hindu, by Swami
    Yogeshananda; *The Way of the Muslim,* by
    M. Iqbal; *The Way of the Sikh,* by W. H.
    McLeod; *The Way of the Christian,* by J. C.
    Allen.

Hodder and Stoughton: *World of Islam* (Picture   (9–13's)
    Reference Library No. 28, 1976)

G. M. James: *The Bodhi Tree* (G. Chapman, 1971)   (10–12's)

J. G. Jones: *Faiths of the World* (Holmes McDougall,   (11–14's)
    1977)

A. Kamm: *The Story of Islam* (Dinosaur Publications,   (8–13's)
    1976)

C. M. Kay: *The Arab World* (Oxford Children's   (9–13's)
    Reference Library No. 13, OUP, 1970)

Zaidee Lindsay: *India* (A & C Black, 1977)   (8–13's)
    Pictures by children with a brief text
    providing background to religions,
    customs and traditions.

S. Lyle: *Pavan is a Sikh* (A & C Black, 1977)   (8–13's)
    What the history, traditions and religion
    of the Sikhs mean in the life of a nine
    year old boy and his family living in
    London.

Longman Group Resources Unit: *Schools Council*   (16–18's)
    General Studies Project (1972–74)
    Religion 1 and *Religion 2* (1974 Units)
    1. *The Vicar; Is this Religion?; Does Life*
       Matter?; Matters of Conscience; Marriage
       East and West; Jewish Family Life; Is
       Your Procession Really Necessary?; Death
       and Dying; Is there a God?
    2. *Religious Experience 1 and 2; Men,*
       Minds and Meditation; Communicating
       Religion 1 and 2; Religion and Art;
       Sacred Books; Myth.

Lutterworth Education: *Thinking About* series, edited   (14–16's)
    by R. Trudgian
    1. *Thinking About Islam,* by J. B. Taylor
    (1971); 2. *Thinking about Judaism,* by M.
    Domnitz (1971); 3. *Thinking about*

Hinduism, by E. J. Sharpe (1971); 4.
Thinking about Christianity, by R. St. L.
Broadberry (1974); 5. *Thinking about
Buddhism,* by D. Naylor (1976).

Understanding Your Neighbour series,   (9–13's)
edited by R. Trudgian
1. *Understanding Your Jewish Neighbour,*
   by M. Domnitz (1974)
2. *Understanding Your Muslim Neighbour,*
   by M & M Iqbal (1976)
3. *Understanding Your Hindu Neighbour* by
   J. Ewan (1977)

Photopaks, by P. Longley and S. Kronen-   (11–16's)
berg (1971)
See page 247 for further details of the 4
packs of photographs.

W. H. McLeod: *The Sikhs of the Punjab* (Oriel Press,   (12–14's)
1970)

K. Milne: *Church, Synagogue and Temple* (Wayland   (13–16's)
Publishers, 1975)

S. A. Nigosian: *World Religions* (Edward Arnold,   (16–18's)
1976)
An introduction to six world religions.

E. G. Parrinder: *A Book of World Religions* (Hulton   (10–16's)
Educational, 1965)

Something After Death? (Denholm House   (15–18's)
Press, 1974)
Second title in the *Search for Meaning*
series.

Asian Religions (Sheldon Press, 1975)   (15–18's)

A. E. Perry: *How People Worship* (Denholm Press and   (11–15's)
E. J. Arnold, 1975)
Worship in the world's religions.

K. P. Roadley: *Questing – Symbol in World Religions*   (11–14's)
(Edward Arnold, 1977)
9 stories of events in the lives of the
founders of major world religions.

Sheldon Press: *Issues in Religious Studies* series, edited   (16–18's)
by P. Baelz and J. Holm (1976–1977)
A series of value to sixth-form students
following 'A' level RS courses.
1. *The Nature of Belief,* by E. Maclaren
2. *Religious Language,* by P. Donovan

3. *The Worlds of Science and Religion,* by D. Cupitt
4. *Evil, Suffering and Religion,* by B. Hebblethwaite
5. *Interpreting the Bible,* by D. Stacey
6. *Ethics and Belief,* by P. Baelz
7. *The Study of Religions,* by J. Holm

B. W. Sherratt and D. J. Hawkins: *Gods and Men. A Survey of World Religions* (Blackie, 1972) (15–18's)

R. Street: *Focus on Faiths* (Nelson, 1974) (14–16's)
One of the *In Focus* series.

R. Tames: *The World of Islam* (Jackdaw Publications, 1975) (9–13's)

D. Townson: *Muslim Spain* (C. U.P., 1973) (12–15's)
Of wider interest than its title suggests.

R. Trudgian: *Who is my Neighbour?* (Denholm House Press, 1975) (14–16's)
The fourth title in the *Search for Meaning* series; explores the different religions represented in a multi-cultural society.

B. Wigley & R. Pitcher: *The Developing World* series (Longman, 1969–75) (11–15's)
See page 247 for further details.

Ward Lock Educational: *Living Religions* series (1970–73) (13–16's)
Short and simple booklets covering origins and development of religions, basic beliefs and way of life.
Hinduism, by Y. Crompton; *Judaism,* by M. Domnitz; *Islam,* by el Droube; *The Orthodox Church,* by S. Hackel; *Roman Catholicism,* by P. Kelly; *Buddhism,* by T. Ling; *Living Tribal Religions,* by H. W. Turner; *Protestant Christian Churches,* by M. Ward; *Humanism* by B. Smoker; *Zen and Modern Japanese Religions,* by M. Pye; *Sikhism,* by W. Owen Cole and P. Singh Sambi.

L. & C. Wolcott: *Religions Around the World* (G. Chapman, 1970) (11–13's)

T. Zinkin: *India and her Neighbours* (Oxford Children's Reference Library, O.U.P., 1967) (9–13's)

E. Christian Studies

J. C. Allen: *The Way of the Christian* (Hulton, 1977) (9–14's)

Sister Audrey: *Jesus Christ in the Synoptic Gospels* (SCM 1972) (14–18's)
For 'O' and 'A' level.

I. H. Birnie: *Focus on Christianity* series (Edward Arnold, 1969/78) (14–18's)
6 books for use with senior secondary pupils either for CSE or general R.E.
1. *The Church in Your Community*
2. *Christians and Social Work*
3. *Four Working for Humanity* (Luther King, Huddleston, Symanowski and Bonhoeffer)
4. *Christianity and Politics*
5. *The Church in the Third World*
6. *Christianity and Youth*

I. H. Birnie (Ed.): *People with a Purpose* series (SCM, 1973 onwards). (10–13's)
Biographies of outstanding Christian men and women.
See page 263 for full details.

R. Bowood: *The Story of our Churches and Cathedrals* (Ladybird Books, 1964) (9–13's)

L. G. Brandon: *What do we know about Jesus?* (Edward Arnold, 1977) (12–14's)

R. St. L. Broadberry: *Thinking About Christianity* (Lutterworth, 1974) (14–16's)

B. Brown: *Making Sense of Living* (Denholm House Press and E. J. Arnold, 1969) (14–16's)
Making Sense of Loving (Denholm House Press and E. J. Arnold, 1969) (14–16's)
The Choice (Denholm House Press and E. J. Arnold, 1970) (14–16's)
The Search (Denholm House Press and E. J. Arnold, 1970) (14–16's)
Project study books on Jesus and the Christian faith suitable for both CSE and general RE.

Christian Education Movement: *Christianity in View* series (1976–78)
Series of posters carrying 8 A4 black and white photos plus Teacher's notes on:–

1. *Christian History;* 2. *Christian Symbols;*
3. *Christian Worship;* 4. *Christian Action.*
Topic Folder Number One – Christianity   (11–16's)
Leaflets on symbols, worship and build-
ings, creeds, Church and Community,
the Gospels, history of the world
Church etc.

Discovering the Church (Dimension 1,   (12–13's)
1973)
Teacher's book and 10 workcards.

Ask About Religion series (1977)

Christian Objects   (9–13's)
Information on bible, water, bread and
wine, the Christmas crib and Easter
garden, candles, light and crosses etc.

C. Chapman: *Christianity on Trial* series (Lion   (15–18's)
Publishing, 1974)
3 discussion books for able senior
secondary pupils.
1. *How can we know if Christianity is true?*
2. *Questions of God, man and the universe.*
3. *Questions about Jesus Christ.*

R. Fice and M. Simkiss: *We Discover the Church* (E. J.   (7–11's)
Arnold, 1972)

R. Glithero: *Discovering Jesus* (Denholm House   (11–13's)
Press, 1970)

M. H. Grimmitt and G. T. Read: *Christians Today*   (9–16's)
(Kevin Mayhew Ltd., 1977)
A thematic approach to teaching
Christianity in R.E.
2 sets of 32 black and white photographs
of:
1. *Christians in their Homes and Churches*
2. *Christians in their Local Community and
World Community.*
Booklet for teachers: *Teaching Christianity
in R.E.* Containing Spiral Curriculum
and Details of Photos.
Book: *Christians Telling* – personal
accounts of Christian faith and beliefs
for classroom use. (1979)

S. Hackel: *The Orthodox Church* (Ward Lock, 1971)   (13–16's)
One of the *Living Religions* series.

260

J. Hencher/C. Herbert/A. Talbot-Ponsonby: *A* (11–16's)
Place to Dream – a new way of looking at
Churches and Cathedrals (CIO, 1976)
A highly original approach most valu-
able to the RE teacher.

F. G. Herod: *Who Cares? – Christianity and modern* (13–16's)
problems (Methuen Education, 1972)

R. J. Hoare: *Our Saints* series (Longmans, 1967) (7–9's)
1. *St. Francis of Assisi;* 2. *St. George;*
3. *St. Columba;* 4. *St. David;* 5. *St.*
Patrick; 6. *St. Nicholas;* 7. *St. Louis;* 8. *St.*
Christopher.

P. J. Hunt: *What to Look For Outside a Church* and (9–12's)
What to look for Inside a Church (Ladybird
Books)

P. Kelly: *Roman Catholicism* (Ward Lock, 1971) (13–16's)
One of the *Living Religions* series.

E. Lord: *Mysteries and Problems* (Longman, 1970) (14–16's)
Investigates the Christian response to
questions of human existence.

Lutterworth Education: *Biography for Today* series (9–13's)
(1972–75)
Biographies of modern Christians. For
details see page 264.

G. O'Mahony and P. Melvin: *Look Further 1 and 2* (11–16's)
(Mayhew-McCrimmon, 1972–73)
Two sets of workcards with a Christian
perspective.

J. Pedley: *Jesus in Our Age* (Blandford, 1972) (13–15's)
The life of Jesus and the relevance of his
teaching for today. Confessional in
tone.

D. Pringle: *Christianity in Action Today* (Schofield & (12–16's)
Sims, 1968)
38 chapters on Christian individuals,
groups and organisations.

R. Purton: *Churches and Religions* (Blandford Press, (9–13's)
1972)
One of 24 class books in the *Approaches*
to Environmental Studies series.
(4 sets of 12 slides are available from the
Slide Centre to accompany this book).

Religious Education Press: *Christian Denominations*   (14–16's)
series (1977–78)
48-page books providing information
about the beliefs and practices of
different denominations.
The Church of England by Jan Baker
The Orthodox Church by Margaret Doak
The United Reformed Church by K. Slack
The Society of Friends by G. Gorman
The Church of Scotland by J. Bulloch
The Baptists by J. Wood
The Methodist Church by J. Bates
The Pentecostal Churches by K. Ottosson
The Salvation Army by C. W. Kew
The Roman Catholic Church by M. Murphy

The Faith in Action series, edited by G.   (11–13's)
Hanks and D. Wallington. (1974
onwards).
Short biographies of modern
Christians.
For details see page 265.

R. W. Thomson: *English Christianity* series (REP,   (10–12's)
1960)
1. *How Christianity Came to Britain*
2. *How Christianity Grew in England*
3. *How Christianity Spread in England*

G. Tolderlund-Hansen: *2,000 years of Christianity*   *(13–16's)*
(Harrap, 1971)

G. Turner: *Christianity – a brief description of the*   (13–16's)
present-day Church (Edward Arnold,
1977)

M. Ward: *The Protestant Churches* (Ward Lock, 1970)   (13–16's)
One of the *Living Religions* series.

B. R. Youngman: *The Four Paths* series (Hulton,   (7–11's)
1973)
1. *The Path of Service;* 2. *The Path of Duty;*
3. *The Path of Healing;* 4. *The Path of
Leadership.*

The New Outlook Scripture (Nelson, 1972)   (11–16's)
For details see page 253.

F. Biography/Christian Lives/Heroes/Religious Leaders
W. Barclay/Zeffirelli: *Jesus of Nazareth* (Collins, 1977)   (12–18's)

262

I. H. Birnie (ed.): *People with a Purpose* series (SCM,   (10–13's)
1973 onwards)
Biographies of outstanding Christians.
1. *Mother Teresa,* by S. M. Hobden
(1973); 2. *Trevor Huddleston,* by I. H.
Birnie (1973); 3. *Helder Camara,* by N.
Cheetham (1973): 4. *George Macleod,* by
S. M. Hobden (1973); 5. *Kenneth
Kaunda,* by R. Trudgian (1973);
6. *Barbara Ward,* by N. Cheetham and
C. King (1974); 7. *James Baldwin,* by D.
Edwards & I. H. Birnie (1975); 8. *Danilo
Dolci,* by J. Ferguson (1975).

M. Bhoothalingam: *Children's Ramayana*   (9–12's)
(Government of India Ministry of Information, 1972, or Independent Press)

B. Brett: *Mohammed* (Collins, 1972)   (11–13's)

N. J. Bull: *Great Christians* series (Hulton, 1972)   (9–13's)
Each book contains 20 short biogra-
phies.
1.*The Early Saints;* 2. *New Life in the
Church;* 3. *Workers for God;* 4. *The Church
in all the World.*

One Hundred Great Lives (Hulton, 1973)   (9–13's)

B. Cooper: *Meeting Famous Christians* (Mayhew-   (14–18's)
McCrimmon, 1977)
Interviews with Anthony Bloom, Helder
Camara, Trevor Huddleston, George
Macleod, Michel Quoist, David
Sheppard, Roger Schutz, Cardinal
Suenens, Sally Trench, Pauline Webb,
Colin Winter, Sheila Cassidy.

N. Frith: *The Legend of Krishna* (Sheldon Press, 1976)   (16–18's)

M. H. Grimmitt (Ed.): *Christians Telling* (Kevin   (9–16's)
Mayhew Limited, 1979)
A collection of short autobiographies,
stories and personal statements of belief
suitable for reading or telling to
children and young people. Part of the
Christians Today materials.

C. Hodgetts: *We will suffer and die if we have to* (REP,   (14–16's)
1969)
A folk play for Martin Luther King, Jr.

J. Kennett: *The Kennett Library series* (Blackie, 1973 (9–13's)
onwards)
Lillian (1973)
Anne Frank (1974)

Ladybird Books Limited: *Series 561* (9–12's)
6. *The Story of Captain Cook;* 7. *Florence
Nightingale;* 10. *David Livingstone;*
16. *Captain Scott;* 28. *Joan of Arc;* 29. *The
Pilgrim Fathers;* 30. *Elizabeth Fry;*
44. *John Wesley.*

Lutterworth Educational: *Biography for Today* series (9–13's)
(1972 onwards)
Brief, attractively written biographies
from a Christian viewpoint.
Prisoner of the Jungle: John Dodd, by D.
Norman.; *The Pilot Who Changed Course:
Leonard Cheshire,* by C. Scott.; *God's Fool:
Toyohiko Kagawa,* by C. Scott.; *Treasures of
Darkness: Helen Roseveare,* by J. Hills-
Cotterill.

C. Mackinnon: *Stories of Courage* (Oxford Children's (9–13's)
Reference Library, O.U.P. 1967)

G. O'Mahoney: *Six Lives* (Mayhew-McCrimmon, (12–16's)
1973)
Posters and teaching notes on Borelli,
Luther King, Hilary Pole, Sue Ryder,
Schweitzer, and Mother Teresa.

W. Mayne: *A Book of Heroes.* (Puffin 1970) (9–13's)

H. G. Moses: *Knights of Jesus* (Blond Educational, (10–13's)
1965)
12 great Christians seen from a
Christian perspective.

M. Muggeridge: *Something Beautiful for God* (14–18's)
(Fontana, 1972)
Malcolm Muggeridge talking with
Mother Teresa and describing her life.

J. O'Neill: *Martin Luther* (C.U.P., 1975) (12–16's)
One of the titles in the *Cambridge
Introduction to the History of Mankind*
Series.

B. Peachment: *The Defiant Ones* (REP, 1971) (14–16's)
Biographical studies of Danilo Dolci,
Father Borelli and Abbé Pierre with syn-
opsis for dramatic development.

264

D. J. Prickett (Ed.): *Special People* series (Denholm   (8–13's)
 House Press, 1975)
 Short biographies.
 Green Book: include Jimmy Saville OBE.,
 Leonard Cheshire, Mollie Harvey,
 Luther King, David Wild, Mother
 Teresa and others.
 Orange Book: includes Sir Francis
 Chichester, Sir Basil Spence, Cliff
 Richard, Reg Dowey, 'Blue Peter', The
 Samaritans, and others.

D. Potter: *Son of Man* (Penguin, 1971)   (16–18's)
 A powerful and controversial view of
 Jesus.

F. W. Rawding: *The Buddha* (C.U.P., 1975)   (12–16's)
 One of the titles in the *Cambridge
 Introduction to the History of Mankind*
 series.

Religious Education Press: *The Faith in Action* series,   (9–13's)
 edited by G. Hanks and D. Wallington
 (1974 onwards).
 Short biographies of modern Christians
 showing how Christian faith has
 influenced their lives.
 Devils' Island (Charles Pean, S. A.) by B.
 Peachment
 The Nun in the Concentration Camp
 (Mother Maria), by G. M. Target.
 Children of Naples (Riccardo Santi), by G.
 Hanks.
 Three Fighters for Freedom (Civil Rights
 Workers), by B. Peachment.
 Friend of Drug Addicts (David Wilkerson),
 by R. J. Owen.
 Down Among the Dead Men (Sally Trench),
 by B. Peachment.
 Arctic Mission (Jack Turner), by J & M
 Burrell.
 Trial of Faith (Richard Wurmbrand) by
 R. J. Owen.
 An Aeroplane or a Grave (John Flynn), by
 B. Peachment.
 Single Ticket to China (Gladys Aylward) by
 D. Hare.
 The Red Cross Story (Henri Dunant), by B.
 Peachment.

Helen (Helen Keller) by G. Hanks.
Island of No Return (Father Damien), by G. Hanks.
Escape from Death (Sundar Singh), by D. Hare.
The Great Doctor (Albert Schweitzer) by N. Martin.
The Tiger of Naples (Father Borrelli), by B. Peachment.
I Wish He was Black (Trevor Huddleston), by R. J. Owen.

K. P. Roadley: *Travelling – Symbol in Story* (Edward Arnold, 1976) (9–13's)
The stories of Theseus, Jason, Rama, Sinbad, Jonah, Tobias, St. Francis, St. Christopher and Suppuraka.

Questing – Symbol in World Religions (Edward Arnold, 1977) (9–13's)
Stories include: Natchez Indians, Krishna, Moses, Gautama, Zoroaster, Master K'ung, Jesus, Muhammad, and Nanak.

J. D. Searle: *Twentieth Century Christians* (St. Andrews Press, 1978) (12–18's)
12 mini-biographies: Gladys Aylward, John Buchanan, Mother Teresa, John Dodd, Leonard Cheshire, Mario Borrelli, Ernest Gordon, Brother Andrew, Martin Luther King, Nicky Cruz, Cliff Richard and Sally Trench.

E. Seeger: *The Ramayana* (Dent, 1975) (14–18's)

R. Shanker: *The Story of Ghandi* (Children's Book Trust, New Delhi, 1971, or Independent Publishing Co.) (9–13's)

J. Troughton: *The Story of Rama and Sita* (Blackie, 1975) (9–13's)

R. J. Unstead: *Great Leaders* (Carousel, 1973) (9–13's)

P. M. Wylam: *Guru Nanak* (Children's Book Trust, New Delhi, 1969 or Independent Publishing Co.) (8–13's)

G. Woodcock: *Gandhi* (Fontana, 1972) (16–18's)

G. Children's Literature in Religious and Moral Education
(24 suggestions for use with 8-13's by Geoffrey Robson)

(i) Direct treatment of religious issues

Alice Comparetti: *The Hammer of Thor* (Lion)

> The struggle between Christianity and Germanic paganism in Anglo-Saxon England seen in the lives of three boys, sold as slaves in Rome, freed and trained by Gregory and sent back to help Augustine and Paulinus in their mission. Several passages verbatim from Bede.

Ann Holm: *I am David* (Puffin)

> David escapes from concentration camp but not from fear, makes his way across Europe in search of his mother under the protection of his self-chosen God.

Zvi Livne: *Children of the Cave* (O.U.P.)

> The children of a Jewish village who survive massacre by the Romans in AD 70 rebuild it as a religiously based Kibbutz-like community.

Elizabeth G. Speare: *The Bronze Bow* (Puffin)

> Daniel, a young Galilean boy, hates the Roman rulers who crucified his father. He joins a guerrilla band to gain revenge, but hears Jesus speak and gradually changes his views.

Geoffrey Trease: *Red Towers of Granada* (Puffin)

> Robin, a young Oxford scholar, driven from his village as a leper in 13th century England is cured by a Jew, shares exile with the Jewish family and, in moorish Spain, seeks a medicine to cure Queen Eleanor. Raises questions of religious tolerance realistically.

(ii) Direct treatment of moral issues

Hester Burton: *Time of Trial* (O.U.P.)

> Radical bookseller persecuted for his 'socialist' views during Napoleonic wars. Raises problems of overcoming prejudice and hostility toward reforming ideals among ordinary people. It has a romantic side as well.

A. Rutgers van der Loeff: *Everybody's Land* (U.L.P.)

> Two gangs of children, one white, one black, prepare to fight for a piece of waste ground to play on; they later join together to defeat adult greed which threatens to 'develop' their land. Racial prejudice and materialism squarely faced with a glance at former Nazi persecution of Jews.

Ian Serraillier: *The Silver Sword* (Puffin)

> A Jewish family is eventually reunited after the children

journey across occupied Germany from the ruins of Warsaw in 1945. War and making friends of former enemies are convincingly handled.

Sylvia Sherry: *A Pair of Jesus boots* (Puffin)

Rocky O'Rourke, from a tough block of flats in Liverpool, longs to be a real crook like his (jailed) elder brother but other people, including his despised stepsister Suzie, help change his ideals.

Geoffrey Trease: *Bows against the Barons* (Brockhampton Press)

Anti-romantic Robin Hood attempts a social revolution in feudal England but dies having failed to right the wrongs of the poor.

(iii) *Indirect treatment of religious and moral issues*
a) *Realism*

Alison Morgan: *Fish* (Puffin)

An unloved newcomer to the small Welsh village, 'Fish', adopts a stray dog, but his friend's farm loses some sheep and Fish's dog is suspected. Raises issues of keeping promises and the 'odd' child's need for affection.

Philippa Pearce: *A dog so small* (Puffin)

Ben longs for a dog for his birthday and is disappointed when all he gets is a picture of one. His imaginary dog becomes a dangerous obsession preventing him from coming to terms with reality. 'Keeping promises' again.

Ivan Southall: *Let the balloon go* (Puffin)

A spastic boy struggles to free himself from the protective coccoon provided by his mother and school mates.

John Rowe Townsend: *Gumbles Yard* (Puffin)

A group of children, abandoned by their 'parents', avoid being taken into care by setting up house in a deserted warehouse in the slums of Manchester. Introduces situation of children who are not properly cared for and brings in the local curate (unsentimentally) as a problem-solver.

Patricia Wrightson: *I own the Racecourse* (Puffin)

A mentally retarded boy is 'sold' the racecourse by a beery tramp. His friends try to convince him of his error until they see the world through his, very different, eyes.

b) *Fantasy and Myth*

Richard Adams: *Watership Down* (Puffin)

Already a 'classic', the rabbits' escape from their threatened burrow leads them through trials and dangers in which prophecy, sacrifice, faith, goodness and even a hint of eternal life are made convincing by the quality of the writing.

Roald Dahl: *Charlie and the Chocolate Factory* (Puffin)
Childish vices are amusingly caricatured. A passive hero does not detract from children's enjoyment of the story.

Ursula Le Guin: *A Wizard of Earthsea* (Puffin)
A search for identity where a young wizard struggles to defeat the evil shadow he has let loose.(Other books in the trilogy are less captivating to younger readers).

Kenneth Grahame: *Wind in the Willows* (Methuen)
Needs no recommendation. The beauty and terror of the natural world, worth of friendship, humour and joy in simple things are communicated through the different animal characters.

Rosemary Harris: *The Moon in the Cloud* (Faber)
Amusing adventures of a Hebrew animal tamer before the Flood. Reflects unself-consciously the ideal of loyalty to God amid the deities of ancient Egypt (Noah and family appear also).

Russell Hoban: *The Mouse and his child* (Puffin/Faber)
The alarming adventures of a clockwork toy mouse and his child in an evil world. Prophecies are fulfilled and good does triumph over evil.

Ted Hughes: *The Iron Man* (Faber)
This frightening creature is treated as an enemy until a boy treats him as a friend. Then, through his challenge to the monster from outer space, the Iron man becomes the Saviour of the World.

C.S. Lewis: *The lion, the witch and the wardrobe* (Puffin)
In this and the other *Narnia* stories, a journey symbolises a search for purpose in the life and the struggle between good and evil impulses within the child's character reflects a cosmic struggle in which victory comes through suffering.

E.B. White: *Charlotte's Webb* (Puffin)
A little girl and a friendly spider save a baby pig from his fate. Delicately raises problem of miracles, death and a life with a purpose.

For other titles, especially of novels and stories with a multi-faith perspective, see W. Owen Cole (Ed.): *World Religions: A handbook for teachers* (3rd edition, 1976, obtainable from the Commission for Racial Equality) pages 31-33 and pages 42-56.

H. Discussion materials

Edward Arnold: *Checkpoints* series, edited by J. L. Foster (1974–78) (14–16's)
16-page investigations attractively presented for use with teenagers of average and below average ability.
1. *Drug Takers;* 2. *Unmarried Mothers;* 3. *The Handicapped;* 4. *The Police;* 5. *Prisons;* 6. *Housing;* 7. *Growing Old;* 8. *From 0–5: The Pre-School Years;* 9. *Tobacco and Alcohol;* 10. *Trade Unions.*

I. H. Birnie: *Encounter* (McGraw Hill, 1967) (14–18's)

I. H. Birnie and J. Elliott: *Confrontation* (McGraw Hill, 1975) (14–18's)

Blackie and Sons: *Investigations* series, by J. Curry (1974) (13–16's)
Investigations into young people's experience of the social environment.
The Colour Problem, The Police, The Mobile Society, Newspapers, City Life, The Health Service, Football, The Home.

Viewpoint series, by D. Ryder (1976) (11–16's)
Explore 'viewpoints' through discussion, role-play, project work.
1. *A Start in Life;* 2. *It's Your Future;* 3. *A Time to Care.*

Christian Education Movement: *Probes Series 2* (1974 onwards) (15–18's)
World Development, Dilemmas in Medicine, Survival, Money, Liberation, Health, Law and Society

J. J. Evans: *Guard Our Unbelief – passages for discussion* (O.U.P., 1971) (15–18's)

Harrap: *New Generation* series, edited by P. Sommer (1972) (14–18's)
Written with civics, social studies, citizenship and politics in mind. Titles revised in 1977: *Information, Becoming a Citizen, Central Government, Local Community, Welfare State, Commercial Life, The Law, World Affairs 1 & 2.*

Issues series, by J. Love and C. Edwards (1977) (14–16's)

Investigations into human dilemmas
using casenotes:
Squatters, Tug of War (foster/natural
parents), *The Doomed Valley, Gypsies*

Counterpoint series, by P. Moss (1974–76)   (14–16's)
Make young people aware of the back-
ground and implications of things they
have always taken for granted.
1. *Media;* 2. *Crime and Justice;*
3. *Medicine and Morality;* 4. *Prejudice and
Discrimination;* 5. *People and Politics.*

A. Harris and G. Gurney: *Argument* (CUP, 1970)   (14–16's)

Hulton: *Breakway* series, by P. A. Sauvain (1973–74)   (14–16's)
Text photographs and picture strips.
1. *People with Problems;* 2. *Finding a job
and settling down;* 3. *World of Adventure;*
4. *Living in Towns.*

D. Konstant and J. Cumming: *Beginnings*   (11–13's)
(Macmillan/Search Press 1970)
A discussion book using extracts and
photos.

Longman: *Occasions* series, by R. Mills (1976)   (14–18's)
Themes of common experience looked
at through extracts from literature,
social reports, film, TV scripts,
children's writing and photographs. 4
topic booklets, a study guide and four
slide sets.
*Births, Weddings, Funerals, Moments of
Truth.*
Visual Discussion series, by D. Adland
(1972, 1974, 1975)
Modern problems and questions pre-   (15–18's)
sented through text and visuals:
1. *I am a Man;* 2. *Which Way?;*
3. *Identity*
Enquiries series, by J. Hanson
Magazine-type social studies topic   (14–16's)
books.
*Courtship, Aggression and Control, Family
Life, Drugs, Pollution and Conservation,
Communication, Learning.*

Thinkstrips series,   (14–16's)
Comics on social and health topics for
less academic.

It's Your Round (drinking); *It'll Never Be
the Same* (young couple with baby); *It's
only Fair* (roles)

Lutterworth Education: *Life Cycle* series, by J.   (14–16's)
    Elliott and E. Payne (1975)
    Collections of readings and visuals.
    Suitable for 'Religion and Life' O and
    CSE syllabuses. Expresses a pre-
    dominantly Christian viewpoint.
    1. *Sex, Marriage and Family Life*
    2. *Education, Work and Death*

    Cross Currents series, by J. Bone (1973)   (16–18's)
    Discussion books for sixth form ethics
    and religious studies.
    1. *Good Thinking;* 2. *Reasons to believe*

M. Lynch: *It's Your Choice,* (Edward Arnold, 1977)   (13–16's)
    6 role-playing exercises on topics of
    social concern.

P. Miller and K. Pound: *Creeds and Controversies*   (14–16's)
    (English Universities Press, 3rd edition,
    1975)
    A discussion book on morality and reli-
    gion.

D. and C. Milman: *What do you think?* (Blackie,   (9–13's)
    1977)
    Uses extracts from children's literature,
    photos and drawings.

Nelson and Son Ltd: *Activity Factsheets,* by D.   (15–16's)
    Church and B. Ford (1973)
    Starting points for project work.
    1. *The Homeless;* 2. *Old Age;* 3. *Local
    Pollution;* 4. *Transport Problems;*
    5. *Unemployment;* 6. *Gambling;* 7. *Crime
    in Towns;* 8. *Fatherless Families;* 9. *New
    Towns;* 10. *Living in New Towns.*

Oxford University Press: *Standpoints* series   (14–18's)
    (1975–77)
    Similar to Penguin *Connexions* series.
    *All in the mind; Don't shoot the goalkeeper;
    Change the street; On the warpath; Death.*
    Other titles in preparation: *India; News;
    Education; Religion.*

Religious Education Press: *Dimensions* series (1977)   (14–16's)
    Thematic anthologies.

Adolescence, by M. Samuda.
Black and White, by J. L. Foster.
Love and Marriage, by M. Samuda.
School by J. L. Foster.

SCM Press Limited: *Living Issues* series, by J.   (14–18's)
Sutcliffe and Philip Lee-Wolf (1971–73)
A study of contemporary issues in the
context of history.
1. *Conflict;*   2. *Communication;*
3. *Behaviour;*   4. *Power;*   5. *Freedom;*
6. *Hope.*

R. Young: *Everybody's Business* (OUP, 1973) and   (16–18's)
Everybody's World (OUP, 1970 – Part 1 of
Everybody's Business).
Extracts dealing with personal, social
and political issues.

I. Worship and Assembly

a) Suggestions for worship and assembly: themes and ideas

J. Bailey (Ed.): *Blueprint 1,2,3 and 4* (Galliard,   (Secondary)
1976–77)
An alphabetic compilation of thematic
material in 4 volumes.

                                       (Primary &
British Humanist Association: *Wider Horizons –*   Secondary)
suggestions for modern assemblies
B.H.A., 13 Prince of Wales Terrace,
London 8

C. Buckmaster: *Give us this Day* (U.L.P. 1964–67)   (Primary &
Vol. 1: *Pattern of Praise* (1964)   Secondary)
Vol. 2: *Times and Seasons* (1967)

M. Brooks and M. Cockett: *Assemblies for Seniors*   (Secondary)
(Kevin Mayhew Ltd., 1977)

J. Bryant and D. Winter: *Well GOD, here we are again*   (Primary &
(Hodder and Stoughton, 1974)   Secondary

A. Bullen: *24 Assemblies for Juniors* (Mayhew-   (Primary)
McCrimmon, 1971)

T. Castle: *Tuesday Again! – 34 Assemblies for Seniors*   (Secondary)
(Mayhew-McCrimmon 1978)

R. Cardwell: *15 Celebrations for under Twelves* (Grail,   (Primary)
1975)

M. Cockett: *36 Assemblies for Seniors* (Mayhew-   (Secondary)
McCrimmon 1971)

F. Dickinson and I. R. Worsnop: *Primary School Assembly Book* (Macmillan, 1972) — (Primary)

R. Dingwall: *Assembly Workshop* (Darton, Longman & Todd, 1971) (with supplements) — (Secondary)

R. Faulkner: *30 Assemblies for Infants* (Mayhew-McCrimmon, 1971) — (Secondary)

S. M. Hobden: *Explorations in Worship* (Lutterworth Educational, 1970) — (Secondary)

Further Explorations in Worship (Lutterworth Educational 1974) — (Secondary)

B. S. Holt: *Looking for Meaning* (SCM Press, 1971) — (Secondary)

R. H. Lloyd: *Assemblies for School and Children's Church* (REP, 1974) — (Primary & Secondary)

More Assembly Services (REP, 1975) — (Secondary)

Sister Jane Maltby: *Focus on Worship* (Kevin Mayhew Ltd., 1978) — (Primary)

F. Martin *et al*: *Gathered in His Name* (Mayhew-McCrimmon, 1973) — (Primary)

A. G. Patston: *Assemblies for Primaries* (REP, 1969) — (Primary)

F. L. Pinfold: *Meeting Points Assembly Book* (Longman, 1973) — (Secondary)

J. D. Pope: *Contemporary Themes in Worship* (Galliard, 1970) — (Secondary)

D. J. Taylor: *Exploration in Assembly with Children* (Lutterworth Educational, 1973) — (Primary)

P. Wetz and P. Walker: *Celebrating Together* (Darton, Longman and Todd, 1974) — (Primary)

E. Wills: *School Assemblies for 5–7's* (Denholm House Press, 1973) — (Primary)

D. Waters: *A Book of Festivals* (Mills and Boon, 1970) — (Primary)

A Book of Celebrations (Mills and Boon, 1971) — (Primary)

A Book of Assemblies (Mills and Boon, 1974) — (Primary)

P. A. White: *Dramatic Assemblies* (REP, 1970) — (Primary & Secondary)

b) Prayers, meditations, readings and stories

E. Banyard: *Word Alive* (Galliard, 1969) — (Secondary)
Prophets in action (Galliard, 1974)

W. Barclay: *Prayers for Young People* (Collins, 1963) — (Secondary)

274

L. Barnett: *Good Times with God* (Hodder and Stoughton, 1975)   (Secondary)

D. G. Butler: *Many Lights* – World Religions: an anthology for young people (Chapman, 1975)   (Secondary)

C. Campling and M. Davies: *Words for Worship* (Edward Arnold, 1969)   (Secondary)

F. Carr: *101 School Assembly Stories* (W. Foulsham & Co. Ltd., 1975)   (Primary & Secondary)

J. Cookson & M. Rogers: *Time and Again Prayers* (OUP)   (Primary)

T. G. Daffern: *Poems for Assemblies* (Blackwell, 1963)   (Secondary)

Denholm House Press: *Prayers to use with* series
    Prayers for use with Under 5's by M. Bacon and J. Hodgson (1976)
    Prayers to use with 5–8's by D. R. Wilton, R. Renouf and J. Murray (1976)
    Prayers to use with 8–11's by M. Putnam, S. Phillips, G. Duncan and J & E Young (1976)
    Prayers to use with 11–13's (1978)
    Prayers to use with young people, by I. H. Jones, A. E. Perry, A. T. Hubbard (1976)
    Prayer-time with Seniors, by V. Pewtress
    Responsive Prayers for Youth, by S. Hedges
    Down to Earth and Up to Heaven, by S. Hedges

    Stories for teachers to tell children series (edited by P. Morton-George)   (Primary)
    Stories for All Seasons (3–4's)
    Stories for Christmas (3–10's)
    Stories for Under Fives
    Stories for 5–8's
    Stories for 8–11's
    Harvest-Tide Stories

H. Elfick: *Folk and Vision Book of Readings* (R. Hart-Davis, 1971)   (Secondary)

B. Frost & D. Wensley: *Celebration* (3 books) (Galliard, 1970)   (Secondary)

A. Gilmore: *Have a Good Day* (Hodder and Stoughton, 1975)   (Secondary)

S. G. Hedges: *With One Voice* (World Religions) (REP, 1970)   (Secondary)

C. Herbert: *The New Creation* (REP, 1971) (Secondary)

D. H. Hilton: *Words to Share* (Denholm House Press, 1974) (Primary & Secondary)

M. Hollings & E. Gullick: *The Shade of his Hand* (Mayhew-McCrimmon, 1973) (Secondary)

The One who Listens (Mayhew-McCrimmon, 1971) (Secondary)

It's me, O Lord (Mayhew-McCrimmon, 1972) (Secondary)

E. S. & P. Jones: *Worship and Wonder* (Galliard, 1971) (Secondary)

J. Lynch-Watson: *A Patchwork Prayer Book* (Hodder and Stoughton, 1976) (Primary)

P. Mullen: *Assembling* (Arnold, 1977) (Secondary)

J. Mascaro: *Lamps of Fire* (Eyre Methuen, 1972) (Secondary)

C. Micklem: *Contemporary Prayers for Church & School* (SCM, 1975) (Secondary)

G. Parrinder: *Themes for Living* (Hulton, 1973) (Secondary)
 1. *Man and God*
 2. *Right and Wrong*
 3. *Society*
 4. *Goal of Life*

R. Purton: *Day by Day* (Blackwell, 1973) (Primary & Secondary)

M. E. Rose: *The Morning Cockerel Book of Readings* (R. Hart-Davis, 1967) (Primary & Seconday)

L. M. Savary *et al: Listen to Love — reflections on the seasons of the year* (G. Chapman, 1970) (Secondary)

D. Thompson: *Readings* (C.U.P. 1974) (Secondary)

c) Songs and Hymns

A & C Black: *With Cheerful Voice* (reprinted 1971) (Primary & Secondary)

J. Bailey: *New Life* (Galliard, 1971) (Secondary)

P. Blakeley *et al: Someone's Singing, Lord* (A & C Black, 1973) (Primary)

H. Clark *et al: Sing Hosanna* (Holmes McDougall, 1973) (Primary)

G. Clifton: *Sing it in the morning* (Nelson, 1975) (Secondary)

In every Corner Sing (Nelson, 1975) (Secondary)

M. Cockett: *Moving — 6 action songs* (Mayhew-McCrimmon, 1970) (Primary)

M. Coyle: *Sing for Joy* – 27 songs for infants (Primary)
(Mayhew-McCrimmon, 1972)

M. R. Cook & M. E. Rose: *Folk and Vision Book of* (Secondary)
Words and Music (R. Hart-Davis, 1971)

C. Hodgetts: *Sing True* (REP,1970) (Primary)

K. Mayhew: *Haul Away* (Mayhew-McCrimmon, (Primary &
1973) Secondary)
Celebration Hymnal (Mayhew- (Primary &
McCrimmon, 1976) Secondary)
20th Century Folk Hymnal (3 vols) (Kevin (Primary &
Mayhew Limited, 1976–7) Secondary)

B. O'Hare: *God's Rainbow* (Mayhew-McCrimmon, (Primary)
1973)

M. E. Rose: *The Morning Cockerel Hymn Book* (R. (Primary)
Hart-Davis, 1967)

R. Rolls: *Everybody Sing* (BBC, 1973) (Primary)

P. Smith: *New Orbit* (Galliard, 1972) (Secondary)

Faith, Folk and Clarity (Galliard, 1967) (Secondary)
Faith, Folk and Nativity (Galliard, 1968) (Secondary)
Faith, Folk and Festivity (Galliard, 1969) (Secondary)

Jesus Folk (Galliard, 1974) (Secondary)

J. Tillman: *Exploring Sound* (Galliard, 1976) (Primary &

J. Tillman & B. Braley: *New Horizons* (Stainer and Secondary)
Bell, 1974)

E. White: *Good Morning, Jesus* – 24 songs for juniors (Primary)
(Kevin Mayhew Limited, 1978)

D. R. Wilton & P. Buzzing: *New Child Songs* (Primary)
(Denholm House Press, 1973)

PART TWO: BOOKS FOR TEACHERS

J. Reports, pamphlets and statements on Religious Education (1970–1978)

The Fourth R (1970): Church of England Commission on R.E. in Schools. National Society and S.P.C.K.

Moral and Religious Education in County Schools (1970) – a report of a working party to the Social Morality Council, 4 York House, London W8.

The Recruitment, Employment and Training of Teachers of R.E. (1972) – a report to the British Council of Churches, 10 Eaton Gate, London SW1 9BT.

A Questioning Generation (1972) – a report on sixth-form religion in Northern Ireland prepared for the Northern Ireland Committee of the Church of Ireland Board of Education by J. E. Greer.

Images of Life (1973) – problems of religious belief and human relations in schools. (*The Bloxham Report:* R. Richardson and J. Chapman, SCM Press)

Changes in Religious Education – some points for discussion (1973) – Schools Council R.E. Committee Occasional Bulletin, Schools Council, 160 Great Portland Street, London W1N 6LL.

Survey of R.E. in Secondary Schools in Lancashire County (1973) – DES/Lancashire Local Education Authority. Reported in *Learning for Living,* May 1975.

Moral and Religious Education in County Primary Schools (1975) – edited by H. Blackham, Social Morality Council, N.F.E.R. Publishing Co., 2 Jennings Buildings, Thames Avenue, Windsor, Berks.

Objective, Fair and Balanced – a new law for religion in education (1975) – British Humanist Association, 13 Prince of Wales Terrace, London W8 5PG.

Religious Education – a considered view (1976): Association of Christian Teachers, 47 Marylebone Lane, London W1M 6AX.

What Future for the Agreed Syllabus? – a document for discussion (1976) – a working party report to the R.E. Council for England and Wales. Obtainable from the Hon. Secretary, R.E. Council, 55 Boundstone Road, Rowledge, Farnham, Surrey GU10 4AT.

The Child in the Church (1976) – a working party report to the British Council of Churches, 10 Eaton Gate, London SW1W 9BT.

Religious Education in County Schools – a discussion document (1976) – a working party report to the Free Church Federal Council, 27 Tavistock Square, London WC1H 9HN.

Ways Whereby Christian Education in State Schools Should be Saved (1976) – a report by the Education Committee of the Order of Christian Unity, 39 Victoria Street, London SW1.

Religious Education in State Schools (1976) – a statement by the Professional Association of Teachers, 5 Wilson Street, Derby DE1 1PG.

Religious and Moral Education of Deaf Children (1976) – the report of a working party, Church House Bookshop, Great Smith Street, London SW1.

Common Ground (1976) – a report of a religious education forum held in Dundee College of Education, November 1976. Obtainable from Learning Resources Department, Dundee College of Education, Gardyne Road, Dundee, Scotland.

Teachers and Religious Education (1976) – a study by J. E. Greer of the attitudes, opinions and practice of teachers in primary schools in Northern Ireland. (Stranmillis College, Belfast.)

A Groundplan for the Study of Religion (1977) – Occasional Bulletin from the Schools Council R. E. Committee, Schools Council, 160 Great Portland Street, London W1N 6LL.

Schools Council 18+ Research Programme (Studies based on the N & F Proposals) (1977) – a report of the R.E. Syllabus Steering Group. Obtainable from the School Government Publishing Company Limited, Darby House, Bletchingley Road, Merstham, Surrey RH1 3DN.

Curriculum Christianity – Crisis in the Classroom (1977) – papers given at the November Conference organised by the Education Committee of the Order of Christian Unity; edited by F. Tulloch, (Unity Press).

Report on Religious Education and Corporate Worship (1977) – Assistant Masters Association, 29 Gordon Square, London WC1. For details of AMA resolutions on R. E. see the Proceedings of the AMA Council (1978).

The Teaching of Religious Education (1977) – a statement from the Association of Assistant Mistresses Executive Committee, 29 Gordon Square, London WC1H 0PX.

Christians asking questions about education (1977) – Christian Education Movement, 2 Chester House, Pages Lane, London N10 1PR.

Education in Schools – a Christian rejoinder (1977) – a comment on the 1977 Green Paper, *Education in Schools – a consultative document* (1977) by the Association of Christian Teachers, 47 Marylebone Lane, London W1M 6AX.

What Future for the Agreed Syllabus Now? – a document for further discussion (1977) – a working party report of the R.E. Council for England and Wales (incorporating the text of the 1976 report). Obtainable from the Hon. Secretary, R.E. Council, 55 Boundstone Road, Rowledge, Farnham, Surrey GU10 4AT.

The Development of Religious Education: a report on the recruitment and training of Religious Education Teachers (1977) – a joint report from NATFHE/CEM/RE Council. Obtainable from the Hon. Secretary, R.E. Council, 55 Boundstone Road, Rowledge, Farnham, Surrey GU10 4AT.

Young People's Beliefs (1977) – an exploratory study commissioned by the General Synod Board of Education of the views and behavioural patterns of young people related to their beliefs. Report by B. Martin and R. Pluck. Obtainable from Church House, Dean's Yard, London SW1.

Religion in Childhood and Youth (1977) – a research report published in 3 parts in *Learning for Living,* Spring 1977, Summer 1977 and Autumn 1977. Obtainable from CEM, 2 Chester House, Pages Lane, London N10 1PR.

RK, RI, RE: Now What? (1977) – a leaflet by the British Humanist Association, 13 Prince of Wales Terrace, London W8 5PG.

Coping with Christianity (1977) – a report of a religious education forum held in Dundee College of Education, November 1977. Obtainable from Learning Resources Department, Dundee College of Education, Gardyne Road, Dundee, Scotland.

Christianity in the Classroom (1978) – papers given at the CEM Easter Conference, 1977. Obtainable from CEM, 2 Chester House, Pages Lane, London N10 1PR.

Design for Religious Education (1978) – a report presented to the R.E. Council, Northern Ireland. Obtainable from Stranmillis College, Belfast.

K. The Theory and Practice of Religious Education (1961–1978)
(Titles in chronological order)

H. Loukes: *Teenage Religion* (SCM, 1961)

R. J. Goldman: *Religious Thinking from Childhood to Adolescence* (RKP, 1964)

R. J. Goldman: *Readiness for Religion* (RKP, 1965)

V. Madge: *Children in Search of Meaning* (SCM, 1965)

V. Madge: *Introducing Young Children to Jesus* (SCM, 1965)

H. Loukes: *New Ground in Christian Education* (SCM, 1965)

K. E. Hyde: *Religious Learning in Adolescence* (Oliver & Boyd, 1965)

E. Cox: *Changing Aims in Religious Education* (RKP, 1966)

F. & P. Cliff: *A Diary for Teachers of Infants* (Rupert Hart-Davis, 1967)

280

N. Smart: *Secular Education and the Logic of Religion* (Faber, 1968)

K. E. Hyde: *Religion and Slow Learners – a research study* (SCM, 1969)

J. W. D. Smith: *Religious Education in a Secular Setting* (SCM, 1969) (Revised and reissued in 1975 by The St. Andrew Press, as *Religion and Secular Education*)

Schools Council Publication: *Humanities for the Young School Leaver: an approach through religious education* (Evans/Methuen, 1969)

Church of England Commission on R.E. in Schools: (National Society and SPCK): *The Fourth R* (1970)

J. R. Hinnells (Ed.): *Comparative Religion in Education* (R.K.P., 1970)

G. Parrinder (Ed.): *Teaching about Religions* (Harrap, 1971)

H. F. Matthews: *The New Religious Education* (REP, 1971)

J. Dean: *Religious Education for children* (Ward Lock, 1971)

Schools Council Working Paper No. 36: *Religious Education in Secondary Schools* (Evans/Methuen, 1971)

J. Wilson: *Education in Religion and the Emotions* (Heinemann, 1971)

I. H. Birnie (Ed.): *Religious Education in Integrated Studies* (SCM, 1972)

J. Tooke (Ed.): *Religious Studies* (Blond Educational Teacher's Handbooks, 1972)

C. Alves: *The Christian in Education* (SCM, 1972)

M. Evening: *Approaches to Religious Education* (Unibooks, 1972)

M. H. Grimmitt: *What Can I Do in RE? – A Guide to New Approaches* (Mayhew-McCrimmon, 1973. 2nd edition, 1978)

W. O. Cole (Ed.): *Religion in the Multi-Faith School* (Bradford Educ. Services/Yorkshire Committee for Community Relations, 1973)

Schools Council Working Paper No. 44: *Religious Education in Primary Schools* (Evans/Methuen, 1974)

J. Holm and A. Matten: *Handbooks on Objective Testing: Religious Studies* (Methuen Educ., 1974)

T. Copley and D. Easton: *What they never told you about RE* (SCM, 1974)
  A Bedside Book for R.E. Teachers (SCM, 1975)

B. W. Hearn: *Religious Education and the Primary Teacher* (Pitman Education Library, 1975)

M. Taylor (Ed.): *Progress and Problems in Moral Education* (NFER Pub. Co. 1975) (the final 4 chapters deal with RE).

J. Hull: *School Worship: An Obituary* (SCM, 1975)

J. Holm: *Teaching Religion in School: A Practical Approach* (OUP, 1975)

N. Smart and D. Horder (Eds.): *New Movements in Religious Education* (Temple Smith, 1975)

A. Harris: *Teaching Morality and Religion* (Allen and Unwin, 1976)

Community Relations Commission/SHAP Working Party: *World Religions: A Handbook for Teachers* (Community Relations Commission, editor W. Owen Cole, 1976)

W. Greenwood and H. Marratt: *New Objective Tests in Religious Studies* (Hodder and Stoughton, 1977)

M. H. Grimmitt and G. T. Read: *Teaching Christianity in R.E.* (Kevin Mayhew Limited, 1977). A 26-page booklet accompanying the *Christians Today* packs of photographs.

Schools Council R.E. Committee Bulletin: *A Groundplan for the Study of Religion* (Schools Council, 1977).

Schools Council Primary R.E. Project Handbook: *Discovering an Approach* (Macmillan Education, 1977)

C.E.M.: *A Bird's Eye View of R.E.* (edited by S. Tompkins, 1977)

T & G Copley: *First School R.E. – A Guide for Teachers* (SCM, 1978)

L. Agreed Syllabuses of Religious Instruction/Education (1966–1978)

Suggestions for Religious Education (West Riding of Yorkshire Education Committee, 1966)

Learning for Life (Inner London Education Authority, 1968)

A Handbook of Thematic Material (Kent County Council/Kent Education Committee, 1968)

Religion and Life (Lancashire Education Committee, 1968)

Fullness of Life: An exploration into Christian Faith for Primary Schools: Life and Worship (Secondary Schools) (Northamptonshire Education Committee, 1968)

Religious Education: Suggestions for Teachers (Cambridgeshire and Isle of Ely Education Committee, 1970)

Suggestions for Religious Education (City of Bath Education Committee, 1970)

Approaches to Religious Education: A Handbook of Suggestions (Hampshire Education Committee, 1971)

Agreed Syllabus of Religious Education (Cornwall Education Committee, 1971)

Guide to Religious Education in a Multi-Faith Community: a supplement to the Agreed Syllabus 'Suggestions for Religious Education' for use in Bradford Schools. (Bradford Metropolitan District, 1974)

Agreed Syllabus of Religious Instruction (City of Birmingham Education Committee, 1975) (Syllabus obtainable from The Education Offices, Margaret Street, Birmingham)

Living Together: A Teachers' Handbook of Suggestions for Religious Education, (City of Birmingham Education Committee, 1975) (Obtainable from The Education Offices, Margaret Street, Birmingham)

The Agreed Syllabus and Suggestions for Teachers (Cheshire Education Committee, 1976) (Obtainable from County Hall, Chester)

Religious Education: Avon Agreed Syllabus (Avon Education Committee, 1976) (Obtainable from Avon House North, Bristol)

Quest – Nottinghamshire agreed syllabus for Religious Education (Nottinghamshire Education Committee 1977) (Obtainable from County Hall, West Bridgford, Nottingham NG2 7QP)

Religious Education in Hampshire Schools (Hampshire Education Authority, 1978) (Obtainable from The Castle, Winchester, Hampshire)

M. Some useful books for the teacher

(i) Religious and Theological Studies

R. Bach: *Jonathan Livingston Seagull* (Pan, 1972)

A. T. Dale: *The Bible in the Classroom* (OUP, 1972)

W. Owen Cole (Ed.): *World Faiths in Education* (Unwin Education Books, George Allen and Unwin, 1978)

Christian Education Movement: *Christianity in the Classroom* (1978)

E. Cook: *The Ordinary and the Fabulous* (OUP, 2nd edition, 1976)

E. Cox: *This Elusive Jesus – The Problem of Gospel Teaching* (Marshalls Educational, 1975)

H. Cox: *The Seduction of the Spirit* (Wildwood House, 1974)

S. Dicks, P. Mennill and D. Santor: *The Many Faces of Religion: an inquiry approach* (Ginn and Co., 1973)

R. E. Davies: *A Christian Theology of Education* (Denholm House Press, 1975)

J. Ferguson: *Religions of the World: A study for Everyman* (Lutterworth Educational, 1978)

N. Frith (Trans.): *The Legend of Krishna* (Sheldon Press, 1976)

H. Gill: *Ian Ramsey* (George, Allen and Unwin, 1976)

A. E. Harvey: *The New English Bible Companion to the Gospels* (C.U.P. & O.U.P., 1972)

J. Hick: *The Centre of Christianity* (SCM Press, 1977)

J. Hinnells and E. J. Sharpe: *Hinduism* (RKP, 1972)

283

J. Holm: *The Study of Religions* (Sheldon Press, 1977)

R. Jackson (Ed.): *Perspectives on World Religions* (SOAS, 1978) (Available from Extramural Division, SOAS, University of London, London WC1E 7HP)

R. Kendrick: *Does God Have a Body? and other questions* (SCM Press, 1977)

E. Maclaren: *The Nature of Belief* (Sheldon Press, 1976)

R. Minney: *Of Many Mouths and Eyes: A study of the Forms of Religious Expression* (Hodder and Stoughton, 1975)

A. C. Moore: *Inconography of Religions – An Introduction* (SCM Press, 1977)

G. Parrinder: *A Dictionary of Non-Christian Religions* (Hulton, 1971)
Man and his Gods – an Encyclopaedia of the World's Religions (Hamlyn, 1972)
Worship in the World's Religions (2nd edition, Sheldon Press, 1974)

G. Parrinder (Trans.): *The Bhagavad-Gita* (Sheldon Press, 1974)

Penguin Books: *The Pelican Gospel Commentaries*
St. Mark, by D. Nineham. (reprinted 1975)
St. Matthew, by J. C. Fenton (reprinted 1974)
St. Luke, by G. B. Caird (reprinted 1975)
St. John, by J. Marsh (reprinted 1976)

J. Prickett (Ed.): *Initiation Rites* (Lutterworth Educational, 1978)

E. Robinson: *The Original Vision* (Religious Experience Research Unit, Oxford, 1977)

SCM Press Ltd: *Religion and Theology 3/4 – A Select Book Guide,* (1978–79)

E. J. Sharpe: *50 Key Words in Comparative Religion* (Lutterworth Educational, 1971)

N. Smart: *Background to The Long Search* (BBC Publications, 1977)

R. Tames: *The World of Islam – A Teacher's Handbook* (Extramural Division of SOAS, Univ. of London, 1977)

J. Tooke and K. Russell: *Projects in Religious Education* (Batsford, 1974)

R. Walton (Ed.): *A Source Book of the Bible for Teachers* (SCM Press, 1970)

R. C. Zaehner: *Hindu Scriptures* (Everyman's Library, 1972)

R. C. Zaehner (Ed.): *The Concise Encyclopaedia of Living Faiths* (Hutchinson, 2nd edition, 1971)

(ii) Educational Studies

George Allen and Unwin: *Unwin Education Books,* edited by I. Morrish.

> No. 12 *Developing a Curriculum* by S. H. & A. Nicholls (1972)
>
> No. 24 *Creative Teaching – an approach to the achievement of educational objectives,* by S. H. & A. Nicholls (1975)
>
> No. 27 *Aspects of Educational Change,* by I. Morrish (1976)
>
> No. 30: *Common Sense and the Curriculum,* by R. Barrow (1976)
>
> No. 35: *The Place of Common Sense in Educational Thought,* by L. Elvin (1977)

L. Cohen and L. Marion: *A Guide to Teaching Practice* (Methuen, 1977)

J. Eggleston: *The Sociology of the School Curriculum* (RKP, 1977)

P. Hirst: *Moral Education in a Secular Society* (Unibooks/University of London Press/National Children's Homes, 1974)

P. Hirst: *Knowledge and the Curriculum* (RKP, 1975)

J. Hartley/I. Davies/K. Major/S. Hawkins: *Getting Started –* Blackwell's Practical Guides for Teachers (Basil Blackwell, 1975)

A. V. Kelly: *The Curriculum – Theory and Practice* (Harper and Row, 1977)

D. Lawton: *Social Change, Educational Theory and Curriculum Planning* (Unibooks/Hodder and Stoughton Educational /Open University Set Book, 1973)

Open Books Publishing Ltd: *Curriculum Studies* series, edited by D. Jenkins.

> *Curriculum: an introduction,* by D. Jenkins and M. D. Shipman (1976)
>
> *Designing the Curriculum,* by H. Sockett (1976)
>
> *Changing the Curriculum,* by B. MacDonald and R. Walker (1976)
>
> *Curriculum Evaluation,* by D. Hamilton (1976)
>
> *Knowledge and Schooling,* by R. Pring (1976)
>
> *Culture and the Classroom,* by J. Reynolds and M. Skilbeck

P. H. Taylor: *How teachers plan their courses* (NFER Publishing Co., 1970)

J. Wilson: *Philosophy and Practical Education,* (RKP, 1977)

M. F. D. Young (Ed.): *Knowledge and Control* (Collier-Macmillan, 1971)

N. Journals and Periodicals for the R.E. Teacher

Learning for Living – The British Journal of Religious Education, published by C.E.M., Four issues per year. (Obtainable from, Christian Education Movement, 2 Chester House, Pages Lane, Muswell Hill, London N10 1PR.)

Review (published by C.E.M.) contains CEM news, articles, reviews.

Common Room (C.E.M. notes for Secondary staff). Resources, short articles for general circulation among Humanities, R.E., English and Social Studies staff. Available through school membership of CEM.

Spectrum – a magazine for Christians in Education. Published termly by the Association of Christian Teachers, 47 Marylebone Lane, London W1M 6AX.

Digest (published termly by the Association of Christian Teachers). Reviews of books, AVA Material, with particular reference to RE teachers, together with assembly outlines.

The New Sower – A Roman Catholic publication, issued quarterly by Mayhew-McCrimmon Limited, Great Wakering, Essex SS3 0EQ. Includes articles, poems, meditations, teaching material, reviews.

Bulletin of the Association for Religious Education – issued as 'volumes' (e.g. volume 10 included Bulletins 24 and 25). Contains general articles, reviews and news about classroom orientated material and books. Issued periodically. Available from The Membership Secretary, A.R.E., 36 Kent Court, Bankfoot, Newcastle-upon-Tyne NE3 2XH.

Together – tends to be more concerned with voluntary religious education but useful for primary schools, especially for assemblies and special services. Issued monthly. Available from The Board of Education, Church House, Dean's Yard, Westminster, London SW1.

The Bloxham Project Newsletter – concerned mainly with boarding schools but of interest to those teaching in voluntary aided Church schools. Issued termly. Available from Elm Cottage, Willows Lane, Rugby, Warks.

AVA Magazine (The magazine of the Film and Visual Aid Group serving the Conference of Missionary Societies in Great Britain and Ireland). Issued in January, April and September. Available from The Subscriptions Secretary, AVA Magazine, 17 Nether Street, North Finchley, London N12.

Lumen Vitae –International Review of Religious Education – issued four times a year and available from 184 rue Washington, 1050 Brussels, Belgium.

Avon Religious Education Bulletin – published termly, contains articles, details of courses and conferences, a calendar of religious festivals, book reviews etc. Available from Diocese of Bristol Education Committee, Church House, 23 Great George Street, Bristol BS1 5QZ.

O. Services to R.E. Teachers

(i) Professional Associations

ACT: *Association of Christian Teachers,* 47 Marylebone Lane, London W1M 6AX. Tel: 01-486-2561. In association with the Scripture Union; various publications, including *Spectrum* and *Digest;* arranges courses for teachers on R.E. Conservative Evangelical in outlook.

ARE: *Association for Religious Education,* Chairman: Rev. G. J. Miller, Overdale, Birches Nook, Stocksfield, Northumberland NE43 7NU. Tel: 06615-3149. Membership Secretary: Mr. C. Dixon, 36 Kent Court, Bankfoot, Newcastle-upon-Tyne, NE3 2XH. Provides forum and advisory services for RE teachers; publishes periodicals and pamphlets on various aspects of R.E; annual conference. Liberal to Conservative in theological outlook.

CEM: *Christian Education Movement,* 2 Chester House, Pages Lane, London N10 1PR. Tel: 01-444-8383. Publishes RE and General Studies materials for teachers and for use in Primary and Secondary classrooms; regular primary, middle and secondary school mailings to individual members and associated schools; facilitates special projects; arranges day and residential conferences on Christian themes for 4th, 5th and 6th form pupils; annual RE conference; advisory service for teachers; publishes *Learning for Living/The British Journal of Religious Education.* Radical/Liberal in theological outlook.

SHAP: *The Shap Working Party on World Religions in Education.*
Annual mailing, calendar of World Religious Festivals, advisory service for teachers, regular conferences, occasional publications. General enquiries to The Secretary, The Rev. John Rankin, S.W.P., West Sussex Institute of Higher Education, Bishop Otter College, College Lane, Chichester, West Sussex. Tel: 0243 – 87911. Advisory service for specific items only, The Rev. Ray Trudgian, West London Institute of Higher Education, Borough Road, Isleworth, Middlesex TW7 5DU. Tel: 01-560-5911. Inter-faith in outlook.

(ii) R.E. Resources and In-Service Training Centres

The following four centres fulfil a national .role. Each centre organises courses, advises teachers and exhibits a comprehensive display of resources to cover all aspects of R.E. Requests for advice should be specific and accompanied by a stamped addressed envelope. A directory of national and local R.E. centres may be obtained from the York R.E. Centre (address below) on receipt of 50 pence plus postage. Many Local Education Authorities now employ a full-time R.E. Adviser or Inspector to whom local enquiries may be addressed.

(a) Centres initiated and supported by the Department of Education and Science

The R.E. Resources and In-Service Training Centre, Westhill College, Selly Oak, Birmingham B29 6LL. Tel: 021-472-7245, Ext. 58 for the school enquiries; Ext. 57 for church enquiries. (This Centre has a separate Church Education Department which welcomes enquiries from clergy and church workers). Enquiries and visits from teachers in the Midlands and the North of England.

The R.E. (In-Service Training and Resources) Centre, Lancaster House, West London Institute of Higher Education, Borough Road, Isleworth, Middlesex, TW7 5DU. Tel: 01-560-5911 (Ext. 39). Enquiries and visits from teachers in London and the South of England.

(b) Centres initiated and supported by the National Society (Church of England)

The National Society's R.E. Development Centre, 23 Kensington Square, London W.8. Tel: 01-937-4241. (Shares a building with the *Westminster Pastoral Foundation* (Methodist) and the *Westminister R.E. Centre* (Roman Catholic).

The York R.E. Centre, College of Ripon and York St. John, Lord Mayor's Walk, York YO3 7EX. Tel: 0904-56771.

P. Suppliers of audio-visual aids, and resource materials.

Filmstrips and Slides

E.P. Group of Companies, Bradford Road, East Ardsley, Wakefield, Yorks. WF3 2JN.

Carwal AVAs Limited, P.O. Box 55, Wallington, Surrey.

BBC Publications, 35 Marylebone High Street, London W1M 4AA.

Focal Point Filmstrips Limited, 35 Cavendish Drive, Waterlooville, Portsmouth PO7 6YX.

Bury Peerless Esq., 22 Kings Avenue, Minnis Bay, Birchington, Kent.

Hulton Educational Publications Limited, Raans Road, Amersham, Bucks. HP6 6JJ.

(Common Ground), Longman Group Limited, Longman House, Burnt Mill, Harlow, Essex.

Visual Publications, 197 Kensington High Street, London W8 6BB.

EAV, Butterley Street, Leeds LS10 3YY.

Edward Patterson Associates, 68 Coper's Cope Road, Beckenham, Kent. (Time-Life Filmstrips; Centre for Humanities Multi-Media Kits etc.)

Concordia Filmstrips, Viking Way, Barhill Village, Cambridge CB3 8EL.

Gateway Educational Films Limited, St. Lawrence House, 29-31 Broad Street, Bristol BS1 2HF.

Woodmansterne Limited, Holywell Industrial Estate, Watford WD1 8RD.

ESL Bristol (as Gateway), 29-31 Broad Street, Bristol BS1 2HF.

St Paul Publications, Middlegreen, Slough SL3 6BT
(St Paul Book Centres: 57 Kensington Church St., London W8 4BA
133 Corporation Street, Birmingham B4 6PH
5a-7 Royal Exchange Sq., Glasgow G1 3AH
82 Bold Street, Liverpool L1 4HR)

The Slide Centre, 143 Chatham Road, London SW11.

Audio-Visual Productions Limited, 15 Temple Sheen Road, London SW14.

Resource Materials

Tapes of BBC Recordings
Stagesound (London) Limited, 14, Langley Street, Covent Garden, London WC2 9JG.

Slide Frame Mounts
The Clear-Vue Projection Company, 92 Stroud Green Road, London N4 3EN.

Slide Wallets and Suspension Bars
Messrs. Diane Wyllie Limited, 3 Park Road, Baker Street, London NW1.

Storage Equipment/General Supplies
Lawtons of Liverpool Limited, 60 Vauxhall Road, Liverpool L69 3AU.

Laminating Materials/Plastic Wallets
Shire Plastics Limited, Snettisham, Norfolk PE31 7PR.

Audio/Visual Aids Information
Educational Foundation for Visual Aids, 33 Queen Anne Street, London W1M 0AL.

National Audio-Visual Aids Centre, 254-256 Belsize Road, London NW6.

Blank Cassettes
Peak Technical Services, St. Alkmund's Way, Derby 3GQ.

Reprographic Equipment/Materials
O.E.M. (Reprographic) Limited, 140-154 Borough High Street, London SE1 1LH.

Storage Equipment and Reprographic Materials
Ofrex Educational Aids, Lansdowne House, 41 Water Street, Birmingham B3 1HP.

Display Boards
Marler Haley Expo Systems Limited, Expo Systems House, High Street, Barnet, Herts. EN5 5UF.

Illustrations/Books on Indian Religions
Independent Publishing Company, 38 Kennington Lane, London SE11 4LS.

Books, Records on Sikhism/Asian Religions
Pam's Sikh Bookshop, 17 Abbotshall Road, Catford, London SE6 1SQ.
Indian Record Shop, 70 South Road, Southall, Middlesex.
Gobind Stores, Asian Records, 60 Bayswater Road, Leeds 8.

Illustrations/Books on Islam
Minaret House, 9 Leslie Park Road, Croydon East, Surrey CRO 6TN.
Muslim Educational Trust, 130 Stroud Green Road, London N4 3RZ.

Materials on Judaism
Jewish Education Bureau, 8 Westcombe Avenue, Leeds LS8 2BS.
Board of Deputies of British Jews, 4th Floor, Woburn House, Upper Woburn Place, London WC1H 0EP.

Materials on Christianity
SPCK Bookshop and Mail Order Service, Holy Trinity Church, Marylebone Road, London NW1 4DU.
Church Missionary Society, 157 Waterloo Road, London SE1 8UU.

Multi-Cultural Education Materials
The Commission for Racial Equality, Elliott House, 10-12 Allington Street, London SW1E 5EH.

Charts
Pictorial Charts Educational Trust, 27 Kirchen Road, London W13 0UD.

Film Distributors
Audience Planners (UK) Limited, 12 Charlotte Mews, London W1P
        Tel: 01-637-8159
Concord Films Council Limited, Nacton, Ipswich, Suffolk IP10 0JZ.
        Tel: 0473-76012
Central Film Library, Government Building, Bromyard Avenue, London W3 7JB. Tel: 01-928-2345.

Connoisseur Films Limited, 167 Oxford Street, London W1R 2DX. Tel: 01-734-6555.

Contemporary Films Limited, 55 Greek Street, London W1R 2DX. Tel: 01-734-4901.

Edward Patterson Associates, 68 Copers Cope Road, Beckenham, Kent. Tel: 01-658-1515.

Guild of Sound and Vision Limited, Woodston House, Oundle Road, Peterborough PE2 9PZ. Tel: 0733-63122.

EMI Film Distributors Limited, Film House, 142 Wardour Street, London W1V 4AE. Tel: 01-437-0444.

Gateway Educational Media, Waverley Road, Yate, Bristol BS17 5RB. Tel: 0454-316774.

National Audio-Visual Aids Library, 33 Queen Anne Street, London W1M 0AL. Tel: 01-636-5742.

Open University Film Library, distributed by Guild of Sound and Vision (see above).

Religious Films Limited, Foundation House, Walton Road, Watford. Tel: 92-35444.

Section E of *World Religions: A Handbook for Teachers* (edit. Owen Cole, December 1976): Available from the Commission for Racial Equality, Elliott House, 10-12 Allington Street, London SW1E 5EH; contains an extensive list of suppliers, useful addresses and publishers (see pp 191-199).

Q. Publishers of titles listed in the select bibliography

Allen and Unwin, George, Limited, P.O. Box 18, Park Lane, Hemel Hempstead, Herts HP2 4TE.

Arnold, Edward (Publishers) Ltd., 25 Hill Street, London W1X 8LL. (Inspection copies from Trade Department, Woodlands Park Avenue, Woodlands Park, Maidenhead, Berks SL6 5BS.)

Arnold, E.J. Butterley Street, Leeds LS10 1AX.

Batsford, 4 Fitzhardinge Street, London W1H 0AH.

BBC Publications, 35 Marylebone High Street, London W1M 4AA.

Black, A & C, 35 Bedford Row, London WC1R 4JH.

Blackie and Sons Ltd., Bishopbriggs, Glasgow.

Blackwell, Basil, 108 Cowley Road, Oxford OX4 1JF.

Blandford Press, Ltd., Link House, West Street, Poole, Dorset BH15 1LL.

Blond Education (Granada Publishing Ltd., P.O. Box 9, 29 Frogmore, St. Albans, Herts. AL2 2NF.)

British and Foreign Bible Society, 146 Queen Victoria Street, London EC4V 4BX.

British Humanist Association, 13 Prince of Wales Terrace, London W8 5PG.

Brockhampton Press (Hodder and Stoughton, 47 Bedford Square, London WC1B 3DP).

Burke Books, The Barn, Northgate, Beccles, Suffolk.

Cambridge University Press, Bentley House, 200 Euston Road, London NW1 2DB.

Chambers, W & R Ltd., 11 Thistle Street, Edinburgh EH2 1DG.

Chapman, Geoffrey, 35 Red Lion Square, London WC1.

Children's Book Trust, (Delhi), Oxfam House, Banbury Road, Oxford.

Christian Education Movement, 2 Chester House, Pages Lane, London N10 1PR.

Church Information Office/CIO Publishing, Church House, Dean's Yard, London SW1P 3NZ.

Collins/Fontana/Collins Liturgical Books Ltd., 14 St. James's Place, London SW1A 1PS. Trade and Orders: P.O. Box 39, Glasgow G4 0NB.

Darton, Longman and Todd, 89 Lillie Road, London SW6 1UD.

Denholm House Press, NCEC, Robert Denholm House, Nutfield, Redhill, Surrey RH1 4HW.

Dent, J.M. and Sons Ltd., Dunhams Lane, Letchworth, Herts. S96 1LF.

Dinosaur Publications Limited, Beechcroft House, Over, Cambridge CB4 5NE.

English University Press, (Hodder and Stoughton Educational), P.O. Box 704, Dunton Green, Sevenoaks, Kent. TN13 2YA.

Evans Brothers Ltd., Montague House, Russell Square, London WC1N 3AU.

Faber and Faber Limited, 3 Queen Square, London WC1N 3AU.

Foulsham, W & Co., Ltd., Yeovil Road, Slough, SL1 4JH.

Galliard (Stainer and Bell Ltd.), 82 High Road, London N2 9PW.

Ginn and Company Ltd., 69 Fleet Street, London EC4Y 1HD.

Grail Publications Ltd., 27 Clerkenwell Close, London EC1.

Hamlyn Publishing Company Ltd., Hamlyn House, 42 the Centre, Feltham, Middlesex.

Harrap, George G., 182-184 High Holborn, London WC1V 7BR.

Hart-Davis Educational, Granada Publishing, PO Box 9, 29 Frogmore, St. Albans, Herts. AL2 2NF

Heinemann Educational, 48 Charles street, London W1X 8AH.

Hodder and Stoughton Educational Limited, P.O. Box No. 704, Dunton Green, Sevenoaks, Kent. TW13 2YA.

Hodder and Stoughton, 47 Bedford Square, London WC1B 3DP.

Holmes McDougall Limited, Allender House, 137-141 Leith Walk, Edinburgh.

Hulton Education Productions Ltd., Raans Road, Amersham, Bucks HP6 6JJ.

Hutchinson Publishing Group, 3 Fitzroy Square, London W.1.

Independent Publishing Company, 38 Kennington Lane, London SE11 4LS.

Jackdaw Publications Limited, 30 Bedford Square, London WC1B 3EL.

Ladybird Books Limited, PO Box No. 12, Beeches Road, Loughborough, Leics. LE11 2NQ.

Lion Publishing, 121 High Street, Berkhamsted, Herts. HP4 2DJ.

Longman Group Limited, Longman House, Burnt Mill, Harlow, Essex CM20 2JE.

Lutterworth Educational Press, Luke House, Farnham Road, Guildford, Surrey.

Macdonald Educational Ltd., Holywell House, Worship Street, London EC2A 2EN.

Macmillan Education, Brunel Road, Houndmills, Basingstoke, Hampshire.

Marshalls Educational, 1 Bath Street, London ECN 9LB.

Mayhew, Kevin Limited, 55 Leigh Road, Leigh-on-Sea, Essex SS9 1JP.

Mayhew-McCrimmon, 10-12 High Street, Great Wakering, Essex SS3 0EQ.

McGraw Hill Ltd., Shoppenhangers Road, Maidenhead, Berkshire SL6 2QL.

Methuen Education Ltd., 11 New Fetter Lane, London EC4P 4EE.

Mills and Boon Ltd., 17-19 Foley Street, London W1A 1DR.

Nelson, Thomas and Sons Ltd., Lincoln Way, Windmill Road, Sunbury-on-Thames, Middlesex TW16 5BR.

N.F.E.R. Publishing Co. Ltd., The Mere, Upton Park, Slough SL1 2DQ.

Oriel Press Ltd., (Now R.K.P.)

Oxford University Press (Educational Division) Walton Street, Oxford.

Penguin Books Limited, Bath Road, Harmondsworth, Middlesex UB7 0DA.

Pemberton Publishing Co. Ltd., (Elek Books, 54-58 Caledonian Road, London N1 9RN).

Puffin Books (See Penguin)

Religious Education Press, Hennock Road, Exeter EX2 8RP. (and A. Wheaton & Co.)

Routledge and Kegan Paul Ltd., Broadway House, Newtown Road, Henley-on-Thames, Oxon RG9 1EN.

Schofield and Sims Limited, 35 St. John's Road, Huddersfield HD1 5DT.

SCM Press Limited, 56-58 Bloomsbury Street, London WC1.

Search Press Ltd., 2-10 Jordan Place, London SW6 5PT.

Sheldon Press/S.P.C.K., Holy Trinity Church, Marylebone Road, London NW1 4DU.

St. Andrews Press, 121 George Street, Edinburgh EH2 4YN.

Stainer and Bell Ltd., 82 High Road, London N2 9PW.

Studio Vista Publishers, (Cassell and Collier Macmillan), 35 Red Lion Square, London WC1R 4SG.

Temple Smith, 37 Great Russell Street, London WC1.

U.L.P. (Unibooks), (Hodder and Stoughton Educational), PO Box 704, Dunton Green, Sevenoaks, Kent. TN13 2YA. 'A.

Warne, Frederick, 40 Bedford Square, London WC1B 3HE.

Ward Lock Educational Limited, 116 Baker Street, London W1M 2BB.

Wayland Publishers, Wayland House, 11 Folleigh Drive, Long Ashton, Bristol BS18 9JD.

Wildwood House Limited, 29 King Street, London WC2E 8JD.